The Living Philosophy of Edith Stein

ALSO AVAILABLE FROM BLOOMSBURY

Spiritual Philosophers: From Schopenhauer to Irigaray, Richard White
Hannah Arendt's Ethics, Deirdre Lauren Mahony
Philosophical Mysticism in Plato, Hegel, and the Present, Robert M. Wallace
The Bloomsbury Companion to Arendt, ed. Peter Gratton and Yasemin Sari

The Living Philosophy of Edith Stein

Peter Tyler

BLOOMSBURY ACADEMIC
LONDON · NEW YORK · OXFORD · NEW DELHI · SYDNEY

BLOOMSBURY ACADEMIC
Bloomsbury Publishing Plc
50 Bedford Square, London, WC1B 3DP, UK
1385 Broadway, New York, NY 10018, USA
29 Earlsfort Terrace, Dublin 2, Ireland

BLOOMSBURY, BLOOMSBURY ACADEMIC and the Diana logo
are trademarks of Bloomsbury Publishing Plc

First published in Great Britain 2023
This paperback edition published 2024

Copyright © Peter Tyler, 2023

Peter Tyler has asserted his right under the Copyright,
Designs and Patents Act, 1988, to be identified as Author of this work.

For legal purposes the Acknowledgements on pp. xv–xvi constitute
an extension of this copyright page.

Cover image: Portrait of Edith Stein (© Bettmann / Getty Images)

All rights reserved. No part of this publication may be reproduced or transmitted
in any form or by any means, electronic or mechanical, including photocopying,
recording, or any information storage or retrieval system, without prior
permission in writing from the publishers.

Bloomsbury Publishing Plc does not have any control over, or responsibility for,
any third-party websites referred to or in this book. All internet addresses
given in this book were correct at the time of going to press. The author and
publisher regret any inconvenience caused if addresses have changed or sites
have ceased to exist, but can accept no responsibility for any such changes.

A catalogue record for this book is available from the British Library.

A catalog record for this book is available from the Library of Congress.

ISBN: HB: 978-1-3502-6556-1
       PB: 978-1-3502-6560-8
       ePDF: 978-1-3502-6557-8
       eBook: 978-1-3502-6558-5

Typeset by Integra Software Services Pvt. Ltd.

To find out more about our authors and books visit www.bloomsbury.com
and sign up for our newsletters.

Contents

Prologue: Why Edith? vi

Part One 'The root and ground' 1

1   An empathetic life 3

2   Husserl's revolution 33

3   'The Problem of Empathy': The foundations of a philosophical psychology 55

4   'Dionysos or the Crucified One?' – Stein, Nietzsche, Freud and Jung 67

5   Stein's anthropology: *Seele* and levels of the self 93

Part Two A life philosophy 121

6   'Light and death once met' – Stein and St John of the Cross 131

7   'A science of the cross' – Stein's symbolic sense of the self 149

8   The duty of the philosopher: Stein and Wittgenstein 167

Epilogue: The author addresses the subject 190
Notes 194
Bibliography 213
Index 221

Prologue: Why Edith?

The spirit of genuine philosophy is alive in every true philosopher, in anyone who cannot resist an inner need to search out the λόγος [logos, reason, word] of this world, its ratio (as Thomas translated the word). The born philosopher – the true philosopher indeed must be born as a philosopher – brings this spirit with her into the world as potency, as I would call it. The potency becomes actualised when they meet a mature philosopher, a 'teacher'. This is the way we reach out to one another over the bounds of space and time.[1]

Who was Edith Stein?[2] A Silesian German Jew. A worker for women's rights who equalled and surpassed her better-connected male colleagues. A brilliant philosopher and theologian. An ardent German patriot with a deep love of the German intellectual tradition and culture. A psychologist at the dawn of modern psychology. An ecstatic mystic whose prayer was indeed 'a longing for truth itself'.[3] A Catholic nun who spent her last days trying to hold the disaster of mid-twentieth-century Germany at bay whilst she sought her soul in the peace of a convent. And finally, the victim of the Holocaust, transported across her beloved Europe in a cattle wagon and murdered at the Auschwitz-Birkenau death camps.

For some years I have thought of writing a book about her, but the glittering kaleidoscope of her character and talents made it difficult to know where to begin. My own interest in her began in 2016 when I finished a book exploring human personhood through a discussion on the nature of the soul.[4] Of all the authors I explored: Plato, Aristotle, St Augustine, John Cassian, Sigmund Freud, Otto Rank, Carl Jung, James Hillman, she was the one who impressed me the most. I found something in her precise yet rhapsodic writing which the other voices had failed to articulate. Here, I thought, was a writer who not only knew what she wanted to say, but also, and perhaps more importantly, knew what couldn't be said about the human person. Like the philosopher Ludwig Wittgenstein, she was able to say clearly what could be said but also leave unexpressed the mystery that lies at the heart of the human person. As I finished that book I wanted to explore her more deeply, especially in respect to her ability to express the need for a 'soulful life' – *ein seelisches Leben* – in our current disturbing times.

Following this impulse an amusing caprice suggested itself to me whilst I sat under the shadow of St Stephen's Cathedral in Vienna during a break in an international conference on the philosophy of Edith Stein held in that venerable city. I imagined, amongst the selfie sticks and milling tourists, two writers conversing on a neighbouring table. On one side, dressed neatly in her slightly formal 1920s clothes, wearing a dove-grey dress, was Frau Dr Stein, listening intently as was her custom and framing each word carefully and deliberately. On the other side of the tablecloth, shabbily dressed and puffing vigorously on an old cheroot, ash of which would fall in his mocha, was Herr Professor Freud. Pleasantly surprised, slightly against his better judgement, by the wisdom of the young woman, but never letting down his guard as he sought to retain a healthy scepticism in the face of the well-chosen arguments of this phenomenologist convert. Of course it was a fun conceit that could not possibly have happened ... and yet ... Stein was often in Vienna, and although she was not an *habituée* of its coffee houses in the 1920s, who knows, the two may have had a chance encounter as she waited for one of the interminable train journeys she undertook at that time or whilst just enjoying the spring sunshine in the Stephansplatz. Regardless, the phantasy encapsulated my overall vision for this book – that Edith's views, especially on the relationship between the psyche and the mind – should once again be taken seriously enough for her to be in robust dialogue with other 'masters' of psychology such as Freud and his collaborator, Carl Gustav Jung. Yet, as the book proceeded I came to see two things – first that Stein's thought cannot be understood in isolation from the prevailing phenomenological movement, of which she was such an essential part. And secondly, that Stein, through her phenomenological exercises, was led to a radical understanding of Christianity such as to revitalize it and restore its relevance for the coming century.

Professor Antonio Calcagno, whose writings have been so helpful in framing my analysis in this book, suggests three reasons for the scholarly neglect of Stein's work since her death (Calcagno 2006: 263–4). The first is that her philosophical collaboration with Edmund Husserl was time-limited, meaning that she did not in this early period have access to the fullness of Husserl's final phenomenological synthesis which we shall explore later in Chapter 2. Secondly, the nature of Steinian scholarship itself, which has tended to concentrate on the religious, and frankly pious, aspects of her martyrdom at the expense of her philosophy. As he points out, Stein saw an intimate connection between her phenomenological approach and her religious views and I have taken this into account as I explore the nature of her philosophical anthropology in the present book. Finally, there is old-fashioned sexism. If Husserl found it difficult to put Edith on a par with his other male students surely, as Calcagno suggests, he too was suffering from an unconscious bias.

Stein's philosophy, suggests Calcagno, has the possibility of presenting 'a universal philosophy of human experience rooted in both reason and accessibility' – a 'poignant encounter' (Calcagno 2006: 264) which explicitly does *not* exclude faith, belief and spirituality. This acceptance of the spiritual dimension of human personhood can sadly be as great a challenge to the modern academic working in the field as much as sexism and anti-Semitism were in Edith's time. Edith, as we shall see, often spoke of her reluctance to mount a lecturer's podium unless she could speak of the transcendent aspect of human life. In an era that wanted, and still wants, to build a 'psychology without soul', Stein's work stands out as that of someone who logically proposed a transcendent aspect to human life and personhood. It is this 'living philosophy of human personhood' which will be explored in this book.

Aspects of Stein

However, little did I know, when I began this book in the summer of 2019, that the very foundations of our world would be shaken by the Covid-19 pandemic. As the world shut down and movements were restricted I found myself spending day after day in Edith's company and discovering what a wonderful companion she was in a world 'turned upside down'. The fruit of the time spent in her company is this book.

She was a very prolific writer and at the time of writing the German *Ausgabe* of her collected works is just being completed – twenty-eight volumes in all.[5] Although she is now getting the attention she deserves in German-speaking lands the Anglophone world still remains somewhat behind. Despite valiant efforts the Institute of Carmelite Studies in Washington DC has only translated two-thirds of her work into English to date, and again, despite considerable efforts by the admirable International Association for the Study of the Philosophy of Edith Stein (IASPES), it remains early days for the scholarly and critical examination of her writings by English-speaking readers. Although precise in her use of her native German, like her fellow psychologist Sigmund Freud, there lies the problem of translation of her particular terms for the self into English. We shall have more to say about this as we go along.

As well as these issues there lie cultural blocks to her reception. First, there is the difficulty mentioned above of categorizing her. Edith does not easily 'fit into a box'. Many readers see her as a Jewish victim of the Holocaust misappropriated by the Catholic Church. Others focus on the burning piety of this great lady destroyed in her prime whilst others prefer to see her as the great phenomenologist, uncrowned heir to Edmund Husserl. Although she died more than half a century ago in 1942, it has taken up to now for these conversations to 'clear the ground' so that we can begin finally to appreciate her writings in their own right. Edith encompasses so many worlds it is perhaps unsurprising that it has taken us so long to decide which, if any, she belongs to. I am conscious that some readers will finish this book and decide, after all, that she is best left in the 'phenomenological philosopher' 'Jewish thinker' or 'Catholic saint' box after all. But my own hope for the present volume is that it might be part of a 'second wave' of Steinian studies, especially in the Anglophone world, where we shall not be so concerned with fitting her into a particular box but rather begin to appreciate the multi-faceted talent of this extraordinary woman who was both philosopher, psychologist and theologian.

The aim of this book

Although I will need to present certain biographical and contextual angles for those not so familiar with her life the main emphasis of this book will be on ideas. Not simply academic ideas that can lie hidden on dusty shelves, but living ideas – ideas that can change lives. At several times the course of Edith's own life changed direction as a consequence of discovering a new idea. Accordingly, I shall in this volume respect the rich sources of Edith's thought whilst opening her up into conversation with a variety of interlocutors. These conversations – some playful, some serious – will be with thinkers who deeply influenced her, such as St John of the Cross and Edmund Husserl; others with people whom she barely conversed with, such as Friedrich Nietzsche, and, finally, some with authors she couldn't have known, such as Gerard Manley Hopkins. I have chosen each of them first to illustrate diverse aspects of Stein's work, such as her views on the nature of psychology and philosophy, but also to present a 'living philosophy', which, according to the programme of my earlier books, needs to embrace unknowing, ambiguity, paradox, creativity, the symbolic and the libidinal – all of which I see are intrinsic to human selfhood. In so doing my aim will be to open up the conversation of her philosophy from narrow academic silos into a broader sweep of thought. Ultimately for Edith the test of a philosophy is how it *affects* the reader – in taking this perspective my aim is to present Edith's thought as a *living philosophy* which is still capable of changing lives in our rapidly changing twenty-first century.

Although there are many excellent biographies of the saint available, which I have drawn upon here, some aspects of her life and work may not be so well known outside the German intellectual world, I shall therefore begin by introducing her life as well as the key sources to understanding her context. Following this the first part of the book will delineate Stein's 'living philosophy' by means of three aspects of her anthropology: first, her articulation of psychology and how she understands it *vis-a-vis* philosophy and theology, secondly her exposition of the human person and how she relates it to what she calls the soul or core of our being and finally her notion of 'levels of the self'. This discussion will have a preface in which we explore the phenomenological 'revolution' of the early twentieth century which was so important in forming Edith's mature philosophical perspectives.

As well as appraising her intellectual contributions to our ongoing debate about the nature of the self the book will have another aim expressed in its second part. Edith, as we have already seen, was a woman of contradictions, very much a woman of our times. I believe therefore that she has much to teach us on how to live a 'soulful life' in our present strange times. This will be presented in Part Two which I have called, following her own term, 'a philosophy of life'. This will explore various aspects of what we might call the 'duty of the philosopher' as we follow her own final steps to the gates of Auschwitz.

Part Two, then, will guide us towards answering the question which is perhaps more pressing than ever – *how do we live a meaningful life in the contemporary world?* We begin this by exploring her engagement with Carmelite thought and practice as exemplified by her teacher in religion, St John of the Cross. We shall follow this with a conversation with the nineteenth-century English poet Gerard Manley Hopkins and the medieval theologian Dionysius the Areopagite as we explore her essential 'symbolic mentality' in relation to psychological and spiritual resilience. The final chapter ends with some reflections on the 'duty of the philosopher' in our present disturbed and disturbing times. This shall take the form of a conversation with her contemporary, Ludwig Wittgenstein.

Strange islands

As I wrote the book some lines of her mentor, St John of the Cross, came often to my mind:

> *My Beloved is:*
> *the mountains,*
> *the lonely wooded valleys,*
> *the strange islands,*
> *the singing rivers,*
> *the whisper of the sighs of love.*[6]

At various moments when asked *why* she had made some of the dramatic choices of her life: from agnostic philosopher to Roman Catholic, from laywoman to enclosed Carmelite nun, from German patriot to refugee from the Reich, she would often answer with some words from the old Latin Vulgate version of the Jewish Book of Isaiah: '*secretum meum mihi*': 'my secret to myself' or 'my secret remains with me'. Despite half a century of exhaustive analysis of texts, documents and eye-witness accounts, many aspects of the life, and death, of Edith Stein will remain forever unknown. As we embark upon this journey to the 'strange islands' of Edith's life and work I would ask you, the reader, to bear in mind that part of Edith shall forever remain a secret, strange if you like, and we must respect that as we explore her.

This approach very much underscores my own treatment of Stein in these pages. Like her Austrian contemporary Ludwig Wittgenstein (1889–1951) she preserves the gentle flow of the personality through the articulation of a philosophy that is at once profound and yet accessible. The aim of this book, then, is to show how this remarkable woman, who took the full force of the European unconscious in the middle of the twentieth century and paid the ultimate price for it, is perfectly suited to be our own guide at an equally tumultuous time for European, and world, culture. When Stein took her religious vows she took the slightly complicated name: Teresia Benedicta a Cruce. Teresa in honour, as we shall see, of her great mentor and inspiration, St Teresa of Avila, who would eventually lead her to the peace of the order founded on Mount Carmel in the Middle Ages. Benedict in honour of the wise and humane sixth-century Patron of Europe – a title she would eventually share with him when it was bestowed upon her by Pope St John Paul II in 1999. Finally, she added the moniker 'a cruce' – 'at or of the cross', for, as we shall see, she realized in her life that only by holding fast 'a cruce' could she survive what was to be thrown at her. This too will form part of the narrative of this book.

Philosopher, theologian or psychologist?

Regarding my dear Master [Husserl] I have no worries. It has always been far from me to think that God's mercy allows itself to be bound by the frontiers of the visible church. God is truth. All who seek truth seek God, whether it is clear to them or not.[7]

Trained as a psychologist and philosopher Edith graduated to theology through her study of Ss John Henry Newman, Thomas Aquinas and Dionysius the Areopagite. Yet for her all three disciplines were part of a 'seamless robe'. As she was unable to exercise her intellectual skills in a university milieu, partly because she was a woman and partly because she was Jewish, she had to develop a 'practical philosophy of life' as she journeyed around the German-speaking countries in the interwar years exhorting and encouraging other laywomen to develop their talents and intellectual skills. These unique circumstances of her intellectual development, as we shall see shortly, explain the extraordinary practical power of her philosophy and go a long way to explaining how she was able to combine all three into what I have called in this book, her living philosophy.

So, then, who was Edith Stein? A saint, a philosopher, a psychologist, a woman, a *human being (ein Mensch)* for our times. I welcome you to these conversations with that remarkable woman, Edith Stein.

A note on translation

One thing she said I shall never forget, when she once gave her reason for an unfavourable criticism of a very free translation: 'A translator must be like a pane of glass, that lets all the light through but is not seen itself.' It was a very characteristic saying.[8]

The publication history of Edith's works is complicated and unfinished. Much of her mature writing was accomplished under trying circumstances. Interrupted by endless travelling in the tumult of Weimar Germany, she was spared the relative leisure of an academic post to compose these works, even whilst in convent life. As paper shortages arose with the onset of the Second World War drafts and final texts would be written on recycled lecture notes, scraps and shopping lists. As a Jew writing in Nazi Germany the very content of her writing, especially her autobiographical *Life in a Jewish Family*, might have caused problems with the Gestapo not only for herself but also for her fellow nuns. Despite all these pressures it is remarkable just how much of her writing has survived. Many of her manuscripts managed to come with her to Holland after her flight there in 1938. After her arrest in 1942 some wise sisters took care of them – at one point evacuating them out of the convent to a farmyard for safe keeping as the bombs of war rained down. These were later rescued and lovingly preserved at archives such as the Edith Stein Archive in Cologne and the Edmund Husserl Archive in Leuven/Louvain, where many are still kept to the present day. After hostilities ceased scholars, friends and admirers set out upon the monumental task of reconstructing and publishing her *oeuvre*, again, not a straightforward task. Herder in Germany and Nauwelaerts in Belgium began the first series of published works in 1950 with their edition of her last completed work, *Kreuzeswissenschaft/The Science of the Cross*. This would become the first volume in a series now referred to as the *Edith Steins Werke* (ESW). This was supplemented when Herder published the first volume of their *Edith Stein Gesamtausgabe* (ESGA) with a volume of her letters in 2000. This massive undertaking under the stalwart directorship of Hanna-Barbara Gerl-Falkovitz is now completing its final stages with, at the time of writing, twenty-eight volumes published in all. The systematic English translation of these series began with the first volume from the proposed complete *Collected Works of Edith Stein* (CWES) from the Institute of Carmelite Studies, Washington, *Life in a Jewish Family*, which appeared in 1986. The series continues to the present day under the stewardship of the Institute including the great American Steinian scholar and Carmelite, Fr John Sullivan O.C.D. At the time of writing just over half of the German translations have reached English eyes with many more in the pipeline. For scholarly purposes I have in the main referred to these editions, occasionally straying from them where occasion demanded. Where an English translation has been available I have been helped by it. Where not, or where I have sought to emphasize a particular point, I have given my own translation, if possible giving the German original in a footnote.

As will become apparent at times the subtle shades of meaning of German terms may require some rather clunky explanation in English. I apologize in advance to German speakers who happen to read this text.

Acknowledgements and dedication

One of the great joys of working on Edith Stein's thought is the fellowship of the worldwide network of Steinian scholars. Without their care, attention and help very little of this book would have been possible. I am particularly indebted to the following for their invaluable comments on earlier drafts of the text: Prof. Antonio Calcagno, Prof. Christof Betschart O.C.D., Dr Rodrigo Lima, Prof. Iain Matthew O.C.D., Prof. Bernard McGinn, Sr Jo Robson O.C.D., Dr Jacob Phillips, Fr John Sullivan O.C.D. and Hymie Wyse. Attendance at the bi-annual conferences of the International Association for the Study of the Philosophy of Edith Stein (IASPES) has been invaluable and I strongly urge anyone who wants to pursue Edith's thought to join this network.

Earlier versions of Chapter 6 appeared in *Edith Stein's Itinerary: Phenomenology, Christian Philosophy and Carmelite Spirituality* (Klueting and Klueting 2021) and *Biblical and Theological Visions of Resilience: Pastoral and Clinical Insights* (Cook and White 2021). I thank, in particular, Professors Kluetig and Cook for their help with those chapters.

I am grateful to Fr Marc Foley O.C.D. and the Institute of Carmelite Studies, Washington D.C. for their kind permission to quote from the English translations of the Collected Works of both Edith Stein and St John of the Cross. I also express my grateful thanks to Alan Brenik and Carcanet Press, Manchester, UK, for permission to quote the lines from Edwin Morgan's *Salvador Dali: Christ of St John of the Cross* in his *A Book of Lives* (Morgan 2007).

As most of the book was completed during the pandemic 'lock-down' I am grateful, as always, to the assistance, support (moral and physical) from countless friends, students and collaborators who 'kept faith' with endless zoom and skype conferences on the complexities of '*Mitteleuropa*', including Dame Gwynneth Knowles Q.C., Archbishop Kevin McDonald, Prof. Steven Payne O.C.D., Dr Joanne Mosley, Dr Patrick Moore F.S.C, Fr Alexander Ezechukwu O.C.D. and his Oxford Centre for Applied Carmelite Spirituality, Julienne McLean, Dr Mary Eaton, Prof. Sara Sviri, Fr Dominic White O.P. and his 'Friends of Sophia', Dr Michael Kirwan S.J. and Srs Melanie Kingston C.R. and Anne Dunne C.R. of the East Molesley House of Prayer. Steven Wolfe of Steven Wolfe Books, Massachusetts, and Fr Kelvin Ekhoegbe O.C.D. of the Carmelite Book Service, Oxford, kept me supplied with valuable texts whilst all libraries were closed for the duration and Ash and family who, as ever, kept body and soul together during the darkest of times.

Finally, I would like to thank especially my editors at Bloomsbury, Liza Thompson and Lucy Russell, who have shown persistent faith in and provided unwavering support for the project throughout its whole gestation.

At the time of going to press as another dark shadow seems to be falling over Europe once again, I dedicate this work to the Steinian scholars and followers yet to come, and those who face down oppression and modern tyranny in all its forms … may you too find 'rest for your soul' in her writing.

Peter Tyler
Centenary of the Baptism of Edith Stein, London, 2022

Part One

'The root and ground'

1

An empathetic life

On October 12, 1891, I, Edith Stein, daughter of the deceased businessman Siegfried Stein and his wife, Auguste, née Courant, was born in Breslau. I am a Prussian citizen and a Jewess.
EDITH STEIN'S CURRICULUM VITAE, WRITTEN IN FREIBURG, 1916[1]

Writing in his 2006 introduction to Stein's philosophy (still a standard work on the subject), Alasdair MacIntyre pointed out that there was no entry on Stein in *The Oxford Dictionary of Philosophy*, *The Cambridge Dictionary of Philosophy*, *The Oxford Companion to Philosophy*, *The Routledge Encyclopedia of Philosophy* and *The Blackwell Companion to Continental Philosophy*. Although some of these omissions have been corrected there is still a widespread lack of understanding of the significance of Stein's philosophy in the English-speaking world. I have mentioned some of the factors behind this already: a lack of critical English editions of some of her works, a tendency to 'pigeon-hole' her as a Catholic or Jewish martyr or a pious nun (which of course she was too). In addition to these there is a difficulty that her works cover a much wider spectrum of thought than can be found in one academic silo. As well as her core writings on phenomenology and anthropology she wrote on the social situation of women, education and a number of focused spiritual meditations.

Some of the problems with her reception also lie in the strangeness of her life. If you look on a map for the great city in which she was born, grew up and loved you won't find it. Breslau, then part of the Second German Reich, is now called Wroclaw and the capital of the Polish province of Silesia. It is, as one of my Silesian friends calls it, a 'liminal place' existing between worlds, empires, dreams and reality. A city situated in that endlessly fought over corner of Europe where the great continental rivers of the Elbe and Oder arise from the towering ranges of the Tatras.² Edith was born in this melting pot, and there is no better place to meet her than in her own account of that city and her upbringing: *Life in a Jewish Family*.³

She began writing her narrative on 21 September 1933 whilst still in her native Breslau. When she entered the Carmelite order in Cologne later that year she took the manuscript with her where she sporadically worked on it until she was forced out of Germany by the growing anti-semitic climate in 1938. At this point she travelled to the convent at Echt in Holland where she resumed writing the text. Fearful that the manuscript would be confiscated when she left Cologne for Echt she left it in the possession of her sisters in Cologne. In February 1939 she asked if anyone in Cologne was prepared to bring it to Echt. Father Rhabanus, a young Mariannhill missionary, bravely drove it over the border, despite being stopped by border guards (having inspected it they assumed it was his doctoral thesis). After the invasion of Holland by German troops in 1940 Edith again felt the discovery of the manuscript might bring opprobrium to her Dutch convent. Accordingly, Sister Pia of Echt recounted later that the two of them buried the manuscript in the garden 'near the cemetery'. Fearing that damp would destroy it they dug it up again three months later when Sr Pia found a safe hiding place for it in the monastery. Edith herself was arrested and deported from Holland in August 1942. Later, as Echt was on the front line of fighting, the remaining sisters decided to leave the monastery for the convent of Herkenbosch where the manuscript was stored in the attic. In spring 1945 Sr Pia retrieved the manuscript and gave it to the care of Fr Avertanus, Provincial of the Dutch Carmelites, who would later place it with the Husserl archive in Brussels. Even then the eventful journey of the manuscript had not ended. In the early 1960s, as international interest in the life and writings of Stein grew, the Dutch publishers felt it was time for the manuscript to be published. However, there was one problem, in a codicil written for a will just before her arrest, Edith had specified that the *Life* not be published 'as long as my siblings are alive' (see Batzdorff 1998: 174).

Accordingly, as the Dutch publishers began the process of publication the sisters at Cologne demanded that it be stopped until permission had been obtained from her surviving siblings, at this point, in 1963, there only being her sister, Erna, alive and living in the United States. Thus began a new period in the editing and redaction of Edith's manuscript as family members asked for changes, deletions and explanatory footnotes, especially regarding the more private and confidential aspects of the family story that Edith would tell.[4] Accordingly, the full manuscript was only published in complete form in 1985, over half a century after its composition. After such a history with so many twists and turns, like so many of Edith's manuscripts, it is indeed remarkable that we can enjoy it today.[5]

In the first pages she gives her motivation for beginning this task during the dark days of 1933 when Hitler had succeeded to the German Reich's Chancellorship:

> Recent months have catapulted the German Jews out of the peaceful existence they had come to take for granted. They have been forced to reflect upon themselves, upon their being, and their destiny ... Repeatedly, in these past months, I have had to recall a discussion I had several years ago with a priest belonging to a religious order. In that discussion I was urged to write down what I, child of a Jewish family, had learned about the Jewish people since such knowledge is so rarely found in outsiders.
>
> (CWES 1: 25–26)

So from its earliest conception *Life in a Jewish Family* was to be, like that other text by her great inspiration, St John Henry Newman, an *apologia*. Not that of an Anglican Divine explaining his conversion to Catholicism, but rather that of a 'German Jew' 'forced to reflect' upon herself, her being and her destiny and perhaps also, like Newman, to explain her own conversion a decade before to Catholicism. The *Life* therefore does not occupy a neutral space and accordingly, like her beloved Breslau/Wroclaw, it was destined to be fought over as succeeding generations of scholars, friends, family members and admirers have struggled to come to terms with that seemingly innocent phrase that carries so much resonance: 'a German Jew'.

Yet, Edith herself states that:

> What I shall write down on these pages is not meant to be an *apologia* for Judaism. To develop the 'idea' of Judaism and to defend it against false interpretation, to present the content of the Jewish religion, to write the history of the Jewish people – for all this, experts are at hand. And anyone desirous of instruction along these lines will find a broad selection of literature available. I would like to give, simply, a straightforward account of my own experience of Jewish life as one testimony to be placed alongside others, already available in print or soon to be published. It is intended as information for anyone wishing to pursue an unprejudiced study from original sources.
>
> (CWES 1:28)

This has the ring of Stein the phenomenologist: stating the experiences as she observed them and leaving others to bracket in and out the context and subtext as they choose.

Accordingly, Edith is presenting us with a portrait of a late nineteenth-century/early twentieth-century German-Jewish family and from the start we are plunged into the bustling life of this large, lively and busy family of Steins and Courants, presided over by the great matriarch at the centre of it all, Edith's mother, Auguste Stein, née Courant (1849–1936).

The earliest records of the Courants arise from the Franco-German borderlands where Edith's maternal grandfather, Salomon Courant (1815–98), was born. It was from here that his parents moved to Peiskretscham, Upper Silesia. He was to become a soap and candle maker, a travelling salesman, and while in Lublinitz (present-day Lubliniec), Upper Silesia, he met Edith's maternal grandmother, Adelheid Burchard (1824–83), who strangely enough to our eyes was twelve years old at the time and he tells us that 'he was attracted to her immediately' (CWES 1: 29).[6] She was one of eleven children: four sons and seven daughters. 'From then on he came every year. When she was seventeen, they became engaged, and the wedding took place the following year, 1842' (CWES 1: 29). Her parents were Joseph and Ernestine Burchard from the Province of Posen (present-day Poznań). For many years Salomon was the cantor of Lublinitz synagogue and led the prayers there on a regular basis. He also had a prayer room in his own house where on holy days the family would congregate for prayers. Whatever the family religious atmosphere of the household within which Edith herself grew up, the elder generation, as for so many German Jews of her generation, continued to keep the ancient Jewish traditions faithfully observed.

When her maternal grandparents married they opened a small grocery stall which prospered. They, too, then went on to have a large family of fifteen. In Edith's account Salomon is portrayed as a jolly, industrious man who was always generous to those around him. Edith's mother, Auguste Courant, was their fourth child. Initially she was educated in public (Catholic) schools but eventually her father founded his own school for his four eldest children and those of other local Jewish families.

Just as Edith's grandparents had met when her grandmother was twelve years old, so her parents met when Auguste was nine, finally marrying when she was twenty-one. Edith's father, Siegfried Stein (1844–93), worked in the lumberyard owned by the Stein family in Breslau. Again, another large family ensued and Edith was one of eleven children, four of whom died in childhood, the family moving back to Lublinitz to earn a living where her older siblings, Frieda, Rosa and Erna, were all born. However the business didn't prosper there so they decided to return to Breslau at Easter 1890. This is where Edith was born at the family house in Kohlenstrasse in 1891 and where she subsequently spent most of her childhood.

Shortly after Edith's birth her father died suddenly of heatstroke whilst out on a business trip surveying forestry in July 1893. Edith later wrote:

> My mother held me in her arms as he bade her farewell when he set out on the journey from which he was not to return alive, and that, when he had already turned to leave, I called him back once more. So, for her, I was the final legacy from my father. I slept beside her, and when, weary after a day at work, she would return home, her first steps led her to me.
>
> (CWES 1: 75)

Frau Stein elder was to become the mainstay and focus not only of Edith's world but of a large proportion of the extended Stein-Courant family centred around Breslau.

The mother

Writing to Gertrud von le Fort in 1933 as she wrote her *Life* and prepared to enter convent life Edith clearly had her mother very much in mind, and she describes her as 'not a person immersed in culture, but rather of a straightforward and strong nature' (ESGA 2: Letter 284, 9.10.33).[7] A few days later she adds:

> She declines anything that is beyond her Jewish faith ... She particularly rejects conversions. Everyone ought to live and die in the faith in which they were born. She imagines atrocious things about Catholicism and life in a convent. At the moment it is difficult to know what is causing her more pain: whether it is the separation from her youngest child to whom she has ever been attached with a particular love, or her horror of the completely foreign and inaccessible world into which that child is disappearing, or the qualms of conscience that she herself is at fault because she was not strict enough in raising me as a Jew.
> (CWES 5: Letter 158, 17.10.33)

Edith, the youngest, had been born on the Jewish solemn holy day of Yom Kippur (the Day of Atonement) which happened to fall on 12 October 1891, and for this, as well as the usual love a mother has for her youngest, there was clearly always a strong bond between the two women, as evidenced in the wrench Edith's conversion and entry into religious life would later make on her. On Yom Kippur she later wrote:

> Although I did not in any way scorn the delicacies served on the other holidays, I was especially attracted to the ritual of this particular holy day when one refrained from taking any food or drink for twenty-four hours or more, and I loved it more than any of the others ... For me the day had an additional significance: I was born on the Day of Atonement, and my mother always considered it my real birthday, although celebrations and gifts were always forthcoming on October 12.
> (CWES 1: 73–74)

After the death of her husband in 1893, Frau Stein, despite opposition from the family, decided to go it alone and run the family business singlehandedly. The tough circumstances of her childhood, Edith explains in her memoir, always shaped a certain frugality in her mother's later approach to dress and personal habits. These never deserted her. Like Edith she was a practical woman, and Edith pithily remarked that 'she had no taste for tedious office work. (I, too, have always considered this the most disagreeable occupation)' (CWES 1: 45). Edith's brother Arno would eventually take over the lumber company from his mother. This no-nonsense Prussian woman was more than capable of dealing with the rough lumberjacks and timber-yard folk. As Edith related: 'she had acquired such specialized knowledge that she had only to pass by a wood to make an accurate estimate of its value as timber' (Posselt 1957: 9). Yet she clearly had a warm heart and, despite these tough surroundings, she could show a concern and sympathy when needed, a trait later inherited by her daughter:

> Most of the people my mother dealt with were craftsmen. She knew each one's family history. She found it out, usually, when they wanted goods on credit or when they could not redeem the notes they had given. My mother repeatedly followed her kind heart in these cases; sometimes she even gave the 'bad customers' some additional cash when they were in need. She was often cheated; and the business was plagued with heavy losses. Despite that, it prospered. My mother always attributed this fact to being blessed by Heaven.
> (CWES 1: 62)

As well as her close bond to her mother Edith always felt close to the nearest sibling in age – her sister Erna. Despite pursuing quite different paths later in life the two formed a twosome in childhood as there was a difference of seven years between Erna and the next oldest child, Rosa. Between Edith and Erna there was only twenty months' difference. 'The older sisters used to say she [Erna] was as transparent as clear water while they called me a book sealed with seven seals' (CWES 1: 52). Erna would later become a doctor influenced by her successful uncle David in Chemnitz. The uncle likewise tried to persuade Edith to pursue a medical career which she steadfastly resisted.

From an early stage Edith cultivated the life of the mind, and when she was finally admitted to the Victoria School at Breslau she commented that 'I almost believe I felt more at home there than in our house' (CWES 1: 67). At an early age she tells us that 'reason took hold' of her:

> The first great transformation took place in me when I was about seven years old. I would not be able to ascribe it to any external cause. I cannot explain it otherwise than that reason assumed command within me. I recall very well how, from that time on, I was convinced that my mother and my sister Frieda had a better knowledge of what was good for me than I had; and because of this confidence, I readily obeyed them.
>
> (CWES 1: 77)

With this sense of reason came dreams of greatness:

> In my dreams I always foresaw a brilliant future for myself. I dreamed about happiness and fame for I was convinced that I was destined for something great and that I did not belong at all in the narrow, *bourgeois* circumstances into which I had been born.
>
> (CWES 1: 79)

Perhaps for a child of lesser talents this may have been seen as hubris or arrogance, but Edith certainly fulfilled the intellectual ambitions she cultivated as a young girl – no mean feat for a woman in a heavily patriarchal, and increasingly anti-Semitic, society.

As her sisters and brothers got married and had children Edith was often enlisted to look after the children, a task which she thoroughly enjoyed. Also, as described in the *Life*, when there were family quarrels, such as the estrangement of her sister Else and her husband Max in Hamburg, she would often be drafted in as the family mediator.[8] On these occasions, seemingly regular occurrences in her large, lively family, Edith often took the role of counsellor or spiritual director before she had acquired any formal training in these roles. She was clearly a naturally born psychologist in the Freudian sense of a *Seelsorge* – 'carer of souls'.

Student years in Breslau

Reflecting on herself as a teenage student Edith later said:

> From early childhood onwards, I was characterized within the entire family network mainly by two qualities: I was accused of ambition (rightly so) and I was called, with emphasis, 'clever' Edith. Both hurt me very much.
>
> (ESGA 1: 81)[9]

She did not like either of these designations, hinting to her of conceit and the idea that all she had was her cleverness (is the *Life* then, perhaps, an *apologia* towards her family too, to demonstrate her ordinariness?) for 'I knew, after all, from my earliest years that it was much more important to be good than to be clever' (CWES 1: 144). These statements reflect her educational progress through her childhood and early teens. Admitted at the precocious age of six to the Victoria School in the Ritterplatz at Breslau she took easily to the regimen and flourished in this environment finding it 'a second home'. Yet despite this swift progress, in her fourteenth year she decided not to continue and prepare for university entrance but instead went to Hamburg for a period to help in the household of her sister Else who had recently married the doctor Max Gordon and was expecting her second child. She later describes them as 'being totally without belief' and that 'deliberately and consciously I gave up praying' (CWES 1: 150) as a fifteen-year-old staying at their house. Much has been made of this statement with interpretations varying from her entering at this point an 'atheistic phase' to a suggestion that her type of praying somehow changed at this point. As pointed out earlier it is probably fruitless to speculate as to the nature of her spiritual life at this time, so little is known of it. Perhaps the best approach is to follow her advice twenty years later to Hedwig Conrad-Martius: '*secretum meum mihi*': 'my secret remains my own' (see comments made earlier in the Prologue).

In her sixteenth year she decided that she wanted to reapply herself to her studies and returned to Breslau in 1907 so that, with her mother's encouragement, she could complete her secondary education and prepare for university – with Erna, the only Stein children to do so. Women had only first been permitted to attend German universities in 1908 so that when Edith eventually joined the Friedrich Wilhelm University of Breslau in 1910 she was one of the first German women to do so. Speaking of the preparation period for university later, she wrote in the *Life*: 'I still remember that half year of continual work as the first completely happy period of my life. For the first time my intellectual powers were functioning at full capacity, at a task which was truly worthy of them' (CWES 1: 97).

The gap in her studies meant that her reading could range where she wished during this year of preparation and what she learnt during this 'gap year' would influence her for the rest of her life. As well as the obligatory Latin and mathematics she had to study, she used the time for reading literature, especially drama: 'I had a lot of free time. I used it principally for reading, preferably drama: Grillparzer, Hebbel, Ibsen, and, above all, Shakespeare became my daily bread' (CWES 1: 152). Also at this time she first became acquainted with Schopenhauer's *The World as Will and Idea*, much to the consternation of her sisters. They 'feared for my mental health; and I had to return the two volumes to the library unread' (CWES 1: 153). Not for the first time, as we shall see shortly, that her study of Schopenhauer would be interrupted. Intellectually, her mind began to blossom: 'when I sat alone at the desk in the room given me for my work, at the time I had no study of my own, I was totally oblivious of all the world outside' (CWES 1: 157). She had to prepare for written examinations in Latin, mathematics, French and English. Of these subjects she was particularly fired by her study of Latin, something that would become a lifelong passion:

> Latin was something else again; far more enjoyable even than studying modern languages, this grammar with its strict rules fascinated me. It was as though I were learning my mother tongue. That it was the language of the Church and that later I should pray in this language never even occurred to me at the time.
>
> (CWES 1: 157–158)

Needless to say, she successfully passed and commenced her *Gymnasium* studies.[10] Here she continued her study of German literature whilst beginning to visit the Breslau theatre where she heard, amongst other operas, *The Magic*

Flute, *Fidelio* (her favourite) and *Carmen* (not to her taste). Of Wagner she later wrote:

> I also heard Wagner and during a performance found it impossible wholly to evade its magic. Still I repudiated this music, with the sole exception of *Die Meistersinger*.
>
> (CWES 1: 174)

Bach was one of her favourite composers, she mentions with particular warmth the 1912 celebrations in Breslau featuring the massive organ in the Jahrhunderthalle of Breslau. As her *Abitur* (the German examinations necessary to enter University) approached she was drawn to the more academic rather than 'practical' subjects:

> German, history and Latin. Though keeping philosophy on my program, I no longer mentioned it since at the time I did not yet know it was a possible subject for these examinations.
>
> (CWES 1: 174)

The examinations took place in 1911 during her twentieth year. She passed with flying colours so that she could enter the University of Breslau in April 1911 where she would stay for two years until 1913.

Life at the University of Breslau

As a student growing up, and as evidenced in the photographs of the time, she formed part of a lively group of young people at the University of Breslau who hiked in the Riesengebirge, discussed Kant and Spinoza, played music and sang together – in short the carefree student life of German scholars before the Great War. Her chief interests in this time were 'Germanistics' (German literature and culture) and history. This was also the beginning of her lifelong interest in women's rights. A novel movement at the time but one that would remain close to her heart for the rest of her life:

> At that time we were all passionately moved by the women's rights movement. Hans [Biberstein, an admirer of Edith and her sister Erna] was a

> *rara avis* among the male students: he spoke up for equal rights for women as radically as any of us.
>
> (CWES 1: 125)[11]

She joined the Prussian Society for Women's Right to Vote: 'it advocated full political equality for women, was made up mostly of socialists' (CWES 1: 193) and would later describe herself at this time as a 'radical advocate for women's rights' (CWES 5: 100).[12] Most of her student friends were originally from Jewish families but 'none kept a kosher household anymore'. Often in her description of her contemporaries (e.g. Paul Berg in CWES 1: 129) we hear the voice of the 'assimilated Jews' of later nineteenth-century Prussia and the type of Jewish culture within which Edith and so many of her friends and colleagues grew up – a Judaism that put religion at the service of the Prussian state and saw themselves very much as children of the Enlightenment rather than the *schtetl*. As well as her awareness of herself as a Prussian Jew she is also aware in these memoirs of the nuances of class that surrounded her. Commenting on her student acquaintance, Willy Strietzel, she remarks:

> He was short, wore his blond hair in a crew cut, had somewhat of a snub nose and spoke with the strong Silesian dialect which was not at all customary in our 'better' circles. The difference in background and of station was immediately obvious, but neither side found this at all disturbing.
>
> (CWES 1: 130)

As for her studies at the University, her first-year courses included: Indo-Germanic; German grammar, both old and modern; history of German drama; Prussian history at the time of Frederick the Great; English constitutional history; and a beginners' course in Greek (CWES 1: 187). Of particular interest for her at this time was a course on the 'Introduction in Psychology' given by William Stern (1871–1938, inventor of the IQ assessment system) and a course in natural philosophy with Richard Hönigswald (1875–1947), concentrating in particular on epistemology and Kant. Of Stern, she later wrote: 'he had always assured us that at heart he was a philosopher (for which reason he vehemently opposed the separation of the faculties for philosophy and psychology)' (CWES 1: 199).

Indeed, of significance for the present book, the first lecture she attended at Breslau University was on Stern's psychology course. In fact she states in her reminiscences that her four semesters at Breslau University were very much taken up with psychology. In winter 1912–13 she became acquainted with the work of the Würzburg School of psychologists[13] and through these writings she became familiar with Edmund Husserl's (1859–1938) *Logische Untersuchungen* recently published. She also heard mention for the first time of Husserl's student Hedwig Martius (1888–1966, later referred to as Hedwig Conrad-Martius) and her husband, Hans Theodor Conrad (1881–1969), also a student of Husserl's. Hedwig was to be the first woman to gain a doctorate in philosophy at a German University. As she read about this Husserlian circle at the University of Göttingen, she later wrote: 'I was convinced even at that time that Husserl was the philosopher of our age' (CWES 1: 221).

Göttingen

She left Breslau University in 1913 in her twenty-first year. As she prepared to travel to Göttingen to spend the 1913 summer semester there under Husserl and his phenomenological circle she had discussions with Stern about a possible doctorate in psychology. His suggestion that she undertake an experimental investigation into child development didn't inspire her, although on her way to Göttingen she did stop off at Berlin to discuss the project with Stern's collaborator, Otto Lipmann, at the newly formed Institute for Applied Psychology. Of this she later remarked: 'paying that visit to Klein-Glieneke was the only step I ever took toward a dissertation in psychology' (CWES 1: 223).

From this meeting with Lipmann and his nascent Institute she expressed her views on the nature of psychology at that point as 'this science was still in its infancy; it still lacked clear basic concepts; furthermore, there was no one who could establish such an essential foundation' (CWES 1: 224). Later she would refer to the ongoing 'battle against psychologism' which helped instigate her move from nascent psychology to Husserl's phenomenology, which, she stated in her *Life*: 'fascinated me tremendously because it consisted precisely in such a work of clarification and because, here, one forged from the beginning the tools of thought required for this work' (ESGA 1: 134).[14] We shall return to these important themes in the following chapters.

In her writings she always speaks warmly of her Göttingen years:

> Dear Göttingen! I do believe only someone who studied there between 1905 and 1914, the short flowering time of the Göttingen School of Phenomenology, can appreciate all that the name evokes in us.
>
> (CWES 1: 241)

At the University, she tells us, philosophy and psychology were separated so she had to make a choice for one or the other – she chose philosophy. The first phenomenologist she encountered there was Adolf Reinach (1883–1917) who was friendly with Theodor Conrad and Moritz Geiger, all former students of Theodor Lipps (1851–1914) of Munich. This group (later including Stein) would become known to posterity as the 'Göttingen School' of phenomenology.

Reinach extended a warm welcome to her which was followed up as she met other members of the circle:

> That close relatives, or friends one had known for years, should be affectionate in their attitude was self-evident to me. But this was something entirely different. It was like a first glimpse into a completely new world.
>
> (CWES 1:251)

From Reinach she had her first encounter with 'the Master', Husserl himself, for whom she gives a finely drawn description from their first meeting:

> Neither striking nor overwhelming, his external appearance was rather of an elegant professorial type. His height was average; his bearing, dignified; his head, handsome and impressive. His speech at once betrayed his Austrian birth: he came from Moravia and had studied in Vienna. His serene amiability also had something of old Vienna about it. He had just completed his fifty-fourth year.
>
> (CWES 1: 251)

As well as 'the Master', Edith provides precise thumbnail sketches of all the founders of the academic study of phenomenology present at the university at the time and mostly known to her. These include Fritz Kaufmann (1891–1958) from Leipzig and Max Scheler (1874–1928). The latter with whom Edith was not very impressed at the time, displaying, for her, too much academic rivalry with 'the Master' (CWES 1: 261). However, from Scheler Edith had her first real encounter with Catholic ideas, Scheler himself having recently returned to Catholicism after a messy divorce and remarriage. It was accordingly through Scheler that Edith first met what she would later call 'the world of faith':

> This was my first encounter with this hitherto totally unknown world. It did not lead me as yet to the Faith. But it did open for me a region of 'phenomena' which I could then no longer bypass blindly. With good reason we were repeatedly enjoined to place all things before our eyes without prejudice, all possible 'blinkers' (*Scheuklappen*) should be thrown away. The limits of rationalistic prejudice within which I had grown up without knowing it, fell, and the world of faith stood suddenly before me.
> (CWES 1: 262, with alterations)[15]

As we shall see in later chapters, both Reinach and Scheler would go on to influence Edith's later philosophical anthropology.

As well as her philosophical studies she pursued her girlhood interest in German linguistics, life and culture. During these lectures, especially those dealing with 'Hannoverian liberalism': 'I became more conscious here than I had been at home of the virtues of the Prussian character; and I was confirmed in my own Prussian allegiance' (CWES 1: 268).

On empathy

Guided by Husserl she made the choice of the subject for her doctoral dissertation – empathy:

> I had no difficulty on this. In his course on nature and spirit, Husserl had said that an objective outer world could only be experienced intersubjectively, i.e., through a plurality of perceiving individuals who relate in a mutual exchange of information. Accordingly, an experience of other individuals is a prerequisite. To the experience, an application of the work of Theodor Lipps, Husserl gave the name *Einfühlung* [empathy]. What it consists of,

however, he nowhere detailed. Here was a lacuna to be filled; therefore, I wished to examine what empathy might be.

(CWES 1: 271)

This, the Master decreed, would take the form of an analytical dialogue with the work of Theodor Lipps for 'he liked to have his students clarify, in their assignments, the relation of phenomenology to the other significant directions current in philosophy' (CWES 1: 271). When a student objected to this approach (the one adopted in the present work):

> He used to say, with a smile: 'I educate my students to be systematic philosophers and then I'm surprised that they dislike any tasks that have to do with the history of philosophy.'

(CWES 1: 271–272)

Edith spent most of the winter of 1913–14 alone, rising at 6 am and going to bed at midnight, eating little and totally absorbed in her philosophy: 'this excruciating struggle to attain clarity was waged unceasingly inside me, depriving me of rest day and night. At that time I lost the art of sleeping, and it took many years before restful nights were granted to me again' (CWES 1: 272). This affected her mental well-being and she entertained suicidal thoughts during this period. As her views on the subject developed she saw how her own interpretation related to those of Husserl and Lipps:

> What Husserl, judging by his brief indications, thought of as 'empathy' and what Lipps designated as such apparently had little in common. For Lipps it was the concept point-blank at the center of his philosophy; it ruled his aesthetics, ethics, and social philosophy; and it also played a role in his theory of knowledge, logic, and metaphysics.

(CWES 1: 279)

During this, her first major study, she also developed the working method towards writing which she adopted for the rest of her intellectual career: 'Books were of no use to me at all until I had clarified the matter in question by my own effort' (CWES 1: 279). As we shall see shortly, the fruits of this struggle were the foundations for the philosophy which she would develop for the rest of the life – in debt to Husserl and Lipps but by this stage distinctively her own. We shall return to the importance of empathy for her philosophy in a later chapter.

The great war

Her work on her dissertation would soon be interrupted by the outbreak of the Great War in summer 1914. Looking back in 1933 to this prelapsarian time she wrote:

> No one growing up during or since the war can possibly imagine the security in which we assumed ourselves to be living before 1914. Our life was built on an indestructible foundation of peace, stability of ownership of property, and on the permanence of circumstances to which we were accustomed.
>
> (CWES 1: 295)

As with some of the other twentieth-century thinkers we shall explore in this book, the Great War was the watershed that changed all their lives, not least in initiating a deeper concern for the social and political circumstances within which they found themselves. Edith was no exception to this as she described the ending of that era in the *Life* thus:

> So, at four o'clock on the afternoon of July 30, I was seated at my small desk, immersed in Schopenhauer's *The World as Will and Idea*. I intended to go to a lecture at five o'clock. Then came a knock at my door, and Fräulein Scharf and her friend, Fräulein Merk, who was also from Silesia, came in. They told me I could save myself the trouble of going. A notice was posted on the bulletin board that a state of war had been declared and all lectures were suspended. Both of them would be returning home that evening. I slammed shut *The World as Will and Idea*. (Oddly enough, I never took up that particular book again).
>
> (CWES 1: 296–297)

On returning to Breslau one of the first things she did was to register for nursing training telling herself: 'I have no private life anymore, all my energy must be devoted to this great happening. Only when the war is over, if I'm alive then, will I be permitted to think of my private affairs once more' (CWES 1: 299).

Later in the present volume we shall encounter the young Ludwig Wittgenstein and his reaction to the outbreak of the war. Like him, Edith at once gave up her philosophical studies, preferring instead to engage in the war effort. For someone who had written so deeply on the subject of empathy, her accounts of her encounters on the Front with an assortment of characters and situations display her ability to empathize herself into very diverse situations:

> I got the impression that the sick were not used to getting loving attention and that volunteer helpers therefore could find endless opportunities to show their own compassion and love of neighbor in these places of suffering.
>
> (CWES 1: 300)

Returning to Göttingen for the winter semester of 1914–15, she met Roman Ingarden (1893–1970), a young Polish phenomenologist who played a significant role in bringing phenomenology to Poland and with whom she developed one of her closest friendships with a man – well recorded in a fascinating correspondence we shall refer to throughout this book. Her time in Göttingen ended with her passing the state examinations that semester.

Nursing

Having completed her nursing training in Breslau, Edith was summoned to the isolation hospital (lazaretto) in Mährisch-Weisskirchen in April 1915 to nurse soldiers of the Austro-Hungarian army, then an ally of the German Reich (the town was then in the Austro-Hungarian Empire, now present-day Hranice in Czechia, near Olomouc). These isolation hospitals in Austria-Hungary had been set up principally by the Breslau-based Red Cross. The hospital dealt with infections such as cholera, typhoid, diphtheria and venereal diseases such as gonorrhoea. As with Wittgenstein, it was her first close encounter with the rough and tumble of life outside the philosophical circles she had inhabited up to then and, like the Austrian, she was filled with censorious disgust for the lewd and rowdy behaviour of those she worked with. As she wrote in the *Life* after one such encounter:

> Nothing had happened to me, nor had anyone said even so much as one improper word to me. But still trembling from revulsion, I was indignant that such behavior could go on under the very roof that harbored such critically ill persons.
>
> (CWES 1: 331)

Again, like Wittgenstein, this was also her first encounter with the diverse nations of the Austro-Hungarian Empire: Germans, Czechs, Slovaks, Slovenes, Poles, Ruthenians, Hungarians, Romanians, Romanies and Italians. The battle of Tarnow and Gorlice (in which Wittgenstein participated) in May 1915 signalled the change of the theatre of war from the Carpathians to Poland. From this time on the Weisskirchen hospital received fewer diseased patients and more who had been wounded in combat. After several months of stressful work treating these patients (including a colourful high-ranking Polish cavalry officer whom she memorably describes in her *Life* as insisting on being treated naked except for his pince-nez) Stein tussled with the idea of taking leave. Always worried that this was an 'egotistical reaction', she wondered:

> Repeatedly I was plagued by the thought: was it wise, after all, to interrupt my intellectual work so long when, actually, there now was an abundance of personnel available for the kind of work I was doing? On the other hand, I suspected I might be having an egotistical reaction.
>
> (CWES 1: 365)[16]

In early autumn 1915 she eventually returned to Breslau to finish her teaching studies and whilst there she heard in October that the Weisskirchen hospital had been closed. She put herself at the disposal of the Red Cross but was not called upon for service again.

Whether she had become disillusioned with the 'war effort' she doesn't reveal (writing in 1933 this was probably wise) but the closure of the hospital seemed to free her troubled conscience enabling her to return to philosophical work (again, the parallels with Wittgenstein are striking, who at the same time after his war service and capture was preparing the last drafts of his *Tractatus Logico-Philosophicus*. We shall return to this later in the book). Accordingly, back in Breslau she could return to her analysis of empathy as begun before the war. She described her research methods, derived from Husserl, at this time as:

> Next to the fine sheets upon which the running text was set down, I always kept a piece of paper on which to make notes of the related questions which occurred to me in this manner. After all, they would have to be treated in their proper place. Nevertheless, page after page was filled. The writing would bring a rosy glow to my face, and an unfamiliar feeling of happiness surged through me.
>
> (CWES 1: 379)

In winter 1915–16 she paid a return visit to Göttingen. As well as social meetings this afforded her an opportunity to share the drafts of her thesis with 'the Master' at his house in the Hohen Weg. Husserl was happy with her progress but his unexpected appointment as professor at Freiburg-im-Breisgau in the Black Forest in early 1916 meant that her plan to be examined by him at Göttingen had to be altered so that she could submit at Freiburg instead.

As she continued her studies she was asked by the Principal of the Viktoriaschule in Breslau if she would act as a classics teacher. She accepted and would continue this life as an academic researcher depending upon income from teaching right up to her entry into religious life in the 1930s.

An interrupted life

At this point Part One of the *Life*, begun in 1933, suddenly ends with her on a train with Hans Lipps (1889–1941) going to Leipzig before she heads over to Freiburg for her doctoral examination with Husserl. Writing in 1935 Edith had by this time entered religious life and was devoting her efforts to her longest work, *Endliches und Ewiges Sein* (*Finite and Eternal Being*). The account was resumed in 1939 after Stein had fled to Echt in the Netherlands following persecution in Germany. Stein worked barely four months on the continuation finishing in April 1939.

Part Two, as stated, resumes with her journey to Freiburg for the examination of her thesis by Husserl. On her way to Freiburg she interrupted her journey to visit Pauline Reinach in Frankfurt. Here an important incident happened in the cathedral which was to have a lasting effect on her:

> We stopped in at the cathedral for a few minutes; and, while we looked around in respectful silence, a woman carrying a market basket came in and knelt down in one of the pews to pray briefly. This was something entirely new to me. To the synagogues or to the Protestant churches which I had visited, one went only for services. But here was someone interrupting her everyday shopping errands to come into this church, although no other person was in it, as though she were here for an intimate conversation. I could never forget that.
>
> (CWES 1: 403)

The Examination was set for the evening of 3 August 1916 which she passed *summa cum laude* (highest grade). This summer was also the occasion of her first meeting with the young Martin Heidegger (1889–1976) and his future wife:

> I liked Heidegger very much that evening. As long as there was no mention of philosophy, he was quiet and unassuming; but as soon as a philosophical question popped up he was very animated.
>
> (CWES 1: 411)

We shall return to her complicated and troubled relationship with him later. After her successful examination it was agreed that she might become Husserl's 'research assistant', on hearing that the Master approved of this suggestion she wrote: 'I do not know which one of us was more elated. We were like a young couple at the moment of their betrothal' (CWES 1: 413). However, as researchers such as Mary Catherine Baseheart, Marianne Sawicki and Antonio Colcagno have shown, the relationship (like her one with Heidegger) was complicated and multi-layered. For many years she had been described as Husserl's secretary, yet as Sawicki has clearly demonstrated, she was far more proactive in the relationship than this and she often took a decisive role creating, in many instances, coherent texts from Husserl's many scattered and diffuse notes (see *inter alia* Baseheart 1997, Sawicki 1997 and Calcagno 2007). At this point the manuscript of the *Life* ends abruptly after her viva as she visits Frau Reinach in Göttingen on her way back to Breslau.

The aftermath of the war

Having been accepted as Husserl's assistant she finished her teaching duties in Breslau in September 1916 with the intention of returning to Freiburg. Spring 1917 saw the publication of Chapters 2–4 of her dissertation under the title *Zum Problem der Einfühlung* (*On the Problem of Empathy*, hereafter *Empathy*) in Halle, Germany. This is the title it bears today, sadly the rest of the thesis is lost.

Frustrated with Husserl's idiosyncratic practices, Edith found it increasingly difficult to continue as his assistant. As mentioned above, scholarly work in the past two decades has convincingly demonstrated that Stein had significant creative input into the formulation of Husserl's *Ideen II and III* which went way beyond merely 'secretarial' duties. As the biographers mentioned above argue, this would be one of the many occasions when Edith clearly suffered from the gender stereotypes of her contemporaries and fellow academics. In a letter to Ingarden she describes one of these 'differences of opinion' with the Master:

> When the Master recently favoured me with a whole set of directions regarding the handling of his manuscripts (in a most friendly manner, but I simply cannot bear that kind of thing), I explained to him (also, of course, in a most friendly manner) that such a procedure 1) is impossible, in principle; 2) if at all valid, could be set up that way for his use only by himself; and that 3) I am especially unsuited for it, and can only continue with occupation if I do something original on the side.
>
> (CWES 5: Letter 19)

Her growing frustration with the arrangement led to her finally resigning her position in 1917, as she wrote in a letter to Ingarden in February 1918:

> The Master has graciously accepted my resignation. His letter was most friendly – though not without a somewhat reproachful undertone. So now

I am free, and I believe it is good that I am, even if, for the moment, I am not exactly happy.

(CWES 5: Letter 20)

In another letter to Fritz Kaufmann in March 1918 she records how difficult it had been working with Husserl, especially as he often expected her simply to undertake menial tasks, 'putting manuscripts in order' without acknowledging her own original contributions to the development of phenomenology (CWES 5: Letter 21).

This also helps explain why her application to teach at Freiburg (her *Habilitation*) was rejected in 1919. Husserl himself, despite the debt he owed to her, was hardly encouraging, writing in summary: 'should the academic profession become open to women, I would recommend Dr Stein immediately and most warmly for qualification as a university lecturer' (see Neyer 1999: 30). Later attempts to gain a teaching position at other universities would meet with a similar reception. This gendered aspect to the reception of her philosophical work is something we shall return to in a later chapter.

As we move from the narrative contained in *Life in the Jewish Family* we encounter the accounts of her early biographers such as Mother Teresia Renata de Spiritu Sancto (Posselt, who had been Edith's Novice Mistress) and the testimony of her letters as they explore the events leading to her conversion to Christianity.[17] We shall explore this for the remainder of this chapter before pausing the biographical narrative to begin our exploration of key themes from her philosophical anthropology in the first part of the book.

Conversion

We have already mentioned the impact that the encounter in the Frankfurt church had had on Edith in 1917 during this impressionable time as she finally finished her doctorate and was recovering from her war experiences. Another of these significant events recorded by her occurred shortly afterwards in 1918 when Edith helped the widow Anne Reinach (1884–1953, née Stettenheimer) of her friend and mentor, Adolf Reinach (who had been killed in action in 1917), to sort out his papers. Edith expected her mentor's widow would be devastated by her loss. Instead, as the Reinachs had become Christians not long before Adolf's death, Anna displayed, in Edith's eyes, such courage and acceptance in her bereavement so as to again force the 'blinkers' from her 'rationalistic' prejudices. Stein marvelled at how stoically Frau Reinach accepted her husband's death in the hope of the resurrection (see Posselt 1957: 59). As she would later tell her first biographer, Mother Teresia Renata de Spiritu Sancto:

> This was then my first encounter with the Cross and the divine strength which it shares with its bearers. I saw for the first time before my very eyes the Church, born of Christ's redemptive suffering, victorious over the sting of death. It was the moment in which my unbelief was shattered, Judaism paled, and Christ streamed out upon me: Christ in the mystery of the Cross.
> (Posselt 1957: 59)

'Which was why', she added in this conversation with Fr Hirschmann shortly before her death, 'in my clothing for religious life I could have no other wish than to be called "of the cross" in the Order' (Posselt 1957: 49–50).

By now we are probably getting used to the kaleidoscopic pictures refracted around our subject. Accordingly, it should be no surprise that there are at least three versions of the events that led to her conversion. The first and most influential is from Posselt's biography. According to this narrative the key moment seemed to have occurred in 1921 when she stayed at the home of her Göttingen friends, the Conrad-Martiuses, near Bergzabern in the Black Forest. Posselt states it thus:

> It happened, however, that during one of these holiday visits the married couple had to go out. Before they left Frau Conrad-Martius took her friend over to the book case and invited her to choose as she pleased. They were all at her disposal. Edith herself recounts: 'I picked at random and took out a large volume. It bore the title: "The Life of St. Teresa of Avila" written by herself. I began to read, was at once captivated, and did not stop until I reached the end. As I closed the book, I said to myself: "That is the truth".'
> (Posselt 1957: 55–6)

This, then, is the 'classic' account of the conversion, as promulgated by Posselt and her first biographers. However, from Pauline Reinach (1879–1974), sister of Adolf,[18] we have another account made in her submission for Edith's canonization process in August 1965. Here she recounted:

> In the summer of 1921, at the end of her visit to us, myself and my sister-in-law asked the Servant of God to choose a book from our library. She chose a biography of Teresa of Avila, written by herself. Of this detail I am absolutely certain.
>
> (*Sacra Congregatio pro causis sanctorum, Canonisationis servae Dei Teresiae Benedictae a Cruce*, Rome 1983, Vol. 3, p.437, para 1066)

She continued that she first heard of Edith finding the Teresa book in the Conrad-Martius house in Posselt's (1957) biography, a story which she had never heard before (see ESGA 3: 11).[19]

Yet another account of her conversion by her later Jesuit confessor, Erich Przywara, emphasizes the role that an early reading of St Ignatius Loyola's *Spiritual Exercises* had on the spiritually questing young soul (see Przywara 1955: 24 and O'Meara 2002: 121).

These three differing accounts of Edith's conversion are a good demonstration of the refracted images of the woman the present book is exploring. However, Posselt's original description of Edith's conversion after having read Teresa of Avila's *Life* in one sitting remains the most quoted containing one of the most memorable scenes in that account:

> Day was breaking. Edith hardly noticed it. God's hand was upon her and she did not turn from him. In the morning she went into the town to buy two things: a Catholic catechism and a missal.
>
> (Posselt 2005: 63)

Whatever happened in that early post-war period following her departure from Freiburg, Edith's life was clearly 'turned upside-down' and shortly afterwards on 1 January 1922 (the Feast of the Circumcision) she would be baptised into the Catholic church at the parish church at Bergzabern with her friend and colleague Hedwig Conrad-Martius as her sponsor and god-parent.

The events leading up to her baptism have the usual Steinian mix of audacity and simplicity. Convinced that she was now ready to receive baptism she had attended the mass at the parish church of Bergzabern (St Martin's) unannounced. Posselt recounts the story thus in Edith's own words:

> Nothing was strange to me. Thanks to my previous study, I understood even the smallest ceremonies. The priest, a saintly-looking old man, went to the altar and offered the holy sacrifice reverently and devoutly. After mass I waited until he made his thanksgiving. I followed him to the presbytery and asked him without more ado for baptism. He looked astonished and answered that one had to be prepared before being received into the Church. 'How long have you been receiving instruction and who has been giving it?' The only reply I could make was, 'Please, your reverence, test my knowledge.'
> (Posselt 2005: 64)

This priest, the seventy-year-old Fr Eugen Breitling, satisfied with her answers, was able to arrange the baptism (see Posselt 2005: 239). The baptism was followed by her first communion on 2 January and finally by confirmation on 2 February that year (the Feast of the Presentation) administered by Bishop Ludwig Sebastian in his private chapel in Speyer. At her baptism she had taken two new Christian names: Theresia and Hedwig. The former in reverence to her spiritual sponsor, St Teresa of Avila, the latter in appreciation of her earthly sponsor, Hedwig Conrad-Martius, her old philosophical friend.

Her decision was a great blow to her family, especially her mother. Posselt gives the unidentified reactions of two of her family members:

> We were all dumbfounded by the news and did not know whether to be more astonished at Edith or at our mother's behavior. Edith's step was incomprehensible to us all. We knew Catholicism only as it was to be found in the lowest social class of our East-Silesian homeland and thought Catholicism merely consisted in groveling on one's knees and kissing the priest's toe. We simply could not conceive how our Edith's lofty spirit could demean itself to this superstitious sect.
> (Posselt 1957: 57)

Soon thereafter, Edith took as her spiritual guide Canon Joseph Schwind (1851–1927), Vicar General of the Diocese of Speyer, and, at his suggestion, she accepted a position at St. Magdalena's, a Dominican Sisters' training institute for women teachers, located at Speyer. She entered the training institute in Easter 1923 and stayed until March 1931. Amongst her other duties she taught German literature to the students there living a quasi-monastic life, including taking private vows of poverty, chastity and obedience. As one of the Dominican sisters of Speyer later recalled to Posselt reflecting on her work there:

> Her educational work was very fruitful; she quickly won the hearts of her pupils. To all of us she was a shining example whose effect we still feel today. In humility and simplicity, almost unheard and unnoticed, she went quietly about her duties, always serenely friendly and accessible to anyone who wanted her help. And not a few did.
>
> (Posselt 2005: 66–67)

At St. Magdalena's, she was able to live with the sisters rather than among the students, living in the gatehouse just outside the enclosure. Meanwhile, Canon Schwind, finding it difficult to answer all her theological questions, introduced her to Erich Przywara. Schwind died suddenly on 17 September 1927. Writing in her obituary of him, Edith paid fulsome tribute to his life and work:

> More than once Cardinal Newman has emphasized that it is relatively easy for us to develop one aspect of our Christian life, strictness, gentleness, seriousness or cheerfulness. But truly Christian perfection is only attained when these contrasted virtues are exercised in unison. Canon Schwind satisfied this condition in full measure.
>
> (Posselt 2005: 77)

In her words of his work as a spiritual director Edith enunciated her own ideal of that role and encapsulated how many would later describe her own work as a spiritual director:

> The way he led the soul was calm, sure and collected, underpinned with wise insight into human nature and decades-long experience of such soul-guidance – at the same time retaining a sacred respect for the working of God in the soul whilst being sensitive yet bold.
>
> (Posselt 1957: 69)[20]

Ceterum censeo

Writing to her former Göttingen colleague, Fritz Kaufmann, to explain her new situation in 1925 Edith shared some moving words as to how she now found her new life:

> For all of three years now I have been living behind the sheltering walls of a convent, at heart – and this I may surely say without any presumption – like a real nun, even though I wear no veil and am not bound by vows or enclosure. Nor, for the present, may I think of contracting such a bond …
>
> I found the place where there is rest and peace for all restless hearts. How that happened is something you will allow me to be silent about today. I am not shy speaking about it and will surely talk to you about it too at the right time, but that is something that must 'arise' itself; I cannot 'report' on it.
>
> (CWES 5: Letter 38a, 13.9.25)[21]

Although she was reluctant to put into words (*'secretum meum mihi'*) there is a sense that by the early 1920s as she approached her mid-thirties, her life had entered a new phase as she began to put behind her the struggles of student years. Some commentators, such as McIntyre (2006), make a clear delineation between her writings pre-conversion and post-conversion; others prefer to see the continuity between the two (see, for example, Betschart 2013). What hopefully will emerge in the present book is how the philosophical foundations laid by her study of phenomenology could have prepared Edith to step into the 'world of faith' that she lived after 1922. Accordingly, biographically, I propose to pause the account of Edith's life at this point as we embark upon the first half of the book looking at her philosophical anthropology. This will allow us at the beginning of the Second Part, as we explore her 'Life Philosophy', to pick up the narrative as she responded to the growing anti-Semitism of 1930s Nazi Germany and journeyed into convent life.

Before we embark upon that exploration I would like to point out one last element of Stein's life as she lived it at this time. This she described as her *ceterum censeo* from the little phrase that Cato used to conclude his speeches to the Roman Senate (it translates as 'furthermore, in my opinion' and was followed by the repeated phrase 'Carthage must be destroyed').[22] Writing to Sr Adelgundis Jaegerschmid in April 1931 about her work as a pedagogue and lecturer she suggested that what lay behind all this work was a certain little '*ceterum censeo*' or motto theme. Here she responded to Sr Jaegerschimd's suggestion that she leave out all reference to the 'supernatural' (*das Übernatürliche*) in some of her lectures:

> But if I could not speak about that, [the supernatural] I would probably not mount a lecturer's platform at all. Basically, it is always a small, simple truth that I have to express: *How to go about living at the Lord's hand.* Then when people demand something else from me and propose very clever themes that are very foreign to me, I can take them only as an introduction in order to arrive at my '*ceterum censeo*.' Perhaps that is a very reprehensible method. But my entire activity as lecturer has hit me like an avalanche, so that I have been unable as yet to reflect on it in principle. Most likely, I will have to do that some time.
>
> (CWES 5: Letter 89, 28.4.31)[23]

This decade from her conversion until entering convent life in 1933 saw her develop a new way of living, a vocation even, that was in response to the unique circumstances within which she now found herself: a German Jew who had now left her religion; a single, laywoman with no 'official' status within the Catholic Church, an acknowledged member of the Göttingen phenomenological circle who, unlike her male colleagues, was unable to find a university position because of her gender and a seeker of truth who wanted to meld together the various strands of her life. Accordingly, this decade would see her first steps in trying to bring together the various strands of her life, not least in what she would regard as an 'intellectual apostolate' to bring the teachings of the church, as exemplified in the writings of thinkers such as St Thomas Aquinas and St John Henry Newman, to the contemporary twentieth-century philosophical world. This was marked initially by a series of notable translations of the works of Aquinas and Newman (some the first in German), in particular Aquinas' *Disputed Questions* (for which she also provided a lexicon of contemporary philosophical terms) and Newman's *Letters* and the *Idea of the University* (see ESGA 21–27). This work, initiated by her contact with Erich Przywara, would be supplemented at this time by lectures and conferences, many of which explored the role of women in contemporary society which we shall return to later. Her renewed attempts to gain a university post resulted in the writing of 'Potency and Act', later to become her magnum opus 'Finite and Eternal Being'. In many ways, then, despite not having a university post, this would be one of the most philosophically fruitful periods of her life. Concerning this 'intellectual apostolate' she wrote in a letter during February 1928 to Callista Kopf that:

> That it is possible to worship God by doing scholarly research is something I learned, actually, only when I was busy with [the translation of] St. Thomas [Aquinas' *Quaestiones de Veritate* from Latin into German] ….Only thereafter could I decide to resume serious scholarly research. Immediately before, and for a good while after my conversion, I was of the opinion that to lead a religious life meant one had to give up all that was secular and to live totally immersed in thoughts of the Divine. But gradually I realized that something else is asked of us in this world and that, even in the contemplative life, one may not sever the connection with the world. I even believe that the deeper one is drawn into God, the more one must 'go out of oneself'(*aus sich herausgehen*); that is, one must go to the world in order to carry the divine life into it (*in die Welt hinein, um das göttliche Leben in sie hineinzutragen*).
>
> (CWES 5: Letter 45, 12.2.28, see also ESGA 2: Letter 60)

This, then, was her recipe for the life of an intellectual apostolate of 'contemplation in action' which we shall explore in the following chapters as we examine how she developed an anthropology that aimed to harmonize her phenomenological studies with the revelations of faith during these fruitful years. For, as she stated in 1928, she never believed that religion 'is something to be relegated to a quiet corner or for a few festive hours', but rather, it should form 'the root and ground of all life (*Wurzel und Grund alles Lebens sein*)' (CWES 5: Letter 45). It is to this 'root and ground', her spiritual and philosophical anthropology, we shall turn to next.

2
Husserl's revolution

Introduction

On encountering Stein's thought for the first time one insuperable obstacle arises for many readers. That is, that much of her early writing is framed within the Husserlian/phenomenological school as a conscious reaction to the preceding 250 years of modern European philosophy. Consequently, we require two acts to understand her thought – we need first to have a mental grasp of that tradition and secondly we need to understand why Husserl's 'revolution' is so important for Stein's thought and the contemporary world. This is made more complicated for the average Anglophone reader brought up in the British Empirical tradition of John Locke, George Berkeley, David Hume, etc., but perhaps unaware of the wider 'continental' tradition that culminated in the early nineteenth century with the writings of Immanuel Kant, the interpretation of whom dominated philosophical discussion in the Germanophone lands for the next century, not least as to what exactly the sage of Königsberg had actually meant. Accordingly, before we look at Edith's unique contribution to that debate it may be helpful to review this tradition and how it was interpreted by Husserl and his followers. To this end I shall concentrate on Husserl's last writings (in particular, *The Crisis in Philosophy*), paying special attention to his reaction to psychology and what he terms 'psychologism' in contemporary philosophical writing.

The crisis

'The Crisis of European Sciences and Transcendental Phenomenology' was the last work that Husserl was working on at his death.[1] David Carr suggests (Husserl 1970: 155) that as his *Cartesian Meditations* had not been published at this point the *Krisis* was to be Husserl's 'definitive introduction to phenomenology' and perhaps the final summation of his thought. Alfred Schutz remembered that 'in the last conversation which the writer had the good fortune of having with Husserl, he repeatedly designated this series of essays as the summary and the crowning achievement of his life work' (Schutz 1940: 165). Although Husserl's thought had famously progressed from the time when Edith had first encountered it in 1913, for contemporary readers *Krisis* thus offers a lasting final survey of Husserl's thought, the direction he wanted to take it and the direction it did in fact take when read and interpreted by influential phenomenologists of the succeeding philosophical generation such as Maurice Merleau-Ponty.[2]

The *Krisis* arose from two sets of original lectures, one given in Prague in 1935 for the *Cercle Philosophique de Prague* and titled 'The Crisis of European Sciences and Psychology' and the other given in May 1935 to the *Wiener Kulturband* in Vienna and titled 'Philosophy and the Crisis of European Humanity'. Both sets of lectures and the final book all describe a 'crisis' in Western culture which immediately draws the attention of the contemporary reader (see Husserl 1970: 193). Husserl's crisis, as described in these lectures, was an interconnected one of European culture, philosophy and Europe itself: 'the European nations are sick, Europe itself, it is said, is in crisis' (Husserl 1970: 270). It is strange to read these words now after recent turmoil within Europe. Just as Husserl addressed his audience in 1930s Prague and Vienna, three years before their invasion by Nazi Germany, so we once again seem to be asking the searching questions about our present European culture as we step into the next uncertain decade of the twenty-first century. For Husserl, Europe, like for so many of the philosophers we shall refer to in this book (including Edith), is the Europe of philosophical thought and primarily that of Greek philosophical thought which for Husserl shapes the contemporary and distinctive 'European' outlook.

What then, he asks, is this *'geistige Gestalt Europas'* – the intellectual shape or pattern of Europe (Husserl 1954: 319)? This for Husserl begins in Greece in the sixth-/seventh-century BCE which for him is the 'spiritual birthplace' (*geistige Geburtsstätte*) of Europe (Husserl 1954: 276). For at this point a new 'mental pattern' (*geistige Gebilde*) fell into place that would become known as 'philosophy' (Husserl 1954: 321). One of its distinctive qualities would be that it emerged as a 'universal science': 'an all-encompassing science of all that is, bound by ideas of universal validity' (Husserl 1954: 321). This 'philosophy' is then an early understanding of a 'universal science' (*universale Wissenschaft*). This universalizing mentality is the birth of our modern 'scientific' viewpoint: 'the universal science, of the oneness of all that is' (Husserl 1954: 321):[3]

> Soon the interest in the All, and thus the question of the all-encompassing becoming and being in becoming, begins to particularize itself according to the general forms and regions of being, and thus philosophy, the one science, branches out into many particular sciences.
>
> (Husserl 1970: 276)

Thus, the origin of philosophy, and with it the following scientific disciplines, is for Husserl the 'original phenomenon of Europe's mind' (*'Urphänomen der geistigen Europas'*) (Husserl 1954: 321). This transformation of outlook will also transform humanity into 'a new type of humanity' (*'einem neuen Mensch'*) (Husserl 1954: 322) – of which we, today, are the inheritors. This new sort of humanity is thus 'one which living in finitude, lives toward poles of infinity' (Husserl 1970: 277). The emergence of this perception is literally a 'revolution' (Husserl 1970: 279) to which we are all heirs.[4]

From this is born the goal of an 'objective science' whereby 'that which is, not as experienced and verified by *particular* persons and civilizations, as it is experienced and can be validated through experience by them, but rather, that which is – for *all conceivable* civilizations' (Husserl 1970: 321). From then on 'a particular kind of motivation is privileged, which is designated by the expression "theoretical interest in objectively real being"' (Husserl 1970: 319).

This 'scientific' attitude can be contrasted, for Husserl, with the 'natural attitude' by which we encounter the world on a day-to-day basis: 'natural life can be characterized as a life naively, straightforwardly directed at the world, the world being always in a certain sense consciously present as a universal horizon' (Husserl 1970: 281). For the 'natural' person is 'directed toward the world in all his concerns and activities. The field of his life and his work is the surrounding world spread out spatiotemporally around him, of which he counts himself a part' (Husserl 1970: 292).[5] Thus, this 'natural attitude' can be contrasted with the scientific 'theoretical attitude' that arises from philosophical *theōria* (Husserl 1970: 282).

Rationalism as recently invented

In Husserl's schema the original Greek vision is thus thwarted at the dawn of the modern world by the scientific or rational/empirical 'turn' of the early modern period for he sees this 'scientific objectification' as a key element in fomenting the present 'crisis': 'the stage of development of *ratio* represented by the rationalism of the Age of Enlightenment was a mistake, though certainly an understandable one' (Husserl 1970: 290). However, he does not see a way out of our problems lying in a return to an irrationalism or something like the 'natural attitude' (a solution we shall explore in a later chapter when we look at the work of Friedrich Nietzsche, Sigmund Freud and Carl Jung). Rather, he feels that the problem arises from a distortion of the original Greek 'theorising attitude' that evolves in the modern world from the eighteenth century onwards. Therefore, he would not have us reject rationalism but rather *rationalism as recently invented* for, he claims, that the phenomenological method he is proposing will take us back to the clarity of Greece and the first arising of the theoretical outlook: 'the primordial Greek sense [of the theoretical] which in the classical period of Greek philosophy had become an ideal, still requires, to be sure, much clarification through self-reflection' (Husserl 1970: 290).

Therefore, Husserl sees phenomenology as a source of 'purification' of reason, especially after the false path he understands it took in the modern era. In this respect he does not want his philosophy to embrace any sort of 'irrationalism' which he saw as a key threat to both the philosophical and political climate of Europe: 'antirationalism and anti-intellectualism were everywhere, and not merely "in the air"; they were explicit elements of Nazi ideology and propaganda. Husserl's blanket indictment gives expression to a clear link in his mind between philosophical antirationalism and political antirationalism' (Husserl 1970: xxvii). In the Prague lecture of 1935 he had connected this antirationalism with an undermining of the ideal of a 'Europe of the spirit':

> The general faith in the idea and the practical ideal of Europe, that of a harmonious unity of the life of nations with its sources in the rational spirit, has been undermined. At present we are faced with the imminent danger of the extinction of philosophy in this sense, and with it necessarily the extinction of a Europe founded on the spirit of truth.
>
> (Husserl 1970: xxvii)

Yet, he argues, does not such antirationalism use rational arguments to convince us? Rather than an irrationalism, might it better just be called 'a narrow-minded and bad rationalism' (Husserl 1970: 16) – 'the rationality of "lazy reason" which evades the struggle to clarify the ultimate data.'

So his final philosophical polemics are two-pronged. On the one hand he attacks resurgent European 'antirationalism' and on the other the distorted 'rationalism' that arose in Europe from the Renaissance onwards reaching its apex in the eighteenth century. This new rationalism as recently invented he characterizes as a *naïveté*, in particular: 'the most general title for this *naïveté* is objectivism (*Objektivismus*), taking the form of various types of naturalism, of the naturalization of the spirit (*der Naturalisierung des Geistes*)' (Husserl 1970: 292/1954: 339).[6]

As we shall see, Husserl understood Kant as having tried to overcome this naive objectivity but he believed the sage of Königsberg had failed to go far enough. Where Kant stopped would therefore be the territory for Husserl's revolution, he would go to the roots of the issue and find the very basis upon which this objective naivety rested. His new reflexivity, as outlined in his phenomenological approach, will thus not only be a new start for philosophy but also a new start for 'European humanity' (Husserl 1970: 292).

The 'objectification' of nature taken over by modern 'reason' thus includes an objectification of the spirit for 'the method of natural science must also disclose the secrets of the spirit' (Husserl 1970: 294).[7] This is the origin of our modern dualist 'psycho-physical picture of the world' (Husserl 1954: 341) which leads to universal objectification, including the spirit if it can:

> One causality, simply split into two sectors, encompasses the one world; the sense of rational explanation is everywhere the same, yet in such a way that all explanation of the spirit, if it is to be the sole and thus universal philosophical explanation, leads back to the physical.
>
> (Husserl 1970: 294)

As he piquantly puts it: 'merely fact-minded sciences make merely fact-minded people' (Husserl 1970: 6).[8] Such fact-minded sciences, and the fact-minded people they produce, cannot, he suggests, answer the existential and deeper philosophical hunger of the modern world (Husserl 1970: 6).

Thus, 'reason as recently invented', had, he suggests (leaning heavily here on the philosophical developments of his pupils Martin Heidegger and Hans-Georg Gadamer), fallen into error by dissociating itself from questions of being. Once this dissociation has happened after the Renaissance the key question for philosophy (and for all sciences) becomes: 'are reason and being to be separated where knowing reason decides what being is?'[9] In contrast to this separation, the phenomenological method would present an approach to *Geist* that provides a 'pure and self-enclosed explanatory enquiry into the spirit' (Husserl 1970: 294).[10]

For Husserl, then, one of the main aims of the philosopher is to root out prejudice and in this case he will root out the philosophical prejudices that lie at the heart of modern Western philosophy:

> If [the philosopher] is to be one who thinks for themselves (*selbstdenker*), an autonomous philosopher with the will to liberate themselves from all prejudices, they must have the insight that all the things they take for granted are prejudices, that all prejudices are obscurities arising out of a sedimentation of tradition.
>
> (Husserl 1970: 72)[11]

And this prejudice is the 'objectivism' of the modern rational/scientific viewpoint that brooks no other perspective:

The objectivism, or this psychophysical world conception, in spite of its apparent obviousness, is naively one-sided and has constantly failed to be understood as such. The reality of mind as a supposed real annex to bodies, its supposed spatiotemporal being within nature, is an absurdity.

(Husserl 1970: 294)

For, 'someone who is raised on natural science takes it for granted that everything merely subjective must be excluded and that the natural-scientific method, exhibiting itself in subjective manners of representation, determines objectively' (Husserl 1970: 295). For, even in psychology, is this 'supposed objectivity' sought, which, he calls in these last writings an 'absurdity'.

Descartes and deception

How then did the 'theoretical outlook' of the Greeks become the distorted 'rationalism' of the modern world? This Husserl traces in detail within his final writing and it is worth outlining this analysis if we are to make sense of Stein's later writing on the subject of personhood, much of which can be seen, like Husserl's, as a reaction to the European philosophical wave that arose from Descartes onwards.

Accordingly, one of his main tasks in *Krisis* is to uncover the prejudices of modern philosophy, especially the 'psychologism' of Descartes and Locke, thereby aiming to establish a 'philosophy without prejudice' (Husserl 1970: 86). In this respect the key to understanding this prejudice comes from Franz Brentano's (1838–1917) return to the 'intentionality' at the heart of human interaction with the world. Descartes' mistake, and the 'original sin' of modern philosophy, for Husserl was to have overlooked this intentionality as he formulated his first investigations of the human psyche:

> How is the life of the soul, which is through and through a life of consciousness, the intentional life of the 'I', which has objects of which it is conscious, deals with them through knowing, valuing, etc. – how is it supposed to be seriously investigated if intentionality is overlooked? How can the problems of reason be grasped at all?
>
> (Husserl 1970: 85)[12]

Descartes' radicalism lies for Husserl in the fact that his scepticism, his 'epoché', would be total: 'encompassing all sciences, including mathematics and the experience of the "life-world"' (Husserl 1970: 76). The radicality of such an epoché means that Descartes moves beyond the Greek scepticism of a Gorgias or a Protagoras to question 'being' itself:

> If I refrain from taking any position on the being or non-being of the world, if I deny myself every ontic validity related to the world, not every ontic validity is prohibited for me within this epoché.
>
> (Husserl 1970: 79)

Therefore the only valid onticity left is the questioning 'I': 'I, the I carrying out the epoché, am not included in the realm of objects, but rather am excluded in principle' (Husserl 1970: 77).[13] Yet, Husserl's main critique of Descartes is that in committing the 'original sin' of modern philosophy he does not *bracket the questioning 'I' too*. It is philosophically insufficient, Husserl suggests, not to examine sufficiently the questioning *ego* of the *cogito ergo sum*: 'for within this self-evidence a great deal is comprised. A more concrete version of the self-evident statement *sum cogitans* is: *ego cogito – cogitata qua cogitate*. This takes in all *cogitations*, individual ones as their flowing synthesis into the universal unity of one *cogitation*' (Husserl 1970: 77).

Descartes, then, has gone too far, or rather has assumed too much. In this case the already existing distinction between a pure '*ego*' and an objective indifferent world: 'is Descartes here not dominated in advance by the Galilean certainty of a universal and absolutely pure world of physical bodies, with the distinction between the merely sensibly experienceable and the mathematical, which is a matter of pure thinking?' (Husserl 1970: 79) for 'does he not already take it for granted that sensibility points to a realm of what is in-itself, but that it can deceive us; and that there must be a rational way of resolving this [deception] and of knowing what is in-itself with mathematical rationality?' (Husserl 1970: 79).

From hereon, after Descartes, a new form of philosophizing thus arises that 'seeks its ultimate foundations in the subjective' (Husserl 1970: 81). Descartes has removed the '*ego*' from 'all that is in the world' such that the '*ego*' cannot be part of what is considered in the world (Husserl 1970: 82), this '*ego*', 'remained hidden to Descartes' with regard to 'what acts, what capacities, belong to it and what it brings about as intentional accomplishment, through these acts and capacities' (Husserl 1970: 82). And this, Husserl supposes, will be the future task to be carried out by his phenomenology.

Therefore, 'in the end, behind the psychological-epistemological problems, do we not find the problems of the "*ego*" of the Cartesian epoché, touched upon but not grasped by Descartes?' (Husserl 1970: 85–6).[14]

The vacuum created by Descartes' 'ego' is filled by Locke's 'ideas' which are then transferred to Berkeley and Hume, thus leaving it to Kant to bridge the growing divide between 'rational logicians' and 'empiricists'. Following Descartes then, Husserl supposes we see a split in European philosophy between what he calls the 'transcendentalism' (or better, perhaps 'ideaism' of Locke, Berkeley and Hume, the 'empirical school', fatally flawed for Husserl by its supposed psychologism), and the Continental rational lineage of Malebranche, Spinoza and Leibniz which will ultimately lead to Kant, 'the turning point' (Husserl 1970: 83).

For Locke, for example, 'only what inner self-experience shows, only our "ideas" are immediately, self-evidently given. Everything in the external world is inferred' (Husserl 1970: 84). This being brought out in Locke's famous analogy of the 'tabula rasa'. Locke's concentration on the 'sense data' as a source of knowledge relegates 'bodies in the external world' to a secondary position (Husserl 1970: 85). Following Locke 'this data-sensationalism, together with the doctrine of outer and inner sense, dominates psychology and the theory of knowledge for centuries' (Husserl 1970: 85). Throughout, as this psychological divide develops, he suggests that we continually find lurking behind it Descartes' 'original sin' of ignoring the intentional 'I': 'In the end, behind the psychological-epistemological problems, do we not find the problems of the "ego" of the Cartesian epoché, touched upon but not grasped by Descartes?' (Husserl 1970: 85/6).

Therefore, Husserl's main disagreement with the empirical approach is that the untouched pure '*ego*' remains untouched by reflection:

How is the life of the soul (*Seelenleben*),[15] what is through and through a life of consciousness (*Bewusstseinsleben*), the intentional life of the 'I' (*intentionales Leben des Ich*) – which has objects of which it is conscious, deals with them through knowing, valuing etc. – how is it supposed to be seriously investigated if intentionality is overlooked?

(Husserl 1970: 85/1954: 88)

The sage of Königsberg

Therefore, following Husserl's analysis, the growing 'transcendentalism' of Hume is what will awaken Kant from his 'dogmatic slumber'. For Husserl, Hume's problem is that his ideation has replaced the 'life-world' which presents itself without Hume needing to rely on Locke's or Berkeley's 'ideas'. Thus in Hume we find that 'the ontic meaning (*Seinsinn*) of the pre-given life-world (*Lebenswelt*) is a subjective structure (*Gebilde*), it is the achievement of experiencing, pre-scientific life' (Husserl 1970: 69) – that is, 'the world within whose obvious validity of being the activities and dealings of humanity untouched by science can take place' (Husserl 1970: 68).

Although Kant famously reacts against this position, Husserl argues that he doesn't go far enough. Like Descartes, Kant fails to address the intentionality that lies behind the 'ego':

> Kant, reacting against the data-positivism of Hume outlines a great, systematically constructed and in a new way still scientific philosophy in which the Cartesian turn to conscious subjectivity works itself out in the form of a transcendental subjectivism.
>
> (Husserl 1970: 95)

Yet Kant, unlike his forebears, is able to return to 'philosophy in the old sense' (i.e. the Greek sense) as in his *Critiques* he sets limits to what the new (eighteenth century) philosophy can claim for the world as we experience it. But also, and significantly for Husserl, he opens 'ways toward the "scientifically" unknowable in itself' (Husserl 1970: 95). Thus, for Husserl, Kant is a prophet, as it were, towards phenomenology. His philosophy is 'on the way' but does not go the whole way: 'it is a philosophy which, in opposition to prescientific [i.e. 'natural] and scientific [i.e. empirical] objectivism, goes back to knowing subjectivity as the primal locus of all objective formations of sense and ontic validities, undertakes to understand the existing world as a structure of sense and reality, and in this way seeks to set in motion an essentially new type of scientific attitude and new type of philosophy' (Husserl 1970: 99).

Therefore, the task for the 'new philosophy' of phenomenology is to return to the authentic contemplation of the world of being via 'a radical inquiry back into subjectivity – and specifically the subjectivity which ultimately brings about all world-validity (*alle Weltgeltung mit ihrem Inhalt*), with its content and in all its prescientific and scientific modes, and into the "what" and the "how" of the rational accomplishments' (Husserl 1970: 70). This alone will make 'objective truth comprehensible' and allow a return to 'the ultimate ontic meaning of the world' (*den letzten Seinssinn der Welt erreichen*) (Husserl 1970: 70). Therefore:

> The whole history of philosophy since the appearance of 'epistemology' and the serious attempts at a transcendental philosophy [i.e. Hume] is a history of tremendous tensions between objectivistic and transcendental philosophy.
>
> (Husserl 1970: 70)

This is no better shown than in the false assumptions of the 'objective scientist' who speaks about 'objectivity' without realizing that 'objective truths and the objective world itself as the substratum of his formulae (the everyday world of experience as well as the higher-level conceptual world of knowledge) are his own life-construct (*in ihm selbst gewordenes Lebensgebilde ist*) developed within himself' (Husserl 1970: 96/1954: 99).

Therefore, the consequence of Descartes' 'turn' is, in Husserl's view, to have created two branches of philosophy: a sceptical science that follows Descartes' lead and another 'actual and still vital one' that 'still has roots' in humanity but 'struggles to keep them or find new ones' (Husserl 1970: 15). It is this struggle that he concludes present-day philosophy has to engage in, a struggle for genuine humanity, and nowhere is this better displayed than in the struggle for the 'soul' of psychology, to which we turn next.

The unique problem of psychology

At the onset of his lectures Husserl had made it clear that the cultural and philosophical 'crisis' he was about to describe was particularly acute in one discipline in particular – psychology (Husserl 1970: 3). Indeed, he thought that psychology had its own 'peculiar crisis' (Husserl 1970: 5) centred on what he calls the '*Rätsel der Subjektivität*' – the 'enigma of subjectivity' which leads in the case of psychology to an 'enigma of psychological subject matter and method' (Husserl 1970: 5). As he put it: 'the tragic failure of modern psychology in particular, its contradictory historical existence, will be clarified and made understandable: that is, the fact that it had to claim to be the basic philosophical science, while this produced the obviously paradoxical consequences of the so-called "psychologism"' (Husserl 1970: 18).

As this will be a central theme of the present book we shall spend a little time exploring what Husserl meant here for it will have a strong impact on how Edith will later develop her views on the subject. Husserl's problem with 'objective psychology' is, in a manner take up by Stein, that it misses the 'life of the soul' of which we are by necessity implicated:

> Because of its objectivism, psychology is completely unable to obtain as its subject-matter the soul in its own essential sense, which is after all the I that acts and suffers.
>
> (Husserl 1970: 296)[16]

Therefore, 'the need for a reform of the whole of modern psychology is felt more and more on all sides, but it is not yet understood that it has failed because of its objectivism' (Husserl 1970: 296). Despite its achievements 'it is not a true psychology'. For an 'objective science of the soul' (*objektive Seelenlehre*) 'has never existed and will never exist' (Husserl 1970: 297).

Thus, in modern psychology it is assumed that the subjective, as for the physicist exploring physical objects, has been excluded so that 'psychic entities' can be investigated as the psychic (*psychisches*) in psychology (Husserl 1970: 295). Yet such an approach, argues Husserl, especially in modern psychology, ignores 'the constant fundament that his – after all subjective – work of thought is the surrounding life-world' (Husserl 1970: 295).[17] It is this constantly presupposed ground of all investigation which will be the special field of phenomenological investigation.

Therefore despite the triumphs of science Husserl sees its approach as fundamentally naive: 'since the intuitively given surrounding world, this merely subjective realm, is forgotten in scientific investigation, the working subject is themselves forgotten, the scientist does not become a subject of investigation' (Husserl 1970: 295). In conclusion, Husserl argues that phenomenology should *replace* modern psychology as a 'final form of psychology which uproots the naturalistic sense of modern psychology' (Husserl 1970: 70).

The new philosophy: The phenomenological reduction

Having analysed the crisis of the modern world and traced its roots to, in his mind, the failed Cartesian epoché, Husserl concludes by giving us what he initially promised – a definitive (and perhaps final?) exposition of the new philosophical approach contained in his practice of the phenomenological reduction. We shall conclude this chapter with this exposition which I shall outline in the form of the ten steps with which Husserl presents it.[18]

1. On an everyday level, from the perspective of our modern, post-Kantian view, we perceive the world as comprising existing objects which will include ourselves:

> In this [everyday surrounding Life-World] we are objects among objects in the sense of the life-world, namely as being here and there, in the plain certainty of experience, before anything that is established scientifically, whether in physiology, psychology or sociology.
>
> (Husserl 1970: 104–5)

This is the 'third-person perspective' of the modern 'objective' scientific outlook. Essentially matter, following Descartes, is objectifiably observed, as is all creation – animals, birds, plants, rocks and other humans.

2. However, on the other hand, we cannot deny our subjectivity: 'we are, on the other hand, subjects for this world, namely as the experiencing, contemplating, valuing and purposely-relating I-subjects' (Husserl 1954: 107).[19] Because, for us:

> This surrounding world has only the ontic meaning (*Seinssinn*) given to it by our experiencing, our thoughts, our valuations etc; and it has the modes of validity (certainty of being, possibility, perhaps illusion etc.) which we, as the subjects of validity, at the same time bring about or else possess from earlier on as habitual acquisitions and bear within us as validities of such and such a content which we can reactualize at will.
>
> (Husserl 1970: 105)

3. According to the accepted view, then, we are therefore perceiving the 'world' on two planes – as the objective world supposed by the Cartesian /'rationalist'/'scientific' world view and the subjective 'I-perspective' composed of intention, volition, conception, etc. However, change of content of a perceived item is possible only through change of attitude from the perspective of the 'I'. 'Thus sensibility, the active functioning of the "I" of the living body or bodily organs, belongs in a fundamental, essential way to all experience of bodies' (Husserl 1970: 106), for:

> If we look straightforwardly toward the object and what belongs to it, [our] gaze passes through the appearances towards what continuously appears through their continuous unification: the object, with its own valid being in the mode of being 'present to itself'.
>
> (Husserl 1970: 105)[20]

4. However, in this reflective attitude towards the presenting world 'we have not a one but a manifold' (*haben wir nicht eines, sondern Mannigfaltiges*) (Husserl 1970: 105/1954: 107) for now 'the sequence of appearances is thematic', in this respect 'perception is the primal mode of intuition, it exhibits with primal originality, that is, the mode of self-presence' (Husserl 1970: 105).[21] In addition, there are other modes of intuition that present modifications of this '*selbst da*' ('itself there') as present to us, that is, recollection or imagination of an object. Which is to say, as we perceive the objects in the world around us

we recollect all the images and memories that the object evokes. This will also affect the objects we perceive.

Sitting in a room, if we are asked to perceive an object we shall select that which our 'presentiments' draw us too. We may gaze out of the window to some trees but the perception and 'picking up' of the trees is itself a perceptual act shaped by our presentiments – as they are perceived the trees may evoke memories of childhood, a playground, some lost experience, here we may recall Gerard Manley Hopkins' phrase 'what you look hard at seems to look hard at you' (House 1959: 204).[22] This move, so essential for the phenomenological 'epoché', Husserl describes thus: 'the first thing we must do, and first of all in immediate reflective self-experience *(in unmittelbaren reflexiven Selbsterfahrung)*, is to take the conscious life, completely without prejudice, just as what it quite immediately gives itself, as itself to be' (Husserl 1970: 233/1954: 236), for once we make this fundamental 'phenomenological step', in this 'immediate givenness' *(in unmittelbarer Gegebenheit)*, 'one finds anything but color data, tone data, other "sense" data or data of feeling, will etc.' (i.e. 'none of the things which appear in traditional psychology'). Instead, we find 'the *cogito*, intentionality, in those familiar forms which, like everything actual in the surrounding world, find their expression in language: "I see a tree which is green; I hear the rustling of leaves, I smell its blossoms" etc.; or "I remember my schooldays," "I am saddened by the sickness of a friend," etc.' (Husserl 1970: 233). Thus, Husserl's interpretation of Descartes' '*cogito*' is at the heart of our engagement with existence. In other words, as human beings we are 'intentionally related to certain things – animals, houses, fields, etc. – that is, consciously affected by these things, actively attending to them or in general perceiving them, actively remembering them, thinking about them, planning and acting in respect of them' (Husserl 1970: 235). So the notion of a dead, inanimate and 'objective' world of 'things' takes a blow, for each moment of sensitive perception is maintained and upheld by the sophisticated field of intentional (or 'conscious') engagement that is the proper field of the phenomenologist's (and thus by extension, the philosopher's) attention. Therefore we move from Kant's 'thing in itself' *(das Selbst-da-seiende)* – the thing which is itself there – to the thing which 'was itself there' *(Selbst-da-seiend-gewesene*, Husserl 1954: 107) or that which 'will-be-itself-there' (*Selbst-da-sein-werdende*, Husserl 1954: 108) and back again. Thus, 'presentifying intuitions "recapitulate" (*wiederholen*) – in certain modifications belonging to them – all the manifolds of appearance through which what is objective exhibits itself perceptively' (Husserl 1970: 105).

5. Participating thus in the world will also, as we have seen, involve our living body (*Leib*). This experience of our body is fundamental to the perception of all other bodies, both actively and through habitual reflexivity, which leads to Husserl's distinction between *Körper* and *Leib* – objectively perceived 'flesh' or 'body' and the living-body. A distinction that we shall see in later chapters will become so important for Edith.

6. Accordingly, this movement to and fro, from past to present and future and within and without the 'I' creates the field of apprehension within which we are immersed:

> The consciousness of the world, then, is in constant motion; (*So ist das Weltbewusstsein in einer ständige Bewegung*), we are conscious of the world always in terms of some object content or other, in the alteration of different ways of being conscious (intuitive, non-intuitive, determined, undetermined etc.) (*anschaulich, unanschaulich, bestimmt, unbestimmt, usw.*) and also in the alteration of affection and action.
> (Husserl 1970: 109/1954: 111)

7. This perception and immersion are also happening as a group. There is a social side to this immersion into the given as there is a personal dimension. The community of humanity presupposes the already existing world.

8. The 'subjective', therefore, can never be 'grasped'. It can 'never be held in view, never grasped and understood' (Husserl 1970: 112). In theological terms we could say that the core of the self is essentially apophatic. For Husserl, Kant gets round this startling fact by 'forms of mythical talk' (*art mythisches Reden*) when he talks of 'faculties', 'functions', 'formations', etc. (*Vermögen, Funktionen, Formungen,* Husserl 1954: 114). But Kant's functions are, for Husserl, 'modes of the subjective' which we 'are in principle unable to make intuitive to ourselves' (Husserl 1970: 114). Like Hume and the empiricists, in Husserl's critique, Kant too had fallen into the 'psychologistic' trap of making an unnecessary distinction between the 'idea' and the 'thing itself'. Rather, like Husserl himself, 'the first

thing Kant should have done if he had taken the everyday world as the world of human consciousness, was to pass through psychology – but a psychology which allowed the subjective experiences of world-consciousness actually to come to expression as they showed themselves experientially' (Husserl 1970: 116). Therefore, Kant's problem, for Husserl, was to have distinguished the 'transcendental subject' from the quotidian I as experienced (which Husserl calls *Seele*) and thus created something 'incomprehensively mythical' (Husserl 1970: 118) which, for Husserl, despite Kant's protestations, was still in thrall to the idea-ism of the empiricists.

9. Therefore, from this confusion, the modern concept of 'scientific' attitude arises as manifest in a 'science' such as psychology, that is, the notion of 'an objective science of the subjective' (Husserl 1970: 126) which leads inevitably to two 'objects' of investigation: 'the life world' and the 'objective scientific world' (Husserl 1970: 130):

> For what has always gone under the name of psychology, at any rate since the founding of modern objectivism regarding knowledge of the world, naturally has the meaning of an 'objective' science of the subjective, no matter which of the attempted historical psychologies we may choose.
> (Husserl 1970: 126)

10. To conclude, then, Husserl presents us with the Transcendental Epoché in its final form as his 'method' to reveal the phenomenological presence of the I in our perception.

The transcendental epoché

Therefore, the move from the 'natural' perspective to the one Husserl is seeking (the truly rational, as opposed to the false rational 'objectivism' of the modern world) is achieved through the following steps.

First, there must be the 'epoché of all objective sciences', that is, to free ourselves initially from the 'myth' of the objective (Husserl 1970: 135): 'what is meant is rather an epoché of all participation in the cognitions of the objective sciences, an epoché of any critical position-taking which is interested in their truth or falsity, even any position on their guiding idea of an objective knowledge of the world' (Husserl 1970: 135). He describes this move in a quasi-religious or 'vocational' way: 'the total phenomenological attitude and the epoché belonging to it are destined in essence to effect, at first, a complete personal transformation, comparable in the beginning to a religious conversion' (Husserl 1970: 137).

Having bracketed out the 'objective' world we now have a choice before us: to enter into the naivety of the 'natural attitude' (*die naiv-naturliche Geradehineinstellung*, Husserl 1954: 146) or the new phenomenological attitude: 'a consistently reflective attitude toward the "how" of the subjective manner of givenness of life-world and life-world objects.'[23] In other words, the 'world' is no longer presented to us as objectified matter but we realize our own participation in the organization of this matter through the participation of the intending 'I':

> In general the world or, rather, objects are not merely pre-given to us all in such a way that we simply experience them as the substrates of their properties but that we become conscious of them (and of everything ontically meant) (*und alles ontisch Vermeinte*) through subjective manners of appearance, or givenness, without noticing it in particular.
>
> (Husserl 1970: 144/1954: 146)

So, by turning our attention to the 'how' of the manner of givenness we are thus able to make new connections and 'acquire a number of new theoretically investigated types'. This is the new 'synthetic totality' of phenomenology 'in which we now discover, for the first time, that and how the world ... acquires its ontic meaning (*Seinssinn*) and its ontic validity (*Seinsgeltung*) in the totality of ontic structure (*in der Totalität ihrer ontischen Strukturen*)' (Husserl 1970: 145/1954: 148).

Again, almost in a religious fashion, Husserl stresses the difficulty of the path and that it will demand a constant need to resist the temptation to fall back into the 'natural' way of seeing the world, this he calls the 'completely unique, universal epoché' (*einer ganz einzigartigen universalen Epoché*, Husserl 1954: 151).

Having thus undergone this epoché the 'gaze of the philosopher becomes fully free' (Husserl 1970: 151) leading, in this final stage of Husserl's thought (the subjective idealism that would eventually turn away his followers such as Stein and Ingarden), to the complete identification of the 'world' with the transcendental 'I':

> And there results, finally, taken in the broadest sense, the absolute correlation between beings of every sort and every meaning, on the one hand, and absolute subjectivity, as constituting meaning and ontic validity in this broadest manner.
>
> (Husserl 1970: 151–2)

Therefore:

> This is not a 'view' (*Auffassung*), an 'interpretation' *(Interpretation)* bestowed upon the world. Every view about …, every opinion about 'the' world, has its ground in the pre-given world. It is from this very ground that I have freed myself through the epoché; I stand *above* the world, which has now become for me, in a quite distinctive sense, a *phenomenon*.
>
> (Husserl 1970: 152/1954: 155)

In striking language, Husserl announces that we thus stand before the gate of Faust's 'realm of the mothers' – (Freud and Jung's 'unconscious' which we shall return to later): 'we stand, through our transcendental reduction, only at the gate of the entrance to the realm, never before entered, of the "mothers of knowledge" (Husserl 1970: 153).[24]

Finally, having thus made the phenomenological leap we are no longer concerned with 'things in the world' or what the things in the world are for 'thus we exclude all knowledge, all statements about true being and predictive truths for it … we also exclude all sciences, genuine as well as pseudo-sciences, with their knowledge of the world as it is "in itself", in "objective truth"' (Husserl 1970: 156). Which will inevitably, and significantly for the present volume, rule out in particular the 'pseudo-science' of modern psychology. For such a science (erroneously for Husserl) directs its attention to so-called 'inner' or 'psychic' experience as much as the extrinsic sciences direct their attentions to 'outer' 'objective' facts. Such a process would create an inexpressible 'pure psychic life' cut off from that 'stream of experience' (such as Descartes and Locke sought). Rather, the 'phenomenological-psychological reduction' that Husserl now proposes sees that what is 'proper to the soul includes all intentionalities, the experiences of the type called "perception"' (Husserl 1970: 236). Thus, rather than concentrating on the supposed or hypothetical 'reality' of things perceived the phenomenological psychologist will concentrate on the perception itself in the perceiving 'I'. This will be the psychological investigation into empathy that Stein takes up in her doctoral thesis and to which we shall turn in the next chapter.

Conclusions and consequences

As we detailed the broad sweep of Husserl's thought in this chapter from the 'hard' object phenomenology of the early Husserl to the 'transcendental phenomenology' of the later Husserl we have seen too the contradictions and problems inherent in his task. On the one hand he argued for a release from the ideated fixation of Descartes and Locke yet ultimately, despite criticizing Kant for this move, there is the danger that he is led into a transcendental I-ism that threatens to destroy the distinction between 'I' and 'the world'. McIntyre, assessing Stein's reaction to Husserl, suggests that philosophers such as Stein and Ingarden sensed that there were in fact two ends towards which Husserl's thought led:

> I have already suggested that disputes about the interpretation of Husserl may be due to the fact that there are in fact immanent in Husserl's writings two incompatible philosophical standpoints. Stein recognised this more insightfully and sooner than anyone else.
>
> (McIntyre 2006: 104)

It was this recognition that led Stein to forge her own way as we shall see. But, from the viewpoint of the rest of this book as we look at Stein's approach, there is no doubt that 'Husserl's revolution' gave her the tools to complete her task of creating a new philosophical and spiritual anthropology for the modern world. Where Husserl seems right is in his critique of the errors of modern psychology. This problem arises, he suggests, from 'the fateful erroneous path forced upon it by the peculiarity of the modern idea of the objectivistic universal science with its psycho-physical dualism' (Husserl 1970: 202). It is this dualism that Stein will seek to redress through her anthropology to which we turn next.

3

'The Problem of Empathy': The foundations of a philosophical psychology

Introduction

As we saw in Chapter 1, 'empathy' became one of the key terms by which Edith defined her understanding of the relationship between philosophy and psychology, and, indeed, the human person. Later we shall discuss the theological implications of her thought following her conversion to Christianity. For now, we shall develop our understanding of the relationship, and definition, of both philosophy and psychology by exploring the concept of empathy she developed in her doctoral thesis, parts 2–4 of which were later published as 'On the Problem of Empathy' in 1917.[1] We shall follow this in the next chapter by exploring how her thought can shape our present-day understanding of the disciplines of philosophy and psychology and the relationship between the two.

Stein and empathy

'At the heart of all controversy over empathy (*Einfühlung*) lies a silent assumption: that there are "foreign subjects" and their experience is given to us.'[2] So begins Edith's discussion of the topic at the outset of *On the Problem of Empathy*. Generally speaking, she continues, we look at the phenomena, occurrences and effects of this 'givenness' (*Gegebenheit*) without fundamentally questioning the *Gegebenheit* itself, but, she suggests, it is imperative that we question this and its nature (*Wesen*). This she will undertake using Husserl's 'phenomenological reduction' as we described it in the previous chapter. The goal of this method, she suggests, 'is to clarify and therefore establish the basis of all knowledge'. Like Husserl she is not content to assume the empiricist divide between the 'knower' and the 'known' – 'I' and 'objective reality'. Even this assumption must be questioned, as she continues:

> Is it based on natural experience then? By no means, for even this as well as its continuation, research in natural science, is subject to diverse interpretations (as in materialistic or idealistic philosophy) and thus stands in need of clarification.
>
> (CWES 3: 3)

Thus at the beginning of her discourse, and her philosophical career, Edith, like her mentor Husserl, throws down the gauntlet before the two dominant philosophical approaches of the twentieth century: on the one hand the German schools of idealistic philosophy stemming from Kant and Hegel, on the other the empiricist materialist schools stemming from the British empirical tradition. Her *Gegebenheit*/'givenness' will thus embrace:

> The whole world encompassing us, the physical as well as the psycho-physical, the bodies and souls of people and animals (including the psycho-physical person of the seeker herself).[3]

Like René Descartes she is happy to apply a sceptical programme to the seeming phenomena we observe in the world around us. But, in common with Husserl, she recognizes the limits of such scepticism: 'there are difficulties in seeing how it is possible to suspend the positing of existence and still retain the full character of perception' (CWES 3: 4), for:

> 'I', the experiencing subject who considers the world and my own person as phenomenon, 'I' am in experience and only in it, am just as indubitable and impossible to cancel as the experience itself.
>
> (CWES 3: 5)

Thus for Stein (and the early phenomenologists), the error of the empirical approach is to concentrate too firmly on the 'appearing phenomena' (the 'foreign subjects' she began with) to exclusion of the experience of the observer herself – the 'I' that accompanies all such phenomena, for:

> The world in which I live is not only a world of physical bodies, there are also outside of myself experiencing subjects and I know of these experiences.[4]

Interestingly, for her later investigations, she refers to these phenomena as '*das Phänomen des fremden Seelenlebens*' (literally: 'the phenomenon of the life of the soul of the other') which is '*da und unbezweifelbar*' ('there and indubitable' ESGA 5: 13). This is translated in the present English edition as 'the phenomenon of foreign psychic life' (CWES 3: 5). For reasons given earlier and ones that I will follow through in the present volume, I would like to suggest that Stein deliberately chooses the word '*Seelenleben*' – life of the soul – here and that it may obscure later understanding of her thought to translate it with the phrase 'foreign psychic life' (CWES 3:5). For, I would like to contend, the introduction of the term '*Seele*' so early into her discussion is necessary for understanding the view of the *Gegeben*/'the given' that she is presenting.[5] That is, in her own words, that:

> The individual is not given as a physical body, but as a sensitive, living body belonging to an 'I', an 'I' that senses, thinks, feels and wills.
>
> (CWES 3: 5)

This 'living body of the I' 'not only fits into my own phenomenal world but is itself the centre of orientation of such a phenomenal world. It faces the world and communicates with me' (CWES 3: 5). We are a psycho-physical continuity and it is not helpful, or philosophical, to separate the 'soul' from the 'matter'. Of all the lessons taught by the phenomenologists at the advent of the twentieth century this was perhaps one of the most important, and one that Edith put at the centre of her approach to the mind/soul.

Thus, beginning with her doctoral thesis and extending into her later investigations, her approach to what we would today call 'mental phenomena' will be to look at all these 'various ways of being given' (*diese verschiedenen Gegebenheitsweisen*) (ESGA 5: 12) and how we situate ourselves within them.

For this '*Gegebenheit*'/'givenness' leads us to the *Grundart von Akten, in denen fremdes Erleben erfaßt wird* – 'a basic ground of acting, in which foreign experiences are grasped' (ESGA 5:13/14). It is these 'radical acts' that she designates as 'empathy' 'regardless of all historical traditions attached to the word' (CWES 3: 6). By taking this 'phenomenological' view of empathy she can thus suggest that:

> Empathy does not have the character of outer perception, though it does have something in common with outer perception: in both cases the object itself is present here and now.
>
> (CWES 3:7)

In other words, empathy has for Stein a quality of *Originarität*/'originality'/'primordiality' – it is basic to our comprehension of that which is given in experience. Empathy is thus 'an act which is primordial as present experience though non-primordial in content' (CWES 3:10) – it is a 'kind of act of perceiving':

> Empathy is the experience of foreign consciousness in general, irrespective of the kind of experiencing subject or of the subject whose consciousness is experienced.
>
> (CWES 3:11)

Thus, empathy and the *Seelenleben* of those around us are intimately connected. Not only this, but surprisingly so early in her philosophical career, Stein connects empathy with the 'the only means' that God can comprehend our 'soul-life':

> Thus people comprehend the soul-life of their fellow humans and so, as believers, they comprehend the love, anger and laws of their God, and God is unable to comprehend their lives by any other means.
>
> (ESGA 5: 20)[6]

Thus, contrasting her own approach to empathy with that of, for example, Theodor Lipps, her notion of empathy, 'strictly defined' thus becomes: 'having experience of a foreign consciousness which is only the "non-basic/original" experience that a basic one announces. It is neither the basic experience itself or one that is "assumed" from it' (ESGA 5: 18).⁷ Thus, 'there is a double-sidedness to the essence of empathic acts: and experience of our own announcing another one. And there are various levels of accomplishment possible' (CWES 3: 19). It is this 'double-sidedness' (*Doppelseitigkeit*) of empathy that gives it its unique character, traversing the realms of 'given' (original, basic) and the 'not-given'.

Psychology and phenomenology: 'The constitution of the psycho-physical individual'

Accordingly, at the heart of our comprehension of the *Gegebenheit* is what Stein calls the πρώτη φιλοσοφία ('the proto-philosophy') (ESGA 5: 24) – the proto-, or what she will later call, the 'perennial' philosophy. Such a philosophy will look for what she terms (following Husserl) the 'essence' of the phenomenon that arises. Such a task, she suggests, cannot be undertaken by what she calls a 'genetic-psychological investigation of cause' ('*genetisch-psychologischen Kausaluntersuchung*'). As she explains in a footnote (no. 31), for her, 'genetic psychology' and 'psychology which explains causally' are synonymous. She does not dispute the importance of such approaches to psychology, but argues for an acceptance that the phenomenological approach will encompass the perceiver as well as the perceived – as I stated above, one of the most important lessons the early phenomenologists had to offer the emerging discipline of psychology. Accordingly, the title of Chapter 3 of Stein's thesis, *The Constitution of the Psycho-Physical Individual*, reminds us of her fundamental view of the individual which, as we shall see, with small modifications, she held for the rest of her intellectual career.

Stein begins her description of the self in this chapter by reflecting on the nature of the self – the 'I'. Here she introduces two key themes that will remain central for her later philosophy. The first is that of the 'pure I' – *das reine Ich* – she characterizes it as that which is the *unbeschreiblichen qualitätlosen Subjekt des Erlebens* (ESGA 5: 37) – 'the indescribable subject of experience with no qualities'. This indescribable nature of the 'I' will remain central to her thought and is something we shall return to throughout this book.

Her second reflection on the 'I' reminds us of Kant's 'unity of apperception', that is, the I as being '*die Einheit eines Bewußtseinsstromes*' (ESGA 5: 38) 'the unity of a stream of consciousness': 'going over these experiences, we continually come upon experiences in which the present "I" had once lived. This is even true when we can no longer directly grasp the experience, finding it necessary to view it through remembering representation' (CWES 3: 39).[8] Therefore, 'the stream of consciousness, is characterised as "it itself and no other" with a nature peculiar to it, resulting in a good sense of precisely limited individuality' (CWES 3: 39).[9] Such a 'quality-less' I combined with the 'stream of consciousness' will provide, she suggests, the conditions for the psycho-physical unity of the self. Yet this 'unified stream of consciousness' does not constitute 'the soul'/*die Seele*. Rather: 'amongst our experiences there is one that lies at the ground of them all, which, with its unwavering qualities, manifests itself in them as their identical "bearer": this is the substantial soul.'[10] This is the first time in her writings that Stein treats of the 'soul' at length and, mindful of the discussion introduced earlier, before continuing it may be worth just stepping back to see what role the term plays in the context of her philosophy and how her exposition fits into a wider Central European 'soul-discourse' of the twentieth century.

The soul in 'the problem of empathy'

Having introduced the term '*Seele*', Edith then goes on to enumerate manifestations of the 'soul' in everyday life such as the sharpness of our senses, the energy of everyday life and in our conduct (this will later become briefly her notion of the '*Lebenskraft*', which we will discuss shortly), the tension and relaxation of our will, the intensity of our feelings and the stirrings of our feelings (*die Aufwühlbarkeit unseres Gemütes*) (ESGA 5: 39). All of these, she suggests, give us clues as to the single unifying nature of the 'soul' that grounds them all.[11] How these various events relate to the 'soul' itself is something she will return to, as we shall see, through all her writing. For now she characterizes the soul as 'a substantial unity which, completely analogous to the physical thing, is built out of categorical elements and the sequence of categories' (ESGA 5: 39).¹² Therefore, from this it follows that 'the distinctive structure of the unity of the soul depends upon the characteristic content of the stream of experience and conversely the stream of experience depends upon the structure of the soul' (ESGA 5: 39).¹³ And, 'this substantial unity is "my" soul when the experiences, within which it manifests itself, are "my" experiences – acts within which my pure I lives.'¹⁴

At this point, Edith leaves discussion of the soul as she moves on to the relationship of the mind with the body. However, as stated, the idea of the soul will persist throughout her writings and we shall return to it for an extended discussion later in the book. However, before moving on it is worth just stressing one more use to which Edith puts the term in contrast to current present English use.

Part of the problem here, and one we shall encounter again, is that the term 'soul' (if not referring to Southern beat music) has unfortunately acquired too many theological and metaphysical associations, which may explain why the English translators demurred from employing the term. On the contrary, the 'soulish'/*seelische* in German is inextricably bound up with the bodily. Stein realizes this even before she has become acquainted with the Thomist tradition later on. As she puts it in *Empathy*: 'this dependence of experiences on the influence of the body is a basic characteristic of the soul'¹⁵ (ESGA 5: 39) for 'the separation, which we have already proposed [of soul and body], was always an artificial one for the soul is always presented to us as a soul in a body' (ESGA 5: 40).¹⁶ This is diametrically opposed to the current English use of the term which, if anything, usually denotes a disembodied entity. It is this contradiction that we must be aware of throughout the present book. If anything, what Stein (and the present author) are suggesting is an alternative anthropology that claims the 'soul' back to discourse as way-station between the 'unknown stream of consciousness' of the I and the sensations of the body. In this respect it is also worth noting that Stein's 'soul' at this point (that which is inextricably bound up with the physical body) is to be distinguished from pure 'spiritual feelings' that would not necessarily have that quality. What Stein calls here 'spiritual feelings' (*geistigen Gefühle*, ESGA 5: 47) would, confusingly enough, probably be closer to what most English-speaking readers would today term 'aspects of the soul'.

Soul and spirit: *Seele und Geist*

Perhaps clarity can be given to Anglophone readers as to Stein's use of *Seele* by looking at how she relates it to the other difficult German term, *Geist*. *Seele*, as we have already seen, she states to be that sphere of the personality that is 'dependent upon somatic influences' (ESGA 5: 47).[17] In this respect then 'the soul' for Stein at this stage is that which guarantees the psycho-physical unity of the person by being the ground of all psychic and physical sensations and experiences: 'as that which manifests the unity of single psychological experiences by means of substantial unity, the soul is grounded in the body and forms the image with it of the "psycho-physical individual" – manifest in the delineated phenomenon of "psycho-physical causality" and in the nature of sensations' (ESGA 5: 47).[18] Whereas that which is independent from the somatic is the '*geistig*', elements of which are not grounded in bodily sensations:[19]

> The term shows us they are accidentally psychological and not bound to the body (even if the relevant psychologists in question would not like to face up to the possibility of this consequence).
>
> (ESGA 5: 47)[20]

Such '*geistig*' acts are, for Stein, to be thought of without bodily dependence. As 'pure spiritual acts' they are not dependent upon psycho-somatic foundations of feeling. Again, Stein is working with very fine distinctions here that may be unfamiliar to the Anglophone reader (without an appreciation of the ambiguity of the German term *Geist*).

Thus the term 'soul' acts for Edith as cipher or symbol of the unity of the individual encompassing both the physical and the non-physical (*geistig und psychische*) and that, in combination, the two (consciousness and physicality) each takes on a new dimension:

> A unifying object in which the consciousness of an 'I' and a physical body are insolubly joined together, from which each acquires a new character: the body becomes animated *Leib* (flesh) and the consciousness as soul manifests a unified individual.
>
> (ESGA 5: 52)[21]

If this view of the nature of self is accepted, then the rest of Stein's argument in *Empathy* flows from this central assumption: that if our own body (*Leib*) and psychological life are unified in the soul then encountering another person will also be encountering a blend of the two: 'thus the foreign living body (*Leib*) is "seen" as a living body. We meet this kind of givenness (*Gegebenheit*) (which we call "co-originality") as we encounter the truth of the thing before us' (ESGA 5: 53).[22]

This 'co-originality' is the ability to see both the exterior and 'the inner' elements of the person at the same time: 'in summary, the whole thing is "seen".' This 'seeing-with' ('*mitsehen*') of the other implies these 'inner tendencies' but their '*originäre Erfüllung*'/'their original fullness' is hidden. Thus:

> Also the 'seeing-with' (*mitsehen*) of foreign fields of sensations implies tendencies, but their original fullness is here in principle closed to us; neither in progressive outer examination nor in moving to bodily perception can they bring me to the original 'givenness'. The only fullness, that is possible here is the empathetic realisation.
>
> (ESGA 5: 53)[23]

Thus empathy, or as she calls it here die *einfühlende Vergegenwärtigung* – the empathetic realization – is the only way we can preserve the 'original givenness' of the psycho-physical unity of ourselves when we encounter another person. By means of this 'co-originality' we distinguish between 'living flesh' and 'dead objects' in our perceptions:

The hand resting on the table does not lie there like the book beside it.

> It 'presses' against the table more or less strongly; it lies there limpid or stretched; and I 'see' these sensations of pressure and tension in a 'co-original' way.
>
> (CWES 3: 58 with amendment)

This 'co-originality' is marked by my ability to move my own hand, in imagination, into the place of the one before us: 'it is moved into it and occupies its position and attitude, now feeling its sensations, though not as original and not as being its own' (CWES 3: 58 with amendment).

By means of such 'co-original' empathy we are thus faced with a very different experience of the world to that which sees my I (the Cartesian *ego*) as the only existing entity and all else as dead matter. The possibility of empathetic realization makes possible our entering into an existing world surrounding us:

> The world, as I fantasise it, is by virtue of the power of its contradiction to my original nature, a non-existing world (without me, living in this fantasy, needing to bring this world into given-ness); the world perceived from the empathetic standpoint, is an existing world – its being posited from the original perception.
>
> (ESGA 5: 57)[24]

The life force

Another term which will occupy Stein later on is also introduced at this point. She talks about one aspect of the co-originality of the living person, what she will later call the 'life force' and here introduces as the 'life phenomena' *Lebensphänomene*, that is: 'growth, development and ageing, health and sickness, vigour and sluggishness, life and death' (ESGA 5: 61). Such phenomena 'fill' the living body and soul – giving 'colour' to every mental and physical act of the individual, being 'seen with' as much as other sensations. We also 'see' such aspects of others in their walk, posture and other bodily movements. In this case, the 'life force' extends also to plants and animals (CWES 3: 69). Interestingly (for the daughter of a lumber merchant) Stein draws the line at a tree feeling pain when being cut down. Something both modern eco-philosophers and non-Western thinkers may dispute. We shall return to Edith's 'life force' later.

The *Kern*

Another key term which will be developed in her later philosophy also makes its appearance in *The Problem of Empathy* – that is 'the core' or '*Kern*'. She introduces her discussion of it as she looks at the nature of the 'spiritual' (*geistig*) self in Chapter 4 of the thesis. She also interweaves into the discussion the ideas of her contemporary Alexander Pfänder, quoting from his *Motiv und Motivation*:

> Strivings and counterstrivings manifesting in the 'I' do not really have the same place in this 'I'. This 'I' possesses an individual structure: the individual *Ichzentrum* (I-centre) or *Ichkern* (I-core) is surrounded by the *Ichleib* (I-body). Now the strivings can exist in the 'I' but outside the *Ichzentrum* in the *Ichleib*, thus in this sense experienced as strivings from beyond the centre.
>
> (ESGA 5: 89)[25]

Stein picks up on Pfänder's distinction between the *Ichkern* and *Ichleib* and will later modify it, as we shall see, into her notion of the *Kern*, at this point it points to her distinction between central and peripheral levels of the self. In the manner of St Teresa of Avila, it is as though the *Ichkern/Ichleib* distinction provides another perspective on the complex nature of the self that supplements the soul/spirit already established by her. We shall return to this in a later chapter.

Thus, when she comes to the conclusion of her thesis she evokes the *Kern* as something we 'glimpse' when we enter into the empathetic realization of another (CWES 3: 109), it is this glimpse which she will develop in her later works as we shall see.

Conclusion

Stein concludes *On the Problem of Empathy* by reiterating that what constitutes the quality of 'soul' in the individual is what enables the 'empathetic realization' to take place with the other, that is, the understanding of the psycho-physical constitution of the individual which enables us to '*mitsehen*' into the co-originality of those around us. This is of course most marked with humans, but Stein, via the 'life force', leaves open the possibility of an empathetic realization of other living creatures such as plants and animals. This ability to empathetically observe the 'life force' in others enables us to perceive the 'soul' of the other:

> Naturally, personal attributes – such as goodness, willingness to make sacrifices, the vigour with which I go about my affairs – will also contribute to the 'soul' of a perceived psycho-physical individual.
>
> (ESGA 5: 92)[26]

They also stand outside the 'psycho-physical' (or 'soul') continuum as aspects of the purely *geistig* aspects of the individual. Therefore, she concludes:

> Not only that the categorical structure of the soul as soul must be retained, but within its individual form we meet an unchanging core – the personal structure.
>
> (ESGA 5: 92)[27]

This *Kern*, as we shall see later, will be of the nature of the 'purely *geistig* structure'. By such means of development of the character, the psycho-physical 'soul' can therefore develop in harmony with the innate 'core': 'so can the psychophysical empirical person come to a more or less full realization of the "*geistig*" one' (ESGA 5: 93).[28]

We have seen in this chapter how '*The Problem of Empathy*', early work that it is, contains the main building blocks of Stein's anthropology of the person, and indeed much of her later philosophy: the role of the soul, the key attribute of empathy, the presence of the life force and the 'core'. We shall now turn in the next chapter to contrast the 'root and ground' of Stein's anthropology as developed in this early writing with that of three of her philosophical and psychological contemporaries: Friedrich Nietzsche (1844–1900), Sigmund Freud (1856–1939) and Carl Jung (1875–1961). In so doing we shall facilitate the next of our conversations regarding the living philosophy of personhood in the contemporary world and the nature of the relationship between psychology and philosophy.

4

'Dionysos or the Crucified One?' – Stein, Nietzsche, Freud and Jung

> *Have you understood me? Dionysos or the Crucified One ...*
> (NIETZSCHE: *ECCE HOMO*: 9)[1]

Stein and Nietzsche

We saw in earlier chapters how Edith was saturated in the late nineteenth-century German cultural tradition of '*Geisteswissenschaft*', in the sense of a study of the universal and global sense of human nature. Whilst, as we saw in the last chapter, her mature thought and work centred on phenomenology and the work of Husserl and his circle, one of the aims of this book is to extend this intellectual conversation to include other representatives of the cultural milieu within which her thought grew. This chapter will begin that process by looking at the 'borderlands' between philosophy and psychology through a conversation with the founders of twentieth-century 'depth psychology'. I have begun that conversation from a possibly unexpected source: the ecstatic, infuriating and fascinating writings of the nineteenth-century seer and philosopher Friedrich Nietzsche (1844–1900).

Whilst Edith was reaching intellectual maturity in the early twentieth century, appreciation and assimilation of Nietzsche's writing were at their height. Although she makes little reference to his work in her mature writings she was clearly well versed in them as she indicates in this incident described in the *Life* during a summer hiking holiday with her student friends in the Riesengebirge:

> We had provided ourselves with an adequate supply of books for the vacation; so, lying outside, each of us would get engrossed in her own. I remember that Rose [Guttmann, a friend] had brought along Nietzsche's *Zarathustra*. Sometimes she would interrupt her reading to call on me for help.
>
> (CWES 3: 133–134)

Nietzsche ended his published and sane writing career with the final line from *Ecce Homo* that I have quoted as a 'motto sentence' for the themes we shall explore in this chapter.[2] And in many respects 'Dionysos versus the Crucified One' summarizes Edith's own struggle between two opposing forces in her own, and in German society's, heart at the beginning of the twentieth century: on the one hand the libido-based energetic theories of Nietzsche which would be harnessed and developed by the pioneers of depth psychology such as Freud and Jung; and on the other 'the Crucified One', and more particularly in Edith's case, the challenge of Christianity, and how this could be lived out in the life and writings of a serious student of philosophy. It is to that dilemma we turn now as we explore the borderlands between philosophy and psychology in both Stein's work and that of her libidinal contemporaries.

Nietzsche and the (re-) birth of Dionysos

Nietzsche's revolutionary thoughts exploded onto the European scene in his first published work, *The Birth of Tragedy from the Spirit of Music*, which was published in 1872. This book, with all the enthusiasms and incoherences of a young man in his late twenties, sets the tone for what Nietzsche would later present in similar keys but never again with quite the same melody. It is that unique melody that we shall explore here, examining its contribution to the foundation of a mindset which will not only influence the whole of *fin de siècle* European culture but will also provide the seeds for the nascent twentieth-century psychological schools.

My argument in this chapter will be that Nietzsche's 'rediscovery' of the libidinal roots of civilization will pose a problem for which two solutions are presented – on the one hand the psychologization of Jung, Freud and the psycho-analytic schools and on the other the spiritual anthropology of Stein. Thus, as will become apparent, Nietzsche's works lay out the battleground for the great twentieth-century 'battle of the soul'. Before he reached the point of incoherent insanity in his final years his writings would wake up the whole of Europe in his fiery denunciations of what he saw as a torpid and decadent culture which, in spiritual matters especially, had fallen asleep and needed 'the madman raving in the marketplace' to rouse it from his slumbers. In seeking a new spiritual (or 'anti-spiritual') path for his fellow Europeans, Nietzsche, like Husserl, effectively bypassed the findings of the Enlightenment and German nineteenth-century Idealism as he forged a path back to what he saw as the heart and *Ursprung* of European culture: 'the Greeks' and ancient Attic culture.[3]

Nietzsche begins the *Birth*, and indeed his public writing career, with his famous distinction between the Apollonian and Dionysian. Famous, and influential, but often misrepresented, to the Anglo-American mind at least. For many in that culture their interpretation is drawn from artworks such as Thomas Mann's novella, *Death in Venice* (1912), later remade and represented by Luigi Visconti in the 1971 film where the fictionalized Aschenbach, here played by the British actor Dirk Bogarde, is changed from a writer to a musician (loosely based on Gustav Mahler) followed by the 1973 Benjamin Britten opera, again of the same name, but this time following more closely Mann's narrative.[4] In all three *Kunstwerke*, Aschenbach's struggle between sensuality and intellectual control is represented by the 'battle' between Dionysos and Apollo that he experiences towards the end of the novella in a dream.[5] Throughout Mann makes continual links between the cholera epidemic in the dying city (a clear metaphor for Mann's *fin de siècle* Europe), Aschenbach's lusts and the 'stranger god' of Dionysos and his 'struggle' with the Apollonian.

Yet, I say 'misrepresented' as the legendary 'battle' between the two forces as presented by artists such as Mann and Britten is not what Nietzsche describes in the *Birth*. Rather, as we would expect, Nietzsche gives a more subtle typology, which, as we shall see, will have a significant impact on the emerging 'science of the soul' in the twentieth-century psychological sciences.

Nietzsche begins his description in the *Birth* by associating the two deities with the difference between the realms of dream (*Traum* – Apollo) and intoxication (*Rausche* – Dionysos):

> To reach a better understanding of these two drives (*Triebe*), let us first conceive them as the separate art worlds (*Kunstwelten*) of dream (*Traum*) and intoxication (*Rausche*), two physiological manifestations (*physiologischen Erscheinungen*) which contrast similarly to the Apollonian and the Dionysian.
>
> (Nietzsche 1993: 14/1990: 19)

Nietzsche's opening – much criticized and much misunderstood – is significant from the perspective he buries in the first line:

> We shall have gained much for the science of aesthetics when we not only through logical comprehension (*logischen Einsicht*) but through the immediate certainty of view (*unmittelbaren Sicherheit der Anschauung*) have come to see that continuous development of art as arises from the duality of the Apollonian and the Dionysian.
>
> (Nietzsche 1993: 14/1990: 19)

Again, as with Husserl, we see here an explicit reaction to Kant's schema but, in contrast to Husserl, Nietzsche does not want to advocate a return to a supposed purified Greek *theoria* but rather a return to something altogether more 'rich and strange'. No longer relying upon the logical comprehension of the *ratio* Nietzsche enlarges his perspective to embrace the 'immediate certainty' of the *Anschauung* that will inform his discourse. Having chosen his path he is clear that the best way is thus not simply to rely on the means of logical discourse, but like the Greeks before him, to embody the *Anschauung* through the mythic figure:

> These terms are borrowed from the Greeks, who revealed the profound mysteries of their art-view (*tiefsinnigen Geheimlehren ihre Kunstanschauung*) not just in ideas/concept (*Begriffen*) but in the vividly meaningful forms of their divine pantheon (*in den eindringlich deutlichen Gestalten ihrer Götterwelt*) to make it comprehensible to those who wish to understand.
>
> (Nietzsche 1993: 14/1990: 19)

With these passages Nietzsche, I would argue, thus ushers in our own world – the 'modern' (or perhaps better 'psychological') world – that seeks to comprehend the world not by reason but via the mythic figures, dreams, drives, shapes and forms of the 'underworld': more familiar to us moderns as Freud's 'unconscious'. The *Gestalten* he will play with in the *Birth* are those of Apollo and Dionysos (amongst others) but what is notable, and what had such a profound effect on the clinicians, psychologists and philosophers who would follow him, is the use to which he puts these *Gestalten* and *Geheimlehren*. They will from now on sketch out the 'drives' of the soul as we go beyond reason to find the source of being itself (Husserl's and Goethe's 'Realm of the Mothers'). This reason, this enlightenment, will later be characterized by Nietzsche in his text as the Socratic, the 'man' of reason who will seek out the answers to the *mysterion* through the use of reason, logic and dialectic alone. Yet, *pace* Mann, Britten and Visconti, the true conflict does not therefore exist between Apollo and Dionysos, but rather between the mythic world view, the world seen through the eyes of the deities (this he will term the tragic view) and the later Socratic dialectic that seeks to end the triumph of the tragic in the Greek world view. In Deleuze's words, Socrates for Nietzsche thus becomes the figure who 'opposes the idea of life', the 'theoretical man, the only true opposite of the tragic man' (Deleuze 1986: 13).

Immature the *Birth* may be, but Nietzsche certainly achieved what he set out to accomplish in this work. He had *shifted the ground*, upon which the West assessed itself and its claims to truth. From the Socratic enthronement of reason Nietzsche had introduced the possibility of a new world view (*Anschauung*) that would recalibrate our view of ourselves. In Freud's words, we would no longer be masters in our own houses, but rather we would have to pay new attention to the drives that arose from the cellars of our personalities.[6]

The symbolic dream-picture

The Apollonian and Dionysian thus become for Nietzsche representatives of '*Kunst Triebe*' (Artistic Drives) that 'spring from nature itself' (Nietzsche 1993: 18/1990: 22) without the mediation of the artist. According to the *Birth* they become manifest through two means – the immediacy of dream and the ecstasy of intoxication. Neither is concerned with intellectual accomplishments or artistic culture (in the case of the dream) or indeed individuality (in the case of ecstasy) which would rather perhaps destroy the individual in the collective destiny of the whole.

The Dionysian, second cousin to Freud's later *Id* and Unconscious, arises from the 'innermost Ground of nature', like the spring, full of *Wollust* and Green (Nietzsche 1993:17). It will 'tear down the veil of Maya' as it leads to the Primal One-ness – *der Ur-eine*. Being touched by it:

> Man is no longer an artist, he has become a work of art ... the artistic power of the whole of nature reveals itself to the supreme gratification of the primal One-ness amidst the paroxysms of intoxication.
>
> (Nietzsche 1993: 18)

Yet, rather than threatening the individual Nietzsche sees what Freud will later term 'the return of the repressed' in the birth of Greek tragedy (and in his own time, soon enough repudiated, in the birth of Wagnerian music drama). For tragedy (and by implication Wagnerian *Gesamtkunstwerk*) reveals the 'symbolic dream-image' to ourselves. This is the 'symbolic dream picture', the archetypes or '*Ur-bildern*' of the self – these symbolic dream pictures of the archetypes being conveyed, according to Nietzsche, through the tragic medium.

Dionysos as portrayed in the *Kunstwerke* of Mann, Britten, Visconti *et al* mentioned above is a rampant destroyer of the cool Apollonian intellect. Yet Nietzsche is at pains throughout the *Birth* to distinguish the raw destructive energy of Dionysos, what he calls the *Hexentrank* – the Witch's Brew – full of '*Wollust und Grausamkeit*' (the same witch's brew that leads King Pentheus to be torn apart limb from limb by his mother and his attendants in Euripides' *Bacchae*), and its *symbolic* mediation of the drive through the medium of tragedy. In this distinction lies the birth of the twentieth-century psychological therapies. As Freud and Jung both recognized (how far they may have been influenced by Nietzsche is a moot point), the destructive drives are best dealt with by means of the mediation of the formulations of the therapeutic counselling room – thus obviating the expression of these gruesome drives in the witch's brew of unmediated expression. In Nietzsche's words, such a mediation 'recalls (the deadly acts) as medicines recall deadly poisons' (Nietzsche 1993: 20). Thus, the psychological therapies, following Nietzsche's formulation, act as homeopathic drugs in recalling the source of poison itself.

Nietzsche's 'new world of symbols' (*neue Welt der Symbole*) (Nietzsche 1993: 21) can thus helpfully be identified with the formulas and arts of the emerging discipline of psychoanalysis. Including, following Nietzsche's prescription, '*die ganze leibliche Symbolik*' – the whole symbol of the body made manifest in rhythm, movement and dance:

> Not only the symbolic of the mouth, the face and the word but the fullness of all limbs in the rhythmic movement of the language of dance.
> (Nietzsche 1993: 21)[7]

In the *Birth* Nietzsche is ostensibly talking about the Attic discovery of tragedy as a means of channelling the destructive Dionysian in society. Yet it is not too far-fetched to see his account as mirroring parallel developments in nineteenth-century European society as I have done here. The full title of Nietzsche's book, *The Birth of Tragedy from the Spirit of Music*, reveals his specific intent of relating the birth of the Attic arts to the contemporary artistic labours of Richard Wagner as he sought to establish a home for his *Gesamtkunstwerk* in Second Empire German society – as Nietzsche makes clear towards the end of the *Birth* with his explicit references to *Tristan* and *Die Meistersinger*. Similarly, as suggested at the beginning of this chapter, we can see the *Birth* as mirroring the concomitant movement in late nineteenth-century European anthropology from the post-enlightenment rule of reason to something more 'rich and strange'.[8]

This post-enlightenment world conjured up by Nietzsche will take many new forms. In the early *Birth* he suggests that the '*mythos*' of the tragic art will act as a mediation from the more extreme forms of the '*Wollust*' allowing them to be channelled into more 'civilized' forms of behaviour. This, at least, is how the psychoanalytic schools of Freud and Jung, as we shall see, will understand his message. Yet, there is something rawer and more brutal too in the Dionysos that Nietzsche imagined in the 1870s. Thomas Mann, looking back on these events after the rise of Nazism in the middle of the twentieth century, suggested that Nietzsche in the 1870s had released 'the German spirit, German music, German philosophy' 'out of Dionysian profundities' as 'tragical drama is reborn'. But this new spirit, however, would turn out to be the spirit of 'a new generation, heroic, temerarious, contemptuous of all weakly doctrines'. For 'this tragic wisdom, blessing life in all its untruthfulness, hardness and cruelty, Nietzsche baptized with the name of Dionysos' (Mann 1973: 360). As Nietzsche developed his ideas after the *Birth*, 'Dionysos' would become something stronger, darker, seemingly opposed to the conscious mind. As he would later put it in the *Gay Science*:

> The problem of consciousness (more correctly of becoming conscious of oneself) confronts us for the first time when we begin to conceive how much we could do without it.
> (Nietzsche 1990: 1.500, *Die Fröhliche Wissenschaft*: 354)

As 'the chamber of human consciousness is narrow' (Nietzsche 1990: 2.268, *Zur Genealogie der Moral* 3:18) Nietzsche increasingly suggests in his later works that the mediating spirit of the 'tragic' is insufficient for 'what does not destroy me makes me stronger' (Nietzsche 1990: 2.327, *Götzen-Dämmerung* 1:8). By the time Nietzsche wrote *Zarathustra*, that we heard Edith reading at the beginning of the chapter, he became increasingly focussed on casting off socialization and social norms to create the free man depicted in *Zarathustra* as he who 'makes knowledge instinctive' (Nietzsche 2001: 37, Book 1:11).[9]

We saw earlier that, like Nietzsche, Husserl questioned the eighteenth-century empirical/rational divide and sought to find the answer to the modern dilemma in Attic Greece. Yet, unlike Nietzsche, he steadfastly rejected the 'irrational', preferring to see the phenomenological move as one that would reform reason returning it to its Greek purity. Likewise, as we shall see, Stein's approach not only concerns itself with the causes of the modern malaise, but like Husserl, she too reveals a different path, that leads away from the over-dominant Nietzschean model, especially as practised in the psychological therapies. Before we turn to Stein's critique, however, it is necessary to continue the narrative of how Nietzsche's Dionysian revelation found its way into the emerging narrative of the psychoanalytic schools, especially in the circles around Sigmund Freud and Carl Jung.

'To a drunken feast of joy'

Nietzsche's influence on the emerging discipline of psychoanalysis is nowhere better seen than in the early correspondence of Freud and Jung. Before their break in 1913 they had worked together on creating the new discipline acknowledging quite openly their debt to the 'Dionysian' climate then prevalent in European culture in the aftermath of Nietzsche's work. In this spirit Jung writes to Freud in 1910:

> Religion can be replaced only by religion. Is there perchance a new saviour in the International Fraternity – we need the eternal truth of myth
> (Jung to Freud 11th November 1910 in Jung 1988: 294)

Thus, from its very beginnings, psychoanalysis explicitly saw itself as replacing Christianity: 'Christianity must be replaced by something equivalent' (*ibid*). Psychoanalysis, writes Jung to Freud (or as they refer to it, from its Greek fore letters: ψα), will provide a new phenomenon to replace religion, and in particular Christianity. To effect this psychoanalysis will draw on the Dionysian spirit popularized by Nietzsche in works such as *The Birth*:

> I think we must give ψα time to infiltrate into people from many centres, to revivify among intellectuals a feeling for symbol and myth, ever so gently to transform Christ back into the soothsaying god of the vine (*in den weissagenden Gott der Rebe*), which he was, and in this way absorb these ecstatic instinctual forces of Christianity (*jene ekstatischen Triebkräfte des Christentums*), for the one purpose of making the cult and the sacred myth (*den heiligen Mythos*) what they once were – a drunken feast of joy (*zum trunkenen Freudenfeste*) where mankind regained the ethos and holiness of an animal.
>
> This way the beauty and purpose of classical religion which from God knows what biological need has become a *Jammerinstitut* [literally, 'an Institute of Woe']. Thus Analysis should be a means to help people get in touch with these Dionysian libidinal impulses.
> (Jung to Freud 11th November 1910 in Jung 1974: 324/1988: 294)

Thus, as Bishop points out, instead of the '*Dionysos gegen den Gekreuzigten*' that we began this chapter with, Jung will 'transform the Crucified back into the God of the grape' (Bishop 1995: 64). This 'Dionysian element' is one to which Jung would constantly return, even after the break with Freud:

> The Dionysian element has to do with emotions and affects which have found no suitable religious outlets in the fundamentally Apollonian cult and ethos of Christianity.
>
> (Jung 1971: 12. 182)

It is noteworthy that in his later 1921 essay on 'The Apollonian and the Dionysian' (in *Psychological Types*) Jung forgoes Nietzsche's 'reconciliation' of the Dionysian and the Apollonian in *The Birth of Tragedy* preferring (like Mann) to emphasize the dark conflict of the Apollonian and the Dionysian in their struggle for dominance. Jung, in typical fashion, 'corrects' Nietzsche's 'error' as he presents a version of the *Birth* that fits more closely to what Jung himself is developing after his break with Freud:

> I must emphasise this point for the sake of clarity in the ensuing discussion, since for some reason Nietzsche has omitted to make it clear, and has consequently shed a deceptive aesthetic veil over the problem.
>
> (Jung 1971: 6. 139)

Jung must retain his 'shadow' if his own theory of the self (his own Jungian anthropology) is to hold true. Rather than the reconciliation of the Apollonian and Dionysian in Attic tragedy Jung reminds Nietzsche that 'the gods of Olympus owe their splendor to the darkness of the Greek psyche' (Jung 1971: 6. 139). Finally, Jung plants his central argument for the reason of the 'error' in the *Birth of Tragedy*, did not 'Nietzsche's later "conversion" to Dionysius best show that the aesthetic substitute did not stand the test of time?' (Jung 1971: 6.141, fn 14).

Thus, for Jung, Christianity was not to be destroyed (how far this remained on Freud's agenda remains another question), but rather to be transformed by helping people to return to the springs of the libidinal – the *ekstatischen Triebkräfte des Christentums* – which Jung felt had been abandoned.[10] So, in Jung, we don't have the destruction of Christianity, but rather the *transformation* of Christianity. Jung is a reformer – he sees much that is good in Christianity but, like Nietzsche, he feels it has lost its connection with the libidinal – for him, the emerging practice of psychoanalysis will restore this.

A civilization adrift

Writing the *Wandlungen und Symbole der Libido* in 1912, which would cause his split with Freud, and during the build up to the Great War, Jung reflected on a civilization that had slipped its Christian moorings. The prospect disturbed him. 'The world has not only lost its gods', he concluded, 'but had lost its soul as well'[11] (Jung 1971: 5.77). Such a collapse of the Christian faith in the general population will, he suggests, lead to the upsurge of an *'antike Raserei'*, the ancient fury/frenzy, and the old problem of *Ausgelassensheit*, licentiousness in a *'Rausch der Entsittlichung'* – an intoxication of depravity (Jung 1912: 222 – 223). For, he suggests, these ancient drives, such as evoked by Nietzsche, are 'the archetypes, the forms or river-beds along which the current of psychic life has always flowed' (Jung 1971: 5.228). Like the English poet, Matthew Arnold, Jung reflects on the mournful roar as the tide of Christianity subsides but also speculates as to why Christianity was adopted by Western culture in the first place. To this his reply is that it was:

> accepted as a means of escape from the brutality and unconsciousness of the ancient world. As soon as we discard it the old brutality returns in force, as has been made overwhelmingly clear by contemporary events. This is not a step forward, but a long step backwards into the past … the beast breaks loose and a frenzy of demoralization sweeps over the civilized world.
>
> (Jung 1971: 5. 230)

Such early warnings were to come to a head in the 1930s as he watched with apprehension the rise of Adolf Hitler and Nazism. This was indeed the return of the ancient *Raserei* and *Rausch der Entsittlichung* – here Dionysos transformed by Jung into Wotan – the inconstant Lord of 'inspiration, madness, intoxication and wildness, the god of the Berserkers, those wild people who run amok' (Bishop 1995: 284). This god will now rule the hearts of the German people and lead them to the brink of catastrophe. But still, beginning with his break with Freud and continued through his life work, he saw 'the return of Dionysos' as something to be countered by the homeopathic influence of therapy. Just as the Attics employed tragedy to tame the wild Eastern gods, now therapy will do the same in our time, as Bishop puts it 'as early as 1912 Jung had set out his post-Nietzschean agenda for the transformation of faith into a secular, psychological religion' (Bishop 1995: 107). As we saw, like Nietzsche, for Jung in some strange way the Dionysian is connected with the realm of the Mothers, the *Urmütter* – the same place to which Faust himself descends. This realm, the realm of the Mothers, is the source of the *Raserei* and libido together. As such it is to be venerated and enshrined at the centre of the psychotherapeutic process:

> [The libido] is that part of us which is immortal, since it represents that bond through which we feel that in the race we are never extinguished. It is life from the life of Mankind. Its springs, which well up from the depths of the Unconscious, come, as does our life in general, from the root of the whole of humanity, since we are indeed only a twig broken off from the Mother and transplanted.[12]
>
> (Jung 1971: 5. 202/1912: 194/195)

For Jung, Faust's 'descent to the mothers' reveals 'the deepest roots of Faust's longing' as he descends to the '*Ur und Allwesen*' of libido (Jung 1971: 5. 205/6/1912: 198/199) here reflecting the '*Urwesen*' that Nietzsche describes in the *Birth* (Nietzsche 1990: 1.17). By tapping back into this *Urwesen* therapy, like religion, goes back to the libidinal roots of humanity. The same libidinal root that Nietzsche designated as the 'mythic root of religion' in the *Birth* that kept religions alive. Once modern religion, he speculated, had abandoned this root, it would wither and die:

> For this is the way in which religions are wont to die out ... the feeling for myth (*das Gefühl für den Mythos*) perishes and its place is taken by the claim of religion to historical foundations.
>
> (Nietzsche 1990: 1.10)

Edith Stein's human education

To conclude this chapter I will put the 'Dionysian psychology' of Freud, Nietzsche and Jung in dialogue with Edith's own approach to psychology and what she will increasingly refer to as 'the soul'. In so doing I will draw upon three main sets of texts. The first were written shortly after her doctorate was completed and whilst she (unsuccessfully) sought a teaching post at a German university (the so-called German *Habilitationsschrift*). These are available in Volume 6 of the *Edith Stein Gesamtausgabe* as *Beiträge zur Philosophischen Begründung der Psychologie und der Geisteswissenschaften* and have received an English translation in Volume 7 of the English *Collected Works of Edith Stein*. The second set of texts date from the period in the early 1930s when she commenced a new phase of her career at the German Institute for Scientific Pedagogy at Münster. Here she worked closely with the Catholic Teachers Association of Germany, lecturing widely on the curriculum and pedagogy of Catholic education, especially in relation to the role of women (we shall return to this in a later chapter). Despite the need to research and lecture on pedagogy the desire to pursue her philosophical anthropology persisted and we shall see how it manifested in her 1932/3 text *Der Aufbau der Menschlichen Person* (available in Volume 14 of the *Gesamtausgabe* but at the time of writing not available in English translation). The final selection comes from the work completed after her entry into the Carmelite Order in 1933: *Endliches und Ewiges Sein/Finite and Eternal Being* (Volume 11/12 of the *Gesamtausgabe* and Volume 9 of the *Collected Works*). Although there is a continuity in her thought one also sees a developing mind, especially in respect to the relationship between the theological and philosophical, the spirit and the self, which I will try to reflect here. In the following chapter we shall go deeper into her anthropology but for the remainder of this chapter we shall explore her response to the 'depth psychology' presented so far built upon the phenomenological foundations we discussed in the previous two chapters.

As both Nietzsche and Jung (and, as we saw earlier, Husserl) had linked hands with Faust in their descent to the 'mothers' so Edith Stein begins *Der Aufbau* by stating that beneath everything we do there stands a guiding *logos*

(ESGA 14: 2). At the outset she signifies the difficulty of rendering '*logos*' into German, citing as her somewhat skittish example Faust's famous attempt to translate '*Im Anfang war das Wort*' from St John's Gospel in his study in Goethe's play (just before the devil appears). Faust famously concludes by declaring his preferred translation to be: '*Im Anfang war die Tat!*' – 'In the beginning was the deed!' (*Faust*: 1.1236 in Goethe 1971: 37). Which is significant in that when she returns in her later work, *Finite and Eternal Being*, to a discussion of the role of *logos* in our lives she stresses that it makes itself manifest in our *actions* as much as our *thoughts*. As she puts it later:

> Another access to the indwelling of God in the soul and to the place where the soul's being appears anchored in divine being is gained – likewise on the basis of inner awareness – by starting out from the experience of what a person *can do* and what a person *should do*, or from the relationship of the freedom of the I (*das Ich*) to the power which commands (*zu Gebote stehenden Kraft*): the power which is at a human being's disposal as an already present possession … Every free act is a performance (*Leistung*) that consumes power.
>
> (CWES 9: 444, ESGA 11/12: 374)

Like Nietzsche and Faust, for Stein '*Im Anfang war die Tat*'. However for Stein, unlike Nietzsche, the self-giving act reveals that our action arises from a source greater than ourselves:

> If then there is an obligation that is beyond the natural power of the I, the source of the additional strength must lie outside the person's nature (*auf eine Kraftquelle ausserhalb seiner Natur*).
>
> (ESGA 11/12: 375, CWES 9: 445)

And for the origins of this source 'faith provides the answer.' Thus, for Stein 'the innermost aspect of the soul'(*das Innerste der Seele*) is a 'vessel' (*Gefäss*) into which God's spirit (the life of Grace – *das Gnadenleben*) streams if it opens itself up to God with its willing power. For 'the spirit of God is meaning and power' ('*Gottes Geist ist Sinn und Kraft*'). This spirit gives the soul new life so that it can perform new acts which by its own nature it would have been incapable. Therefore she concludes:

At its base, then, every 'meaning'-full demand which is made upon the soul with obligatory force is a 'word of God'. For there is no 'meaning' that does not have its eternal home in the *logos* and anyone who willingly receives such a word of God simultaneously receives the divine power to comply with the demand.

(ESGA 11/12: 375, CWES 9: 445)

Stein therefore presents us with a fascinating anthropology. Like Goethe and Nietzsche (and Wittgenstein in his *Philosophical Investigations*) she asserts that '*Im Anfang war die Tat*' but for Stein the *Tat* is that which reveals to us God's action (his 'grace') in the ground of our soul. Once we have opened up the soul to this grace it increases with strength so that:

Every increase in grace leads in addition to a strengthening of the human being's spiritual being and opens up to the soul a richer and more penetrating insight into the divine word, into the supernatural meaning that underlies every event and that becomes articulate in the innermost aspect of the soul as an 'inspiration' (*Einsprechung*).

(ESGA 11/12: 375, CWES 9: 445)

The *logos* is therefore for Stein an '*objective Ordnung*'/ 'objective ordering' of beings which is revealed through our deeds (ESGA 14: 2). As we shall see in the next chapter, this is a lifelong task of acting so as to reveal the inner nature of what she will increasingly refer to as the soul. The nature of the self will thus determine what will be manifest in the acts of our life in a similar way to, for example, the type and nature of leather which, she tells us, will determine the type of shoe that will be made from it. Thus, the idea of the individual person, the anthropology, is inescapably linked for her with our relations to the world and those around us – our action in the world.

She develops this idea by stressing the key elements of German idealism as it has developed up to then in the hands of Gotthold Lessing (1729–81), Johann Herder (1744–1803), Friedrich Schiller (1759–1805) and Goethe (ESGA 14: 4). Such a person as portrayed in this tradition (as can be seen in Nietzsche for example) is free and called to develop 'perfection'. This Enlightenment turn (without the shadows we saw cast by Husserl in his account of the period) is characterized for her by an optimism and 'activism' (*Optimismus und Aktivismus*) seeking especially the perfection of humanity through the perfection of each individual. Here she cites in particular Herder and his call to classical antiquity for this 'perfection' (*Vollenderung*). From this spirit arose the educational reform movements of the eighteenth and nineteenth centuries which urged the educators and young alike to take their places in this great positive goal for the betterment of humanity (and from which she herself benefitted so much). Reason itself is central to this programme and enthroned as the guiding principle of the work (here she notes the influence above all of Jean-Jacques Rousseau, 1712–78). Such a search, as indeed Freud and Nietzsche both note in their own ways, leaves, she states, the 'darker' urges and feelings in the shadow to be suppressed. Yet, in the depths she notes that these 'dark forces' continue to be 'at work' (ESGA 14: 5).[13] For many Germans, she points out, these darker urges were first revealed in the Russian writings of Lev Tolstoy (1828–1910) and Fyodor Dostoevsky (1821–81) and it is the description of these darker drives that is later taken up by the psychologists – the irruption into daily life of the dark movements of the depths (ESGA 14: 5). Yet, for Stein, it was the Great War ('the great fiasco') that brought these dark depths out into the open from beyond the pages of the Russian novelists and off the Viennese couches: 'the powers of the depths were revealed to all the world in the War and the madness that followed it' (ESGA 14: 5). In this madness, humanity, reason and culture were all subsumed. The initial optimism of Nietzsche's post-enlightenment programme has thus clearly evaporated for her at this stage. Instead of the perfectable 'super-man' of *Zarathustra*, the Great War had rather revealed the return of Nietzsche's (and Jung's) ancient *Raserei* and *Wollust*.

Writing in the 1930s, Stein sees the then dominance of psychoanalytic views as proof of the triumph of this notion that we are controlled by dark forces from below (*Triebe*). She depicts the analysts arguing as to which are the strongest drives, and whether overall there is unity to personhood: 'can we know a unity to the soul which controls the drives or whether the soul's life, on the surface and in depth, will not be led into chaos?' (ESGA 14: 6). Therefore, in contrast to the old Idealism of Goethe and the poets she sees the new twentieth-century psychoanalytic view as the dethronement of the intellect and the free-acting will, as well as the objective unity of the self and the cultural *telos* to which it once strove. In such a world, following the psychological world view, the goal of life (and education) is to mould a 'normally functioning' human being who can balance these lower drives, all to be discovered by the abstractions of psychoanalysis. Once analysed and identified the drives will need to be either suppressed or fed. Consequently, she views the whole process and glorification of analysis (and consequently human drives) as a hindrance rather than a help in creating a fully rounded *'menschliche Ausbildung'* – 'the formation of the human person' (the title of her book) – not only for the individual but for society itself (ESGA 14: 26–7).[14]

Stein's (post) modern Christian anthropology of personhood

Therefore, we can see that in contrast to the views of Freud, Jung and Nietzsche, Stein presents a third alternative for a (post) modern anthropology. To formulate this in the *Aufbau* she begins with the thoughts of her contemporary Martin Heidegger, whose ideas, as we have seen, were beginning to dominate German philosophy in the 1930s. A philosopher also fascinated and influenced by Nietzsche, whom he interpreted as searching for the root of being (*Sein*) amongst the pre-Socratic philosophers. Thus, paraphrasing Heidegger's latest ideas in *Sein und Zeit* (1927) and *Was ist Metaphysik?* (1930), she states that for him: 'the great question of metaphysics is the question of the nature of Being' (ESGA 14: 7).[15] In Stein's view, Heidegger's search for *Sein* in everyday life inevitably leads to existential 'angst' as to the nature of humanity's place in the cosmos, emphasized by life itself constantly being bounded by inevitable death. From this, Stein points out that at the heart of Heidegger's approach lies a question about *Geist* and freedom. Yet, she suggests, he leaves us wanting. Apart from posing the question of 'being and non-being' he does not present us with a solution to the *Angst* within which we find ourselves (ESGA 14: 8). The individual, for Heidegger, is free insofar as they align their life with the fullness of Being; however, what will be the consequences of that? With great prescience, she questions what will happen when such a rampant 'idealism' will smash away all idols – for what will be left to follow? Heidegger's shameful behaviour under the National Socialist regime certainly vindicates her alarm here.

Stein begins her exposition of her 'third way' between Idealism and Reductionism by stressing that her Christian anthropology shares with Idealism certain characteristics, namely, the conviction that human nature is fundamentally orientated towards the good, the potential for individual freedom and choice, our call to perfection and appreciation of the underlying unity of humankind (ESGA 14: 9). However, although this may appear similar to a Christian anthropology, such as the one she proposes, the two approaches fundamentally differ as to the origins of respective goals. For a Christian anthropology presupposes that we are created in the image of God and it is this image that imbues our beings with goodness, the search for perfection, unity and so on. In this respect Stein follows in the footsteps of possibly one of the first 'Christian psychologists' – St Augustine of Hippo (354–430). For, like him, she sees contained within the human person the *Bild*/picture of the Christian Trinity, something we shall return to in the next chapter. Behind and supporting all this, for both Stein and Augustine, is love, the fundamental basis of human personhood: 'humanity *is* only through God and, *what* it is, through God. Because the human being is spirit, and as spirit is equipped with the light of reason (i.e. the figure of the divine *logos*), then she can know.'[16] Likewise as the spirit is will, so the human being has freedom. Thus spirit (*Geist*), knowledge and will become the pattern of the Father, Son and Holy Spirit within the individual, reflecting their Trinitarian nature in the interactions of the human self.[17]

In contrast to the play of the Dionysian urges behind the superficial day-to-day 'consciousness' that we find in Nietzsche, Jung and Freud, she points rather to the underlying, what may be called, 'moral' nature of the human soul which reflects its creative source in the Divine Trinity (ESGA 14: 10). In this 'moral' account of the self we were originally good but are fallen – our drives rebel against the spirit, reason is darkened and the will weakened. However, although subverted, reason and will are still there even in a weakened state and can still perform the function for which they were originally created – to draw us back to communion with the God-head. Each then has the possibility of returning to the God-head as it battles with this 'lower nature'. Such a view of the human self perceives an overall 'unity of apperception' when it recognizes within itself its divine original image.

She therefore presents a Christian *Bild* of the person, in Betschart's words, 'neither totally integrated (the idealistic trap) nor totally fallen (Freud), but redeemed by Christ and from his perfection a call comes endlessly' (Betschart 2014: 200). From this perspective, therefore, pursuit of the Nietzschean or Freudian Dionysian drives in themselves will not lead to freedom for: 'humanity has no power over the forces of the deep and cannot find its own way from the depths to the heights' (ESGA 14: 11).[18] Like Karl Kraus (1874–1936), what worries her about both the materialist and idealist positions is the concomitant lack of individual moral choice.

For Stein, Christ alone, as Son of God, can lead us through these drives to the light of will, reason and freedom that we seek as the original picture of the soul. In this respect Christ contains the unity of apperception, that is, the human soul restoring the *Bild* of God into the human soul:

> The natural light of our reasoning is strengthened through the light of grace and is better protected against being led astray if not also made secure against it, and above all, the spiritual eye is opened to recognize everything in this world which witnesses to another World.
>
> (ESGA 14: 11)[19]

The Christian baptism, the *metanoia*, that changes the *nous*/'soul' of the one who participates in it, is that which redirects our passions and drives back to their origins in God (ESGA 14: 12 see also Tyler 2017). This connection between *metanoia* and confession is one particularly emphasized, of course, by Augustine. Paraphrasing Augustine she reminds us that 'within the human person lies truth' (ESGA 14: 12)[20] and that this truth *is* the Divine Being of God: '*that* is the truth, which one strives for within and goes to the Ground. The soul comes to know itself and thus knows God within itself' (ESGA 14: 12 c.f. Augustine's *On the Trinity* 10.5.7).[21] Like Augustine, she evinces a deep scepticism for a 'self-knowledge purely based upon natural means' (ESGA 14: 13). No Wotan, 'soothsaying God of the vine', *Führer* or Dionysos can rescue us from the place we are in. Only, she suggests, can this happen by recognition of the light of truth that enters the self from the image of the God-head planted deep within ourselves. She therefore argues that we naturally and inevitably strive for the transcendent and that the Christian anthropology she presents, rather than destroying our desires to be complete human beings, fulfils them. This fulfilment thus becomes for Stein only possible once we face the divine light shining on the Dionysian depths of the soul.

Thus the human being, for Stein following Aquinas, is a 'microcosmos' which holds together in itself 'all the realms of the created word in unity' (ESGA 14: 26).[22] Accordingly her *Bild* of the person, her anthropology, cannot be separated from philosophical, theological and metaphysical questions as indeed, I have argued here, can ours, whether we are a philosopher, teacher, counsellor, psychologist, minister, pastor or general caregiver. For her the pastoral care flows from the anthropology and the anthropology flows from the philosophical and theological foundations that underpin it.

As we shall explore later in this book, from this fundamental view comes her understanding of the person which will underpin all her later writings. Thus, the human person straddles two worlds, the spiritual and physical, and because of this exists on several levels at once. We shall return to these levels of the self in the next chapter. For now it suffices to emphasize that the Christian anthropology she presents us with is held together by her notion of the 'soul-centred' (*seelische*) nature of the human. The word, 'soul', indeed, far from being a distraction or anachronism, is actually central to her exposition of a Christian anthropology. If we follow her arguments carefully she is presenting an escape from, on the one hand, the Charybdis of Freudian (or materialist) reductionism, and on the other the Scylla of transcendental idealism (Heidegger's pursuit of Being leading to the frenzied Idealisms of the modern world). Rather she wants to restore the integrity of human personhood that encompasses the physical, emotional, mental and spiritual aspects of the self.

We are material things and exist in a material space but we are not just a material element (ESGA 14: 29/30) but as living entities we also have a '*Seelenwesen*' – 'soul-nature'. As to the nature of this soul, she states that at this point in the *Aufbau* she will not elaborate, and taking our cue from her we shall return to this in the following chapter.

The life force (*Lebenskraft*)

Before we turn in the next chapter to the key Steinian psychological concepts of 'soul' and 'levels of self' we shall conclude this chapter exploring her relation to psychology in an exposition of an important element of self that we encountered in the previous chapter and one that she develops in one of her earlier works still dominated by phenomenology: *Psychische Kausalität*, completed in 1918 at the close of the Great War.[23] In the light of the discussion above of the Dionysian *Triebe* that so obsessed Nietzsche and Freud, her exposition of what she calls the *Life-Force (Lebenskraft)* is fascinating because it relates particularly to these 'Nietzschean' themes.

Stein begins her exposition by describing, as it were, the 'field' of experience – the original stream of consciousness (*der ursprüngliche Bewusstseinstrom*) (ESGA 6: 11), which for her is 'a pure becoming' (*ein reines Werden*) from which comes the field of being out of which experience streams. It is a continuous stream without links. Within this field she gives her definition of the 'I' as:

> The current is *one* because it streams from *one* I. Thus, what from the past into the future lives, in every moment, feels new life springing forth and carries the whole trail of the past with it – that is the 'I'.
>
> (ESGA 6: 15)[24]

However, within this unity of apperception which is the I, she is at pains to distinguish the 'life force' from 'consciousness'. She makes this distinction by noting the differences between states of being (*Lebenszuständen*) and states of feelings (*Lebensgefühlen*) (ESGA 6: 21).[25] The states of feeling in consciousness can be different from a state of being, such as a 'weariness that is present without us being aware of it', for, 'it is definitely possible that I feel invigorated without there actually being the state of refreshment really present – the future will give a better knowledge of this' (ESGA 6: 21). Thus the feelings give us a momentary glimpse of the nature of the I and the underlying *Lebenskraft* within it (ESGA 6: 22). Even in this relatively early work, her phenomenological analysis shows Stein the fundamental unknowable nature of the I as a transcendental category.

This is to be distinguished from the 'I' that collects around the feelings in the 'stream of life':

> The I that possesses this real property is naturally not to be confused with the pure I, which is the radiating point of the pure experiences originally lived.
>
> (ESGA 6: 22)[26]

The I is thus only experienced as a 'bearer of properties' – in itself it lies mysterious and ungraspable (as we saw earlier was the case with Husserl, a point we shall return to in the next chapter). As noted, it is this notion of the mysterious unknown centre of self that Stein will later enshrine, as we shall see, in her later philosophy as the essential unknowing that lies at the heart of the self. This 'real I' (and thus apparently caught up in the Life Force) is what she now designates as the 'psychical' (*psychische*) in contrast to the stream of consciousness of feeling – the conscious I:[27]

> We now see that consciousness (*Bewusstsein*) and the psychical (*psychisches*) can be fundamentally distinguished from one another: consciousness as a realm of 'known' pure experience and the psychical as a sphere within which experiences and their contents witness to a transcendent reality (*bekundenden transzendenten Realität*).
>
> (ESGA 6: 22)

Following good Kantian principles Stein resists the urge to define the transcendent realm in itself pointing rather to its 'witness' via the epiphenomena of consciousness. Therefore what generates consciousness is not the everyday 'life feelings' (*Lebensgefühle*) but 'rather the modes of life-force' (*Lebenskraft*) that are witnessed by those life feelings (ESGA 6: 23). 'Life-force' is thus an underlying force that undergirds our every day 'experiences' or feelings of self.

A year later Stein will take up her consideration of the life force in her next published work *Individuum und Gemeinschaft* (1919, also in ESGA 6). Here her focus shifts from the individual to society; however, she wants the two to resonate or mirror each other so that the basic anthropology she presented in the earlier work will be reflected in her analysis of society. Central to this consideration is the role that *Lebenskraft* plays in 'the total composition of the community' (ESGA 6: 164). Again she reminds us that the individual psyche is 'rooted' in the *Lebenskraft*. The properties reveal themselves in *sinnliche* (sensory) and *geistig* (spiritual/mental) properties which reveal a 'split in the *Lebenskraft* itself' (ESGA 6: 165) into sensory and mental *Lebenskraft*. All this reveals the 'original layout' (*ursprungliche Anlagen*) of the psyche that is manifest and unfolds itself in daily life. Time and again she returns to the notion of human development being about the unfolding of innate dispositions of the soul to which we will return in the next chapter.

From this connection between everyday experiences and feeling and an underlying psyche or soul rooted in life force comes another key phrase in the Steinian lexicon which we introduced in the previous chapter – the *Kern*, core or nucleus. We shall give a fuller account of this in the following chapter, suffice to say at this point she relates the *Kern* to the psyche and *Lebenskraft* thus: 'the structure of the *psyche*, as we have depicted it up to now, has still not accounted for its ultimate core' (ESGA 6: 200).[28] It is to that 'ultimate core' and its relationship to the 'soul' we shall return in the following chapter.

Nietzsche or the Crucified One?

In this chapter we have seen how Stein delineates her approach to human personhood from that of her contemporaries. As has been pointed out, it is significant that Stein undergoes her investigations against the backdrop of the development of German psychology operating, as I have argued, within the shadow of Nietzsche. Like Freud, Jung and Nietzsche she too has a 'life force' that is operating beneath the surface of day to day sentient life. How the four thinkers discussed in this chapter approach this life force and what they do with it determines, in a way, their approach to the psyche and psychology.

Nietzsche, as we have seen, sees the life force as an unstoppable force of nature that is dammed at our peril. The Greek genius, in his eyes, had been to amalgamate the Dionysian and Apollonian life forces in the great sacred act of the tragic drama. This had been sadly perverted by the growth of the Socratic dialectic and the cult of reason. In his early work he saw the return of the tragic muse in the sorcerer of Bayreuth – Richard Wagner – who at this high point in his career hoped to rebirth the Attic tragic on his 'green hill' in the Franconian countryside. Attending the opening of the Bayreuth festival in 1876, Nietzsche (not for the first or last time) was sorely disappointed as he observed the gross and crude behaviour of his fellow Germans – markedly untransformed by the power of Wagner's *Gesamtkunstwerk*.[29] Towards the end of his life Nietzsche increasingly replaces the opposition of Socrates and Dionysos that he had developed in the *Birth* into the opposition between Dionysos and 'the Crucified One' with which we began this chapter. As he would write in *Ecce Homo*, his last completed work: '[Christianity] negates aesthetic values, the only values recognized by the *Birth of Tragedy*; it is nihilist in the most profound sense, whereas in the Dionysian symbol the ultimate limit of affirmation is attained' (*Ecce Homo* in Nietzsche 1967: 271). Leading to his final denunciations of Christianity in some of the last things he wrote:

> Christian morality – the most malignant form of the will to lie, the real Circe of humanity – that which *corrupted* humanity ... it is the lack of nature, it is the utterly gruesome fact that *antinature* itself received the highest honors as morality and was fixed over humanity as law and categorical imperative.
> (Nietzsche 1967: 332)

Nietzsche's Dionysian legacy remained after his lapse into insanity, however, and, as I have argued here, it slowly transformed itself into the quest for the life force in his successors. On the psychological side Freud finds a convenient designation for Nietzsche's life force in his own notion of the *Id/Es* and the unconscious (*das Unbewusste*). Suppressed, this time by the overactive I and over-I (*Ich* and *Über-Ich*) that seek to thwart its destructive aspects, leaving the individual psyche to be thrown into a perpetual psychic conflict between *das Ich* and *das Es*. The sad consequence of this is '*das Unbehagen in der Kultur*', as he will finally call it – the sense of unease in our civilization as the 'civilized' person suppresses the original libidinal (or indeed Dionysian) drives in the goal of creating civilized society.[30] The repressed finally re-emerges towards the end of Freud's life in his native Austria as he and his family are persecuted by the triumphant Nazis, who, ironically, also claimed cultural justification through the doctored works of Nietzsche (and the racist intellectual circle that had grown up around Wagner's Bayreuth).[31]

Meanwhile, Jung followed the 'soothsaying God of the vine' to re-enter the world of Gnostic Christianity as he sought a return to the underworld which he explored in the fantastical journey described in the *Red Book* (see Jung 2009 and Tyler 2015). His journeys into the archetype, so inspired by Nietzsche, will direct his own thought towards the development of the new science of analytical psychology.

For Stein, following Kant and Husserl, the life force exists too, underlying and forming our conscious lives to the same extent at Freud. Yet for her the unknowable thing remains just that: a transcendental presupposition that lies at the heart of the self. After her discovery of Christianity she finds what she had earlier intuited: the divine unknowing of the Christian mystical tradition to which we will return in a later chapter. Thus, from the same philosophical roots as her contemporaries, she is able, too, to construct an anthropology which will preserve the mysterious unknowing that lies at the heart of human personhood. This will coalesce around her later 'soul-psychology' to which we turn next.

In one of her last lectures given before she was forced to retreat from academic life following the Nazi rise to power, she returned to her lifelong love: the German classics and especially Goethe's *Faust*. Like Husserl, Nietzsche, Freud and Jung she concluded this lecture by reflecting on the 'realm of the mothers' – '*das Ewigweibliche*' – that draws us above from the conclusion of Part Two of *Faust*. Here she finds a representation of the healing power of the feminine that we shall return to in a later chapter. This healing power, she concludes, arises from 'the foot of the cross' (ESGA 16: 168), a healing power that will become increasingly important for her as she stepped into the darkening world of 1930s Germany.

Conclusion

We have seen in this chapter how Nietzsche in the *Birth* prefigures the twentieth-century move from an anthropology of the self based on reason to one that seeks its origins in the drives. Freud himself is somewhat circumspect as to the origin of these drives, sometimes favouring a biological root, following

Darwin, at other times talking of shadier metaphysical entities such as *Eros* and *Thanatos*. For Nietzsche, on the other hand, they are manifestations of the *Ur-Eine* seen so dramatically and viscerally in the coming of spring as represented by the Greeks in the ubiquitous figure of the Satyr. Where, however, Nietzsche is prophetic is in his prediction of the end of scientific rational discourse as the 'psychological' tips over into that which lies beyond reason (Husserl's *Irrationalismus*):

> Only after the scientific spirit has been taken to the limit and has been forced by the demonstration of these limits to renounce its claim to universal validity, can we hope for the rebirth of tragedy.
>
> (Nietzsche 1993: 82)

What all the thinkers discussed in this chapter hold in common is a shared belief in the limits of traditional empirical enquiry to discover the ultimate source and home of the human psyche. Freud, as we have seen, preferred to explore the shadowy underworld of the *Id*. Jung moved into the Gnostic truths of myth whilst Heidegger settled with the primeval force of Being. Stein radically returns to the Christian tradition via phenomenology.

Nietzsche had predicted in 1872 the 'gradual awakening of the Dionysian spirit in our contemporary world' (Nietzsche 1993: 94) as an 'entire cultural epoch (the Socratic-Alexandrian) comes to an end' (Nietzsche 1993: 97). As Husserl so forensically examined it, this 'crisis of civilization' overcame European culture in the mid-twentieth century in successive waves of fascist, communist and nationalist enthusiasms that swept the world and still continue to influence us today. In this respect, his prediction of the rise of irrationality seems unnervingly prescient. As we continue to observe the tumults around us we can see the predictive value of Nietzsche's wild writing: Dionysos is unbound and stalks the earth again. Stein, as we have seen, charted her own course through the turbulent waters of the twentieth century. Her alternative vision of the self, her spiritual anthropology, returns to the humane and humanistic roots embedded in the Christian Trinitarian view of the human soul. It is perhaps unsurprising then that these self-same Dionysian forces, whipped up and directed by the National Socialist Party in German, should ultimately be the source of her own destruction in Auschwitz.

5

Stein's anthropology: Seele and levels of the self

Introduction

We now come to the heart of this book, and the heart of Stein's philosophy – her philosophy of the self or soul. Throughout our discussion various definitions and ideas of personhood have arisen – it is now time to try to bring them together. This is no easy task. As numerous commentators have pointed out,[1] one of the first problems is that Stein herself (like Freud and Jung) develops her idea of personhood throughout her writing career. After her conversion to Christianity she incorporates new metaphysical layers into phenomenological analyses previously undertaken, Yet, as commentators such as Betschart and Ales Bello demonstrate, the foundations for her later positions *can* be found in her earlier philosophical work and stressing the discontinuity between the two may lead to an overly artificial division in her work as philosopher and theologian. A move we shall try to avoid here.

Secondly, as re-iterated throughout this book, there is the problem of the status of the documents she produced. As her editor, Beckmann-Zöller, points out: 'Stein's theological anthropology, unfortunately, remains in draft form and was not made ready for publication: it ends in mid-sentence, but it nonetheless allows us to glimpse into Stein's intellectual "workshop"' (Beckman-Zöller 2008: 63). Like her contemporary Wittgenstein, the majority of the writings available to us today were never published in her lifetime and she thus probably displays a greater philosophical fluidity in them than perhaps she would have allowed had they been final drafts.

Finally, as we have encountered throughout this book, there is the problem of translation. Not only are there the difficulties of the English words for key German concepts such as *Seele, Geist* and *Ich* but there is the question of 'translation' of a whole other world of thinking – early twentieth-century German discourse around, for example, *Geisteswissenschaften*, which presents problems for the average Anglophone reader today.[2] With this in mind it might be worth reiterating the reasons I have retained the not uncontroversial term 'soul' in my translations and its significance for the psychological genealogy within which Stein was working.

The return of the soul?

As I wrote earlier my first interest in writing this book was primarily to explore the philosophical and psychological (and ultimately pastoral) implications of Stein's 'philosophical psychology of the soul'. Accordingly, it is appropriate to dedicate a whole chapter to this demanding subject before we explore the implications of this 'living philosophy' for pastoral care in the concluding Part Two of the book. This may at first sight appear a little perverse – why bother ourselves with a term that has largely become obsolete in the twenty-first century? Surely the term belongs either within archaic ecclesial discourse or Southern beat music gatherings? For if the term is used at all today it will probably have a great deal of theological freight or connections to contemporary movements in music. And yet, despite its unfashionability the soul has made a surprising comeback in recent years. This began on the wilder fringes of contemporary transpersonal psychological discourse, notably in the writings of the maverick Jungian James Hillman (1926–2011) and the former monk turned new age guru, Thomas Moore (b.1940). What both had in common was a sense that the current mind-centric practice that we call 'psychology' had drifted far from its roots in the humanities and the sacred sciences. For both, 'soul-language' became a banner under which they could rally their cause – the sense of meaning in everyday life, irrespective of the pathologization of contemporary psychology. In this respect what they were advocating was a new form of what we would now call 'positive psychology' (for an extended commentary on this movement see Tyler 2016).

When I wrote 'The Pursuit of the Soul' in 2016 I was particularly concerned with constructing a psychological and philosophical response to the co-opting of soul by those outside the traditional folds of religion and theology. For just as theologians in the second half of the twentieth century had shied away from too much overt talk of the soul (especially when this might imply a dangerous neo-Platonic spiritualizing of the self) so psychologists had equally forbidden their followers from introducing too much spirituality into psychological discourse. Within this void left by the two spheres of psychoanalysis and theology a new form of 'soul-language' has developed in the past few decades, seemingly separate from the old dualisms that the word often evokes.

The complexity of the problem is compounded by the fact that as well as there being issues around the English word 'soul', so the German word '*Seele*' has an equally varied and challenging etymology, making it just as difficult to extricate from its prevailing cultural matrices as its English equivalent. No better example of this is found than in the works of Sigmund Freud, and in the English translation of his work. The Austrian psychoanalyst, Bruno Bettelheim, famously explored in his *Freud and Man's Soul* (Bettelheim 1982) how the English translation of Freud's work had created a certain Anglo-Saxon tone somewhat alien to the thrust of the German original. As he stated 'the English translations of Freud's writings distort much of the essential humanism that permeates the originals' (Bettelheim 1982: 4). He stressed that Freud himself wrote clearly and elegantly on his themes, and one of the sources of the later success of his work undoubtedly lay in his finely wrought German prose style. By the 1920s his fame had spread across Europe, as well as his notoriety, and in Britain there was the desire to have English versions of his writings available. The task of translating this work fell to a member of the Bloomsbury group – James Strachey (1887–1967) – brother of the famous Bloomsbury aesthete Lytton Strachey, who had sought analysis himself with Freud in Vienna. Because of Freud's scandalous reputation (his writings on sexuality had earned him a certain notoriety in Vienna), Strachey felt it necessary to medicalize and impersonalize Freud's prose as much as possible to make it more acceptable to the scientific and medical communities in Britain.[3]

Nowhere is this shift more apparent, argues Bettelheim, than in the translations of Freud's terms for the self as a whole. For here Freud's preferred terms are *die Seele, seelische* and *Seelenleben*, literally, 'the soul', 'soulish'/'concerned with the soul' and 'soul-life', all of which Strachey replaces with 'the mind', 'mental' and 'mental life'. The effect of this, argues Bettelheim, is to replace Freud's 'direct and always deeply personal appeals to our common humanity' with an 'abstract, highly theoretical, erudite and mechanized – in short, "scientific" – statements about the strange and very complex workings of our mind' (Bettelheim 1982: 5). Psychology, argues Bettelheim, thus becomes 'a purely intellectual system – a clever, exciting game' rather than the invitation to explore the richness and darkness of the individual soul-life.[4] Freud's own vision for the future of the modality he had initiated was neither a profession in hock to the scientific-medical establishment (hence his defence of non-medically trained analysts in *The Question of Lay-Analysis*, 1926) nor a form of life dominated by the clergy and religious ways of thinking (hence the genesis of his *The Future of an Illusion*, 1927). As he wrote to Oskar Pfister in 1928:

> I do not know whether you have guessed the hidden link between 'Lay Analysis' and 'Illusion'. In the former I want to protect analysis from the doctors, and in the latter from the priests. I want to hand it over to a profession that does not yet exist, a profession of secular ministers of souls (*weltlichen Seelsorgern*), who don't have to be doctors and must not be priests.
> (Letter to Oskar Pfister 25.11.1928)[5]

Thus, the battle for Freud's soul – or more specifically his translation of *Seele* – can be seen in the wider context of the battle for the soul of psychology: whether it was to become a medically or clerically dominated profession or neither. As he wrote to Pfister in 1909: 'in itself psychoanalysis is neither religious nor non-religious, but an impartial tool which both the spiritual and layman (*der Geistliche wie der Laie*) can use in the service of the sufferer' (Freud 1963: Freud to Pfister, 9.2.1909). Freud was particularly aware in this context of the American tendency to 'turn psychoanalysis into a mere housemaid of psychiatry' (Bettelheim 1982: 36). Oskar Pfister, the Swiss Protestant pastor with whom Freud corresponded most of his life, put it succinctly in one of his letters:

Your substitute for religion is basically the idea of the eighteenth century Enlightenment met in a proud modern guise. I must confess that, with all my pleasure in the advance of science and technology, I do not believe in the adequacy and sufficiency of this solution of the problem of life.

(Freud 1963: Pfister to Freud, 24.11.1927)

For Bettelheim, there is no reason for the (mis-)translation of Freud's *Seele* by 'mind' apart from 'a wish to interpret psychoanalysis as a medical speciality' (1982: 76) and his retention of the word 'soul' in his interpretation of Freud preserves for him facets of Freud's project lost by the overemphasis on 'mind', as he put it:

Freud uses *Seele* and *seelisch* rather than *geistig* because *geistig* refers mainly to the rational aspects of the mind, to that of which we are conscious. The idea of the soul, by contrast, definitely includes much of which we are not consciously aware.

(1982: 77)

By not providing us with a precise definition of 'soul', argues Bettelheim, Freud is deliberately reflecting the ambiguous nature of the *psyche* itself. Thus Bettelheim's 'soul' is a cipher for all that is ambiguous and indecipherable in the *psyche*. It is, as we shall see in the work of Stein, a call to the 'unknowing' that lies at the heart of the psyche and psychological life.

Stein's story of the soul

As with Freud, Stein increasingly uses the word '*Seele*' when discussing the nature of the person in her writing career. And, as with Freud, I think it important that this terminology is respected even when she is discussed in English. As pointed out, one of the problems from the English perspective is that this discourse, since the Enlightenment, tends to associate the term with something perhaps gaseous and fuzzily religious. Nothing could be further from Stein's use of the term. Following Husserl and her training in phenomenology, the body, and bodily experience, is always paramount in her understanding of self. As Fuentes puts it: 'following the phenomenological approach, we can say that the human person perceives herself as an embodied being, as a living body, and as a psychophysical subject … My body is always present here and can be grasped. Even though I may be unable to see, touch or hear it, the body is always present as completely "my own corporeality"' (Fuentes 2016: 88). Thus, beginning with *On the Problem of Empathy* Stein recognized that 'soul' would *by necessity* have an embodied element that gave it its very nature. As an embodied self, soul is, as we have seen, part of the constitution that contributes towards self-identity.

Throughout her subsequent writings Stein never strays far from this phenomenological approach and thus we find her analysis of self often weaves in and out of that of Husserl's, which we covered earlier in the book, with some important differences. This is no better illustrated than in Part Six of the *Aufbau der Menschlichen Person* (ESGA 14) where she discusses the nature of the relationship between the I and the soul and the significance of the two terms. Expecting a metaphysical treatise we instead get the following:

> I think now about this problem and at the same time I hear a noise from the street, I see the piece of paper lying before me, my desk and other things lying before me. I am directed to the problem; what I see and hear passes me by, it only disturbs the periphery. I am truly turned towards the problem, I rest before it and fix my mental gaze firmly on to it. However there is something else in me, which I am not now giving space for, which I don't turn towards and which won't leave me: an unrest, a worry (*eine Unruhe, eine Sorge*). It is there and I am aware of it, perhaps it has been there a long time and persists 'under' everything else, whatever plays on the surface this remains 'in the ground of my soul' (*auf dem 'Grunde meiner Seele'*).
>
> (ESGA 14: 85)

In Chapter 3 we recalled how our choice of objects in our perceptual field (e.g. Husserl's trees) would lead to an examination of the questioning I that sought them in the first place. In a similar fashion in this phenomenological exercise Edith takes us from our awareness of the 'mental' (or cognitive?) problem before us, to the sensations of sight and sound, to this nagging anxiety (*Sorge*) that lies in the 'ground of the soul'. The choice of words is instructive and reflects those used by Husserl when he paraphrased the famous Heraclitean

Fragment in the *Crisis*: 'You will never find the boundaries of the soul, even if you follow every road, so deep is its ground' (Heraclitus: Fragment 45).[6] Commenting on the passage Husserl suggested:

> Indeed, every 'ground' that is reached points to further grounds, every horizon opened up awakens new horizons, and yet the endless whole, in its infinity of flowing movement, is orientated toward the unity of one meaning; not, of course, in such a way that we could ever simply grasp and understand the whole; rather, as soon as one has fairly well mastered the universal form of meaning-formation (*Sinnbildung*), the breadths and depths of this total meaning, in its infinite totality, take on valuative (*axiotische*) dimensions.
>
> (Husserl 1970: 170)

This 'universal ground' within which the I moves is common to both phenomenologists – Husserl and Stein. Both respect the infinite process and its self-implicating nature. Yet, following her conversion to Christianity, Edith will increasingly apply the term 'soul' to this territory, a move that her 'master' does not take. In as far as he follows her on this he would talk of a 'transcendent I' but this is a very different concept from Stein's 'soul'. As Ales Bello states: 'one speaks of I, the pure I, consciousness, soul, psyche, spirit but how ought one to organize these notions and to what do they correspond? There is no doubt that Edith Stein with her "didactic" capacity helps us much more than does her teacher, but even so the reading and ordering of his analyses is not an easy undertaking' (Ales Bello 2008: 148). Yet where master and pupil agree is that the engaging I cannot be removed from the matrix of subjectivity (like the piece of paper) within which we are immersed. For, as with Wittgenstein's reflections on consciousness to which we will return later, we cannot approach these matters as an accomplished 'fact' or 'objective science' (*pace* modern psychology). We are immersed in the stream of life and consciousness and, to paraphrase Wittgenstein, we must make alterations to the machine whilst it is still running. As Edith put it in her *Einführung in die Philosophie*: 'Consciousness is not a chest that collects lived experiences in itself. Rather these same lived experiences constitute, one following the other, the flow of consciousness' (ESGA 8: 90–1).[7]

Accordingly, we can now begin to see where the phenomenological view of the self differs from, on the one hand, the quasi-objective scientism of twentieth-century psychology and, on the other, the 'drive psychology' of Freud and Jung. In contrast to both there are no 'fixed' entities, whether they are drives, archetypes or neurons – mind (and soul) creates itself through itself. As Ales Bello puts it: 'this means that the self is not given at the beginning as a willing, available object. Rather, it comes to itself, makes itself, and for this reason, the apperception by which we say "I" constitutes the subjective side of something that presents itself as an object' (Ales Bello 2008: 154). This 'self-formation' takes place through our constituent being as '*Geist*'. As *geistige* beings we perceive and are perceived, we are created and creative. This complexity of self, encompassing material, emotional, affective, intellectual and spiritual aspects is what Edith will ultimately call 'soul' – not so much an entity, an X, but rather, as Ales Bello refers to it 'a tension' (Ales Bello 2008: 156).

Thus, by the 1930s Stein had developed an anthropology that, on the one hand, wanted to resist the over-materialization of the emergent behaviourist schools of psychology ('*Psychologie ohne Seele*') and on the other the over-spiritualizing of the 'return of Dionysos' in the mass movements of ecstatic abandonment such as Nazism. For her this middle point was held by her 'psychology with soul' which acts as mediating force between physical matter and *Geist*.

Development of the soul

Recent scholarly research has helped to clarify the genesis of the documents which come after *On the Problem of Empathy* and develop the notion of soul presented there which we looked at earlier. As part of her aim to seek employment at a German university two '*Habilitation*' papers were written which are now both found in Volume 6 of the *Gesamtausgabe*: *Psychische Kausalität*, completed in 1918, and *Individuum und Gemeinschaft*, completed the year after. Both were first published in Husserl's *Jahrbuch* in 1922.[8] The third text I will refer to, *Introduction to Philosophy* (ESGA 8), appears to have been begun whilst completing her doctoral studies and then continued for several years later, incorporating changes evolving from the publication of the other two essays; accordingly, as we shall see, its redaction history is somewhat complicated. One of the important influences on her development of 'soul-language' during this time were her conversations with her fellow phenomenologist (and god-parent) Hedwig Conrad-Martius. In a letter to her friend, Roman Ingarden, in 1917 she first mentions the influence of Conrad-Martius' ideas which had first appeared in the journal *Summa* in that year under the title *Von der Seele* (see CWES 12: 77). Conrad-Martius' 'dialogues on the soul' would finally reach publication as *Metaphysische Gespräche* ('Metaphysical Conversations') in 1921 (see Conrad-Martius 1921). In these years from 1917 to 1921, following the completion of her doctorate, these ideas will begin to percolate as they coincide with her own move to explicit acceptance of the metaphysical perspectives of Christianity.

Her new ideas about soul find their first expression in *Individual and Community* (1919) where she introduces her new concept of *Seele* influenced by her conversations with Conrad-Martius. As Betschart puts it, from this point onwards 'the soul is understood as the innermost part of the whole psycho-physical individual'[9] as for the first time she begins to understand there is an unchanging reality at the heart of the person for which she gives the name 'soul' which more or less engraves itself upon everyday experience (Betschart 2014: 92). As we saw earlier, she also increasingly uses the term *Kern* or 'core' of the self which, like the soul, shapes individual personality and character. As she puts it in 'Individual and Community':

> What this mysterious entity, the soul, is, we must approach closely to seek. Following H. Conrad-Martius' *Conversations of the Soul*, the distinctive quality of being which the soul has, in contrast to the basic elements of *Geist* (to which idea belongs only bodily-*geistige* figurations), is a heaviness and fixedness in itself. Whilst *Geist*-elements are carried by the sphere of the *Geist* to which they belong, the person lives out of their soul, which is centre of their being.
>
> (ESGA 6: 191)[10]

Or, returning to the 'blank piece of paper' with which we started this chapter, this is the nagging *Sorge* that lies behind the phenomenal experiences of sensations and intellectual ideas with which we experience the world. From this point onwards, then, Stein's notion of 'soul' is intimately connected with her idea of 'levels of the self'. These ideas shift and move throughout her philosophy as she develops it. As Ales Bello puts it:

> The treatment of soul is one of the more complex ones in Stein, and this for a variety of reasons. First, the same word *Seele* is used to convey a multiplicity of meanings, sometimes indicating the psyche as sometimes the unity of spirit and psyche. At other times *Seele* connotes a completely autonomous dimension. Her analysis is so subtle and sometimes expressed in such remarkably lyrical terms that one is both surprised and bowled over.
> (Ales Bello 2008: 152)[11]

This notion of 'levels of the self' that she pursued after her doctoral thesis is well illustrated in one of her chatty letters to Roman Ingarden:

> I want to give you a detailed report of my condition in order to tie together some loose ends: physically *(körperlich)*, as always, excellent; mentally/intellectually *(geistig)*, with sufficient expenditure of energy, quite reasonable; on the level of soul *(seelisch)*, extremely unsteady but never totally bad; psychologically *(psychisch)* (my term, but you usually translate it as 'nerves'), constantly miserable.
> (CWES 12: 162)[12]

The letter contains information about the imminent completion of *Individual and Community*, and it is a striking example of how she translated the theoretical 'levels' into a practical and phenomenological analysis of her own self. As in the passage from *Individual and Community* above she is at pains to distinguish the '*geistig*', the intellectual and cognitive, from the '*seelisch*', and this again from the '*psychisch*'. As she continues that passage:

> This central positioning does not mean the whole totality of the I stems from the soul, which rather unfolds in soul, body and *Geist* together – taking form and meaning. Rather the soul grows out of a root to which the whole being of the individual soul-nature in all its dimensions belongs. If we regard this root or 'core' as the formative from which the being of the individual is shaped, so must we also clearly see from this that not

everything on the bodily and psychological levels has being and becoming in the 'core', is shaped by the core. There are physical and psychological processes which are unimportant with regards to the unifying form, the 'personality' and do not bear its stamp. That does not hold for the soul. Everything to do with the soul is rooted in the core.

(ESGA 6: 191)[13]

As we have seen, in her doctoral dissertation the term 'soul' had referred to the unity of aspects of the person especially as relating to material existence. Claudia Mariéle Wulf, in her edition of the *Introduction to Philosophy*, which was written by Edith during the same period, notes how Edith changed the word 'soul' to 'psyche' sixty-five times in the final version manuscript so that 'soul' would take on a new meaning than it had done hitherto, now 'soul' begins to mean 'the total personal qualities borne by the personal I' (Wulf in ESGA 8: xxxi). In these redactions Betschart, for one, sees growing acceptance of Conrad-Martius' view of the soul as Edith gives more weight to the term (Betschart 2016: 82). Thus, the descriptions of 'Seele' in these middle works go further than that presented in '*The Problem of* Empathy' but act as transitions to her final exposition in *Endliches und Ewiges Sein*.

This new understanding of soul is 'weighed down and settled in its own self' being 'the centre of a person's being' (ESGA 6: 191, terms borrowed from Conrad-Martius) – the *Sorge* that lay behind our contemplation of the piece of paper. And from this point onwards *Seele/Kern* will become identified with the '*Wesen/Sein*' of the person.[14] So, as well as distinguishing the 'soul' from the body and the 'psychological' she is also at pains, as we saw in her letter to Ingarden, to distinguish it from *Geist*:

With the mind (*Geist*) we simply engage with the world. But the soul takes the world into its self, in (the soul) the world 'strikes a chord', in every individual soul in a special manner.

(ESGA 6: 193)[15]

The soul can be lived as a 'mental actuality' within the *Geist*, but 'what the soul is, the *individual* soul, so to speak, cannot be expressed by distinct properties.'[16] For the actions of the soul show themselves in our daily lives, but what it is in itself remains unknowable by the intellect: 'its [the soul's] being is like that of the core in which it is rooted – as such in this respect individual, unresolvable and unnameable' (ESGA 6: 193).[17]

Although we cannot 'name' the soul's individuality we are aware of what she calls its 'resting qualities' (*ruhenden Qualitäten*) which are manifested in action as, for example, purity, goodness and refinement (*Reinheit, Güte und Vornehmheit*). These the soul exhibits when it is 'home alone' (*Beisich sein*) and they arise from the being of the soul, outward actions revealing these inward aspects of the soul. Although the character of the soul is not immediately apparent at the beginning of someone's journey its character will slowly emerge in interaction with the outside world – this is the unfolding of the soul which will preoccupy us throughout our lives:

> Under the surface of psychological development, the soul ripens and presses its stamp on this development, without itself being affected by this development.
>
> (ESGA 6: 195)[18]

Again, as throughout her anthropology, within this too lies an essential apophasis: 'what can help the soul in its awakening is completely unsayable'. 'Anything and everything' ('*Alles und jedes*') can suddenly strike the soul in its depths. When this happens: 'the complete realm of the soul pours out into the actuality of life and comes to light – life now for the first time becomes "soul-full"' (ESGA 6: 195).[19] It is difficult to read passages such as this, knowing what we do of Edith's life at the time and the 'miserable' and 'unsteady' time she was going through, not to see her own biography bursting through here as she received the 'soul-full' revelations of 1921/22 that led to her conversion to Christianity. For, as she continues, to live 'soulfully' now means; 'nothing else than that actual life reflects the qualities of the soul and also *pours out* your soul and is *its* life' for 'the soul itself is a source of life' as it 'catches fire' (ESGA 6: 196).

However, the new anthropology of the soul that she develops here is not without its problems, some of which related to our earlier discussions of the unique nature of Steinian psychology. For example, Stein talks of the I descending into the core in these passages suggesting that she has not resolved at this point whether the 'I', or indeed the 'core', is a separate category.

The core

The writings of 1918–21 introduce new key terms to Stein's thought which, as we have seen, will undergo further change as her thinking develops. One such, as we have seen, is the idea of '*der Kern*', already in the doctoral dissertation but not developed, which could be variously translated in English as 'nucleus, core or centre'. All three are found in English translations.

In 1931, towards the end of her time at Speyer she sought once again a post at a German university, this time writing a new *Habilitationsschrift* which survives for us today as *Potency and Act/Potenz und Akt* (ESGA 10). From the point of view of the development of her thought it is an important milestone for it incorporates Thomist understandings of anthropology derived from her recent translation of the Angelic Doctor's *Disputed Questions*. This is apparent in her development of the notion of '*Kern*' where she uses Thomistic categories to further explore what had been introduced in the earlier works. '*Kern*' here denotes the Thomistic 'potential' from which the 'acts' of our everyday instantized selves derive. As Betschart puts it: 'as in the early works, Stein means by *Kern* neither sensory or intellective acts, nor sensory or intellective potentials, rather that which lies beneath the changes of the person and which in the context of scholastic philosophy is termed "substantial form" or "substance of the soul"' (Betschart 2014: 167). At this point Betschart sees the unresolved dispute between *Kern* and *Seele* from earlier works remaining, possibly due to the fact that she hasn't resolved the respective influences of nature and grace on the soul, even though both are under the influence of an undisclosed supernatural source – unnameable and ungraspable – which lies at the heart of human nature. In this respect Betschart suggests at this point in her intellectual development *Kern* identifies more closely with the *Wesen* (nature) of the self whilst *Seele* links to the *Sein* (being) of the I. This reflects her growing preoccupation after her encounter with Thomas with metaphysical questions. In particular she focuses on four in these later pages:

1. Is the core of the person something actual or potential?
2. Is it something simple or differentiated?
3. Is it something changeable or unchanging?

4   Is the actual life of a person totally or partly anchored in the *Kern* – or can it operate totally without participation in the *Kern* (impersonally)? (ESGA 10: 145–6)[20]

To these four questions she responds:

1   The *Kern* of the person is the place of 'being', where the individual soul reflects the 'likeness' (similitude, c.f. Genesis 1) of the Godhead. It is actual being as opposed to potential. However, it is not an '*actus purus*' but 'actuality' showing that a fullness of being is possible.

2   Similarly, through the *Kern* we have a reflection of the indivisibility of the God-head. It is an 'undivided Quale' without 'differentiated qualities or potentialities' (ESGA 10: 146). All that is experienced in the *Kern* is co-terminus with the unlimited potential of eternal being.

3   Regarding 'changeability', the individual personality may change as a person develops and in this respect reflects the teleological end of the '*Kern*'. In the unfolding of personality this is revealed, therefore:

4   The actual life of a person is not totally rooted in the *Kern* but relies on interactions with the outside world and other people as, in Aquinas' words, the potentialities of the *habitus* are developed through interactions with the world around us. (ESGA 10: 146–7, see also Betschart 2014: 168–70)

Thus, here in *Potenz und Akt*, we find Stein moving from the borderlands of philosophy and psychology to the borderlands between philosophy and theology as she uses this analysis to introduce teleological questions of the soul's *habitus* and development derived from Aquinas. As we move into the core from the soul we encounter the *telos* we hold as human beings created in the 'image and likeness of God':

Thomas distinguishes sharply between the total potential, habitual and actual existence of the soul and its 'nature', the promise of which as inner forming principle we have: potential and nature of the soul cannot possibly be identical, for the nature is simple and the potentialities multivalent, corresponding to acts. They are not the nature in itself but the natural properties that are grounded in its nature.

(ESGA 10: 174)[21]

Thus, following Aquinas and Aristotle she also now identifies the 'soul' with the '*entelechy*', '*telos*' or 'purpose' of the person:

The unfolding of the soul, the increase of its inner riches, manifests itself in the subsequent acts in life and moulding through habit (that is, in its development). The complete unfolding is drawn out as *telos* in the *entelechy* – the original core of the person.

(ESGA 10: 263)[22]

Although Stein at this stage often blends the use of her terminology Betschart, for one, identifies three key aspects: *Kern der Person, Wesen der Seele* and *Innerstes der Seele* (Betschart 2013: 173). Although this differentiation is helpful he cautions that the nuances between them here are fine and perhaps it is only later, in *Endliches und Ewiges Sein*, that Stein will resolve these tensions, if resolve them she does, echoing Ales Bello's words earlier that part of the strength of Stein's analysis of the person is to maintain the tension between the various pulls and poles of the self in accordance with the Heraclitean Fragment as cited by Husserl earlier in the chapter. In Betschart's words she 'uses three different concepts to speak about one and the same aspect of soul with three nuances'.[23] First, how it relates to the development of personhood in general (*Wesen*), secondly how it corresponds with individual perspective (*Kern*), and finally the development of *telos* through engagement with the world (*Seele*) (see also Betschart 2013: 175–6).

Whereas the other authors we have surveyed in this book have their own ways of navigating this psychological tension, Stein, as mentioned above, will in her later works increasingly locate the mystery at the heart of human personhood, and the relations of its component parts, within the Christian concept of the Trinity. By equating the mystery of this tension within the elements of the soul with the Christian notion of the Trinity she thus follows the example of earlier writers such as St Augustine to find the anthropological resolution she has been seeking.

These developed notions of *Seele* can be seen in the lectures she gave in the late 1920s and early 1930s collected in *Bildung und Entfaltung der Individualität* (ESGA 16). Here she contrasts the 'metaphysical psychology' of the scholastics such as Aquinas with the 'empirical psychology' of today (ESGA 16: 10). In this former type of psychology the soul is simple and '*geistig*'; however, it has within itself a double function as 'form of the body' as well as root of 'all sensible and *geistige* life' (ESGA 16: 10). Thus, as above, in the 'unfolding of life' the various aspects of the soul are revealed through the 'habit' (*habitus*) of daily life. As she puts it in her lecture of 1930, *Zur Idee der Bildung*, the natural form of the soul is a 'ground-plan' (*Grundform*) which unfolds throughout life:

> Similarly in the way seeds develop into plants. There is in this sense a centre and a periphery, a surface and a depth (we have no other possibility of describing what is in purely *Geist* and beyond space in terms of pictures from the world of space and visibility).
>
> (ESGA 16: 43)

In this respect the human person is, as we have seen, a 'microcosmos' resting between the animals and the angels. For 'humanity is made in the image of God' (ESGA 16: 49)[24] but we only see partly what God alone sees in fullness.

As we have seen, in her earlier writings she had talked of the soul acting as a 'seal' on the personality, stamping its image on our day-to-day activities. Now she will increasingly refer to the soul as bearing the impression of 'God's seal' (*Gottessiegel*). She also speaks of the soul as containing the 'picture/image of God' (*imago Dei, Gottebenbildlichkeit*) and the 'capacity of God' (*homo capax Dei, Gottfähigkeit*). All metaphors with a long and distinguished history in Christian anthropology, but ones that Stein will recover for the contemporary world through her own phenomenologically inspired interpretation (*see* Betschart 2014: 1).

Following writers such as Aquinas and Dionysius she never forgets the mystery that lies at the heart of the human person. This mystery can only be seen and understood by God alone. In this respect the mystery of the self equals the mystery of the Christian Trinity (the individual soul being made in the image of God). As she will put it in the challenge of her last great work on the subject: *Endliches und Ewiges Sein*:

God created human beings in his image. The Creator-God is a triune or tri-personal God. We have attempted to penetrate into the mystery of the Most Holy Trinity, and we have tried to draw the picture of the human being. Will we now succeed in bringing to light the image relationship that exists between human beings and their creator?

(CWES 9: 447)

And it is to that final synthesis we turn now.

Final synthesis: *Finite and Eternal Being*

As we have seen, *Potenz und Akt* was written as an attempt to gain a lectureship in Freiburg University in the early 1930s. Once Edith had decided to join the Carmelite Order in 1933 she took this manuscript with her and, after obtaining permission from her superiors, was able to work on the text which was eventually published after her death in 1950 and known to us as *Endliches und Ewiges Sein*. Apart from 'The Science of the Cross', to which we will turn in the next chapter, it is therefore significant as a final statement of her thought on the subject of the *Seele*.

Here we can find the fullest expression of themes that had been emerging throughout the 1930s. Thus she states now that the *geistliche* nature of the soul presupposes its union with God (ESGA 11/12: 387) but as befits its nature existing between spirit and matter it also has to assist in the unfolding of its nature, as we have seen, through the *habitus* of life and actuality. For, 'as the form of the body, the soul occupies that intermediate position between spirit and matter which is peculiar to the forms of corporeal things' (CWES 9: 460). But now she emphasizes that *Geist* and *Seele* are not separate entities in the human person but rather 'the one spiritual soul unfolds its being in several ways' (CWES 9: 460). In this respect, the soul now has three 'tasks' to perform: 'form itself by unfolding its own essence or nature', 'to form or inform the body' and 'to ascend above itself in union with God' (CWES 9: 460). Thus, as well as presenting itself in an unconscious or unknown fashion it also 'steps forth from itself (i.e., transcends itself) in personal freedom' (CWES 9: 460).[25] The 'one spiritual soul' reveals itself then in three different but interconnected ways, this will incorporate the different Thomist aspects of *Geist* as *mens* and *intellectus (Verstand)*. For 'the soul is spirit (*spiritus*) in its innermost nature, and this underlies the development of all its "powers"' (CWES 9: 460).[26]

As we have seen, Stein was increasingly unhappy with the 'psychology without soul/*Psychologie ohne Seele*' (ESGA 11/12: 521) that had been growing in popularity in the German-speaking lands of the mid-twentieth century. In *Bildung und Entfaltung der Individualität* she had contrasted this empirical approach with the 'metaphysical psychology' of the scholastics such as Aquinas (ESGA 16: 10). The empiricist reductionism of the self was for Stein a grave element that threatened to destroy the unity of the self. In contrast to this movement Stein recognized a 'Living-being/*Lebewesen*' at the heart of the human self (ESGA 11/12: 523) that sought expression through 'the soulish'/*das Seelische*. Only the person with a 'hot heart/*heisse Herz*' (ESGA 11/12: 524) who had seized the world, could, she suggests (clearly in autobiographical terms but also reflecting Ss Augustine and Teresa of Avila) really appreciate the *Leben* that lies at the heart of the self. Thus, she concludes, the soul 'is a personal-spiritual picture within which is expressed the innermost and most actual, the essence, from which the person's strengths and ability to change arises. Not then an unknown X that we seek to clarify through experienced facts, but something which enlightens us and can be felt whilst always remaining mysterious.'[27]

And this is exactly the point where Stein makes the same move as Augustine – that is, to see in the inner contradiction and mysterious tension of the soul a reflection of the Trinity itself. Thus, Stein's solution to the problem of the soul in postmodern context is essentially that envisaged by Augustine in *De Trinitate* and places her writing firmly in the Augustinian tradition as she says herself in the Introduction to *Finite and Eternal Being*. For her, the multiplicity of perspective of the soul is held in the unity of apperception which is Christ. Christ is the unity of perception that holds together all the contradictions, the tensions of the psyche:

> It should be pointed out, first of all, that the spiritual life of human beings, too, must be regarded as threefold and triune. We are indebted to St Augustine for his pioneering work in exploring these dimensions of the

human intellect. He designates as both three and one: 1. Love as such; 2. Mind, love, and knowledge; and 3. Memory, intellect and will.

(CWES 9: 448)[28]

Thus, following Augustine, the ability of *Geist* to 'love itself' allows 'the lover and beloved to become one and love (as pertaining to both mind and will) is one with the lover' (CWES 9: 448):

> Mind, love and knowledge (*Geist, Liebe und Erkenntnis*) are thus three and one. They are held in proper relationship when the mind is loved neither more nor less than is its proportionate due, i.e., not less than the body and not more than God. These three (mind, love and knowledge) are one because both knowledge and love reside in the mind, and they are three because love and knowledge are distinct in themselves and related to one another.
>
> (CWES 9: 448–9)

So self knowledge exists for the human being 'as the Son is born of the Father'. The individual soul is thus a reflection of the divine Triune life and holds within itself Christ as the apperception of the totality of *Geist, Seele* and body:

> Here the natural bond of the soul with the body which makes the soul a soul, is combined and intermingled with the sovereign rulership of the Divine Person which is far superior to the personal freedom of all created spirits.
>
> (ESGA 11/12: 388/ CWES 9: 461)[29]

Thus the soul for Stein consists of a choreography of *Geist*/spirit and *Leib*/body: 'the spiritual life of the human person rises from a dark ground. It rises like a candle-flame that illumines itself nourished by non-luminous matter' (CWES 9: 364). The 'non-luminous matter' of the human body is to be distinguished (in true phenomenological fashion) from the matter which we perceive in the world around us. For, in contrast, *our* matter is matter that is *felt, experienced and innerly sensed*. This, for Stein, constitutes an essential layer and part of self – which is why she refers to it as *Leib* rather than *Körper* (CWES 9: 366, referencing Husserl as we saw earlier). Thus, the human self, as a composite of matter and spirit, is what for Edith is determining of the term 'soul' and reflects the Trinitarian nature of God: 'therefore the human soul is not a mean between spirit and matter but a spiritual creature – not only a formed structure of the spirit but a forming spirit' (ESGA 11/12: 360).[30]

This human choreography of *Leib* and *Geist,* held together in the embrace of *Seele*, is for Stein the reflection in the human person of the Triune God of Christianity. In this respect *Seele* holds this Trinitarian nature as it fulfils its three function as 'form of the body', 'form of the soul' and 'unfolding of the spiritual life' (CWES 9: 462). For the formative power of the soul, based in the body, can also 'rise to a spiritual life of equal rank with the life of pure spirits' (CWES 9: 463). Therefore: 'the threefold formative power of the soul must be regarded as a tri-unity, and the same is true of the end product of its forming activity: body-soul-spirit' (CWES 9: 463). Thus:

> If we attempt to relate this tri-unity to the divine trinity, we shall discover in the soul – the wellspring that draws from its own sources and molds itself in body and spirit – the image of the Father; in the body – the firmly designed and circumscribed expression of the essence or nature – the image of the Eternal Word; and in the spiritual life the image of the Divine Spirit.
>
> (CWES 9: 463)

If, therefore, the person can see this when 'it then opens itself in its innermost being to the influx of divine life, the soul (and through it the body) is formed into an image of the Son of God' (CWES 9: 463) – which includes the ability to be a 'creating spirit' as well as a 'created spirit'. For, once we recognize our sources in the Divine Creative spirit, we once again become 'capable of cooperating in the task of the restoration of creation' (ESGA 11/12: 391/ CWES 9: 464). Hence her designation earlier of the human soul as not just a 'formed picture of the Divine spirit' but also a 'creating spirit'.

Die Seelenburg

We have mapped in this chapter Edith's developing notion of *Seele* throughout her intellectual career. As we have seen the term inhabits all her texts from her earliest to her last writings. We have also seen in this chapter how her thought moves from what we can broadly call philosophical psychology towards a spiritual anthropology or philosophical theology. To conclude this survey and prepare for the second part of the book where we shall move into the 'life philosophy' that she developed in the Carmelite order we shall turn our attention to a short text she wrote as an appendix to *Finite and Eternal Being*: *Die Seelenburg*.[31] Written as a commentary on St Teresa of Avila's sixteenth-century Spanish text, 'The Interior Castle', the *Seelenburg* reveals Edith's mature intellectual engagement with the Carmelite mystical theology that had upended her life in the early 1920s.

We read earlier in the book of the account of her conversion given by various authors, the common element being the importance she attached to Teresa's works. Although Posselt, for example, stresses the role that Teresa's *'Book of the Life'* played in her conversion it seems that Edith may well have been acquainted with the texts even before the celebrated incident at Bergzabern recalled by her novice mistress. The Edith Stein archive in Cologne has an account of Stein's work shortly after returning to Breslau following her collaboration with Husserl and before her conversion in 1921, by a young Jewish student, Gertrud Koebner. In this account Koebner tells us that Edith was already acquainted with Teresa's works having become dissatisfied with the writings of Kierkegaard she was reading at the time:

> She read the books {of Teresa] aloud over a period of time, more as if she were praying them than reading them. I remember how she often told me that these books contained something she had never been able to find in her Jewish religion, though she had seen it truly and faithfully practiced in her mother's home. Because of this, she said, she would have to live and act according to whatever she discovered in them, out of obedience to the Eternal Truth.
>
> (Herbstrith 1992: 70)

As we shall see in the following chapter the Carmelite spirituality that she first encountered at the time of her conversion would continue to play a significant role in the development of her later 'living philosophy'. However, reading the '*Seelenburg*' it is striking how in her description of the seven stages of Teresa's journey of the soul to God contained there she seems to recapitulate her own journey in 'soul-understanding' that we have charted in this chapter.

Thus, she begins by reiterating the point that she has maintained from '*The Problem of Empathy*' onwards that the symbol (*Kennzeichnung*) of the soul is 'in the middle of the whole body-soul-intellect picture that we name "person"' (ESGA 11/12: 501).[32] In this respect the first step to understanding the soul is 'self-knowledge' with which title she paraphrases Teresa's first mansion. Here, again reflecting her own journey, she stresses that self-knowledge will inevitably lead to knowledge of God: 'knowledge of God and self-knowledge support each other. Through self-knowledge we come closer to God' (ESGA 11/12: 503).[33] Do we hear here the words of the young phenomenologist, searching for the epistemological truth in the school of Husserl which led her to her experiences of the transcendent? This comes in the second mansion, 'God's call', which is presumably what she received at the time of her conversion. At this point: 'the soul continues to live in and with the world, but this call penetrates into her innermost part and urges her to self-examination.' After the conversion we are called in the third mansion to rest awhile with God whilst placing our affairs under the will of God. Again, we are reminded of the Speyer years where Edith sought to find whither God was calling her as she adopted her 'intellectual apostolate' during the 1920s. In the Fourth Mansion the soul experiences the 'comforts' (*Tröstungen*) and 'sweetnesses' (*Süssigkeiten*) of God as grace, as we have seen, begins to flow into the soul. At this point the person comes to the 'middle-point of the soul', a phrase that reflects the increasing importance Stein gives to the soul from the 1920s onwards. The Fifth Mansion describes the 'gift of union' which at this point Edith says was embodied for her in Carmelite life. A place of '*Sorglosigkeit*' (lack of anxiety) in contrast to the *Sorge* we heard she experienced during the 1920s. At this point Teresa compares the soul to a silkworm that has grown fat and now spins a cocoon before the 'beautiful white butterfly' emerges from the silk. Again, is this a reference to Edith's own transformation as she would emerge clothed like a butterfly in the Carmelite habit of her final years? This Teresa describes in Mansion Six as the 'spiritual marriage' – again, a striking autobiographical reference for Edith who, as we shall see shortly, underwent a symbolic marriage to

Christ as she entered the Carmel in Cologne in the 1930s. Not without its troubles, this spiritual marriage endures into eternity as described in the Seventh Mansion. This she characterizes, as she does in *Finite and Eternal Being*, as a reflection of the union in the soul with the Trinitarian nature of God for, as we saw above, at this point 'all three Persons share themselves with her'.

Edith concludes the '*Seelenburg*' again in an autobiographical fashion by stressing how reflection on human personhood cannot but lead from the philosophical to, as we have put it here, the theological. Dilthey, she reminds us, was continually interested in questions of 'Protestant Theology', Brentano had been a Catholic priest and even Husserl had spent his whole career with a lively interest in the great tradition of 'philosophia perennis' (ESGA 11/12: 522). As in the text of *Finite and Eternal Being* she refers favourably once again to her old colleague Alexander Pfänder whose '*Die Seele des Menschen*' (Pfänder 1933) she had asked to be sent to her whilst working on the text at the Cologne Carmel. From here she mentions Pfänder's notion of 'a drive within the soul for self-generation which is rooted in the nature of the soul'.[34] This '*Seelentrieb*' is a useful antidote to the Freudian '*Triebe*'/drives which we have explored and once again underlines the fundamental difference between her 'picture of the soul' and that of her psycho-analytic contemporaries. The *Seelentrieb*, the drive towards ensoulment, is, as she makes clear in these last important works, a drive that is creatively endowed upon us but also generates our creativity from within:

> [The soul] is by nature created and not the creator itself. It does not generate itself but can only draw its generation out from itself. At the deepest point it is bound to the lasting creative ground of itself. It can therefore only fully generate as long as it lies in contact with the lasting creative ground.
>
> (Pfänder 1933: 226)[35]

By adopting Pfänder's phrase she concludes with what ultimately is a positive picture of the human soul as a creating and creative force. This is no dark Freudian battleground between conflicting primeval (Dionysian?) drives of sex and death but rather the location of the divine creative spirit that will continually enable humanity to renew itself, even after the disasters of the twentieth century.

Conclusion

We have seen in this chapter that in most of her writing Stein understands the language of the soul as that which fosters union and wholeness in the self – it is a locus where body, mind, heart and spirit can be usefully identified and held in creative tension. This is the libidinal creativity of soul-language that I mentioned at the outset of the present volume. From her early writings, then, she creates a picture of the soul where all four categories of being can be held together. In her late work, *Die Seelenburg*, she attempted a synthesis between her own phenomenological anthropology and the medieval Christian writing she had come to admire so much (including, as well as that of Teresa of Avila, that of Thomas Aquinas and Dionysius the Areopagite). From Aquinas she accepted the Aristotelian notion of the soul as form of the body, whilst from Dionysius she saw the essential unknowing that lies at the heart of the human self. This she deftly combined with what she saw as the dynamic sense of self that Teresa of Avila provides in her notion of the 'Interior Castle'. As she put it in *Endliches und Ewiges Sein*:

> The soul is often spoken as a sort of 'space' (*Raum*) with 'depth' (*Tiefe*) and 'surface' (*Oberfläche*). In such fashion belongs the picture (*Bild*) of the 'castle of the soul' (*Seelenburg*), that has outer and inner chambers and ultimately an innermost abode. The 'I' (*Ich*) inhabits this castle, and it may choose to reside in one of the outer chambers, or it may retire into an innerer one. The examples cited can help us to understand the sense of these pictures (*diese Bilder*): they remain however always a necessary help (*Notbehelf*) to grasp relationships which are fully without space (*sie bleiben ja immer ein Notbehelf, um völlig unräumliche Verhältnisse zu veranshaulichen*).
>
> (ESGA 11/12: 365)

Over-concretization or literalism is for Stein the enemy of grasping the nature of self and she understands that 'soul' (*seelische*) language will undermine the concretization of empirical and pseudo-scientific methods of understanding the self. As we saw, like Husserl, she realizes that to separate the 'observing I' from the 'soul-I' is to make a serious category error:

> The I that seeks to find truth, observe and work upon itself like another external thing clearly is not located in the 'innermost'. It almost seems as though it had left the castle in order to observe itself from outside. That is basically not possible, for the observation of oneself is 'life of the I' (*Ichleben*) and the I has no life that is not a life of the soul – unconnected from it [the soul] the I is nothing.
>
> (ESGA 11/12: 365)[36]

We began this chapter with the new understanding of soul that has emerged in recent decades, mainly within psychology. However what is striking, reading Stein's account of the soul in this chapter, is how close her analysis anticipates these contemporary movements, especially in her move away from the old dualisms that the word often evokes. Stein, with her embodied, phenomenological experience of the self, realizes that '*Geist*' or 'mind' will not embrace the complexity of self that she recognizes at the heart of human anthropology. As MacIntyre puts it:

> The word 'mind' would not have served her purposes, since she was concerned not only with phenomena that are usually classified as mental, but also with aspects of our bodily existence that are inseparable from them, and with the nature of the relationship between these.
>
> (MacIntyre 2006: 110)

Stein, reflecting upon the Christian approach to the self, as epitomized in the lineage represented in the writings of Ss Augustine, Thomas Aquinas and Teresa of Avila, is able to preserve the integrity of the self whilst also allowing it to keep its window on the transcendent – something that was always problematic for the emerging psychological perspectives that she wanted to challenge. In this alternative picture of the soul, presented first by Augustine, the multiplicity of perspective on the self – immanent and transcendent – is held in the unity of perception which is Christ, for the individual self reflects the nature of the Trinity within its own self. Accordingly, the conception of the Trinitarian nature of self held in the unity of Christ espoused by writers such as Stein seems to come closest to the symbolic sense of self that I would like to suggest lies at the heart of the contemporary return of soul-discourse. Despite their Gnostic leanings, I suspect that modern psychologists who champion the 'return of the soul', such as Hillman, would also agree that an overly scientific psychologization of the self misses the gossamer-light warp and weft of a performative soul-language that by its nature moves from the transcendent to the immanent and back again – in Stein's language 'the coming to terms of the soul with something that is not the soul's own self, namely the created world and ultimately God' (CWES 9: 434). In this respect I would see the postmodern return of the soul as holding five elements that were always important in the Christian tradition, but perhaps downplayed after the emergence of modernism yet central to Stein's conception of the self.

First, that the term 'soul' is a perspective on the transcendent rather than an 'entity', soul-language introduces a 'third perspective' between spirit and matter that holds both in tension. Secondly, that at the heart of the soul-project lies an essential unknowing. Hillman termed the Freudian desire to replace 'It' with 'I' the 'strip mining of the psyche' (Hillman 1983: 46) and Edith's counter-move suggests an approach to the 'unknown thing' that accepts the unknowing at the heart of our being. Of course such 'unknowing' is deeply set within the Christian mystical tradition and will find a natural home in the writings of writers such as St John of the Cross to whom we shall turn in the next chapter. Third, that the contemporary soul-maker must live in the realm of ambiguity that is the soul's true home. Whether with a client, facing a dream or working on the self, the demands of the soul require an openness to the ambiguity that lies at the heart of the human personality. In this respect, creative imagination becomes the place where the self overcomes the straightjacket of the overly intellective 'I'. Fourth, that our future understanding of the soul will be based on that which is creative, symbolic and artistic. For Hillman the symbolic is indicative of that mode of consciousness that 'recognises all realities as primarily symbolic or metaphorical' experienced through 'reflective speculation, dream, image and fantasy' (Hillman 1975: x). This is Stein's 'creative ground' that soul-work brings us in touch with. The symbolic sources of the soul thus lie very close to the sources of creative and artistic endeavour and thus the pursuit of the soul will often manifest itself through these means. Finally, soul-making is at heart a relational process. The relationship between the soul-seeker and soul-maker is at the heart of the matter. Despite our misgivings about the dualist nature of soul-language, as Edith's work demonstrates, the soul is found not in flight from the body but in the very embrace of its ambiguity and libido (the *Lebenskraft* we explored in the previous chapter) worked out through community life. In this respect Stein's work can be seen as heir to that strand in Christian thought that is not life-denying or anti-libidinal. Indeed, I would argue that Stein's work lays the possibility for an alternative future relational and libidinal anthropology to flourish. In conclusion, I think that the contemporary 'return of the soul' to theology and psychology alike is an inevitable consequence after a century-long attempt to banish the transcendental perspective from human anthropology. The return of soul-language, as explored by Edith, by allowing us to gaze at both the transcendental and the physical simultaneously has, I would like to suggest, only just begun.

Part Two

A life philosophy

Having given an overview of Stein's anthropology the second part of the book looks at how her 'living philosophy' may be lived out, especially in a new 'age of anxiety'. Part One saw Edith's dialogue largely with secular thinkers, in this second part we shall bring her into conversation with thinkers who jointly hold a 'religious point of view'.

Discernment to enter Carmel

We left Edith at the beginning of Part One having embarked upon her new 'intellectual apostolate' following her conversion to Catholicism. We mentioned earlier the intellectual formation she received from Erich Przywara; however, mention should also be made of the other key influence on her life at this time: Abbot Raphael Walzer and the Benedictine community at Beuron Abbey. On the suggestion of Przywara she spent Easter 1928 at Beuron where the splendour of the Holy Week liturgies had a profound effect on her. Edith soon found a kindred spirit with the progressive abbot and after their first meeting it was decided that he would become her new spiritual director. Posselt suggests that after 1928 Beuron became her *Seelenheimat*/soul's home (Posselt 1957: 70). The peace and help she received from Abbot Walzer and

Beuron as the years darkened during the next decade are testified by the fact that, as we have seen, when she finally came to take her name in religion on entering Carmel she chose 'Benedicta' as part of it, thus incorporating the founder of Western Monasticism and Patron of Europe into her new identity (see Sullivan1998).[1]

Yet, although she loved the Benedictine ethos of Beuron she remained convinced, despite resistance from Walzer, that her final resting place in religion must be the Carmelite order. That initial impression received from Teresa of Avila never seems to have been wiped away. The key document that charts her move to Carmel is '*How I Came to the Cologne Carmel*' completed by Edith on the Fourth Sunday in Advent (18th December) 1938 having just taken her permanent vows in the Order and just before her departure from Cologne for the Carmel in Echt, Holland (reproduced in Posselt 2005). In this important document she relates how the darkening political situation of the early 1930s personally affected her. For example, she tells how one evening in Münster in 1933 she ended up talking to a Catholic layman who told her about American reports of atrocities against Jews in Germany. Her reaction is telling:

> Now it dawned on me that once again God had put a heavy hand upon His people, and that the fate of this people would also be mine. I did not allow the man who sat opposite me to notice what was going on inside of me. Apparently he did not know about my Jewish descent.
>
> (Posselt 2005: 115)

Although, as a woman and Jew, she had enjoyed relative freedom over the past decade since her conversion it was clear by the early thirties that political circumstances were now changing dramatically for someone such as herself. We shall analyse her reactions to these political events and her own sense of her Jewishness later in Part Two of the present book. For now it is worth noting how the changing political climate of the early thirties was beginning to enter into her own personal discernment of what direction her life should take in the light of these events. In '*How I Came*' she relates an important 'vision' she received whilst contemplating the cross during her first visit to the Cologne Carmel on Thursday 6 April 1933 (Thursday of Passion week) with

Hedwig Spiegel (whom Edith had sponsored on her conversion from Judaism to Catholicism). She felt immediately drawn to the religious atmosphere of the convent and during the service she relates how:

> I talked with the Savior and told Him that I knew that it was His Cross that was now being placed upon the Jewish people; that most of them did not understand this; but that those who did, would have to take it up willingly in the name of all. I would do that. He should only show me how. At the end of the service, I was certain that I had been heard. But what this carrying of the Cross was to consist in, that I did not yet know.
>
> (Posselt 2005: 116)

The new Reich laws of 1933 made it increasingly clear that she could not continue with her job at Münster, and despite an offer of a new teaching position in South America, her discernment in prayer increasingly led her back to the idea of entering the Carmelite Order. As she put it in her recollections:

> Might not now the time be ripe to enter Carmel? For almost twelve years, Carmel had been my goal; since summer 1921 when the 'Life' of our Holy Mother Teresa had happened to fall into my hands and had put an end to my long search for the true faith.
>
> (Posselt 2005: 118)

Although doubts were expressed by her spiritual director, Abbot Walzer, she decided to persevere in prayer on the matter even going so far as to 'demand an answer' from God in prayer:

> On 30 April – it was Good Shepherd Sunday – the Feast of St. Ludger was observed in St. Ludger's Church with thirteen hours of prayer. In later afternoon I went there and said to myself: 'I'm not leaving here until I have a clarity as to whether I am now permitted to enter Carmel.' As the final blessing was given I had received assent (*das Jawort*) from the Good Shepherd.
>
> (Posselt 1957: 100)

After this experience she asked Abbot Walzer for permission to enter Carmel which he granted in mid-May 1933. Her friend, Dr Elisabeth Cosack, arranged an introduction to the Cologne sisters for her to join them which she did on 21 May. Here at the grille she would meet Mother Abbess (Mother Josepha) and for the first time Mother Teresia Renata de Spiritu Sancto (Posselt) (1891–1961), her contemporary and later novice mistress whom, as we have seen, would later write the first biography of the saint.

The charism of Carmel

What was this religious order she was joining and why did it appeal to her so much? The order she was joining which had been a home to such illustrious members as Ss Teresa of Avila, John of the Cross, Simon Stock and Thérèse of Lisieux traces its origins to the Jewish 'School of the Prophets' traditionally established by Elijah on the sides of Mount Carmel near Haifa in present-day Israel. Varied etymologies are suggested for the origins of the word including that from the words *krm* and *l* suggesting 'a vineyard', others include 'a scrubby area'. Today it remains a green verdant place that dominates the Mediterranean landscape for miles around. As well as its Jewish and Christian associations, for the Muslims it is associated with *Khidr* – 'The Green One' or 'Verdant One', another name given to Elijah in this tradition. Thus the cave of Elijah, situated adjacent to the present-day Carmelite Priory of 'Stella Maris' and currently a synagogue, has during its 2,500-year existence been a church, a mosque, a synagogue and possibly a Roman shrine (see: Giordano 1995 and Florencio del Niño Jesús 1924).[2]

Thus, the mystical mountain maintained and maintains a pull and a power for Christian, Jewish and Muslim people alike and throughout the history of the Carmelite order the metaphors and tropes of Elijah and his mountain continue to recur: the ascent of the mountain, the chariot, the raven, the fire, the cloud from the sea, the desert and the vineyard.

Historically the origins of the order are cloudy. The eleventh and twelfth centuries had seen the first significant medieval encounter between Islam and Christianity known as 'The Crusades' begun with the First Crusade preached by Pope Urban II in 1095 at Clermont-Ferrand in France and continuing throughout the twelfth century. By the early thirteenth century we begin to hear reports of groups of former Crusaders settling on the 'Holy Mountain' near the Wadi 'ain es-Siah associated with Elijah. Thus we find Jacques de Vitry, Bishop of nearly Acre, writing around 1216: 'others after the example and in imitation of the holy solitary Elijah, the Prophet, lived as hermits in the beehives of small cells on Mount Carmel … near the spring which is called the Spring of Elijah' (Smet 1988: 1:3). It was this disparate group, of whom we know so little, who approached Albert of Vercelli, Patriarch of Jerusalem, for a Rule sometime between 1206 and 1214. This Rule, the original form of which is not known,[3] was finally promulgated by Pope Innocent IV in his 1247 Bull *Quem honorem Conditoris*.[4] After 1214 the fortunes of the young order underwent another twist as increasing Muslim incursions into the Christian lands around Acre had made it necessary for the group of hermits to leave the Holy Land in 1238. A General Chapter of the Order in Aylesford, Kent in 1247 eventually produced *Quem honorem Conditoris*. Thus this final version of the Rule holds all the contradictions and tensions that the fledgling order had experienced up to this point. In it we find echoes of the free-range hermits of the Holy Land, the small group who wanted to live as a community on the Sacred Mountain and the final manifestation of the order as a European mendicant order akin to the well-established Franciscans and Dominicans. It is these tensions and contradictions that make the *Rule* such a fascinating and potentially controversial document. As Kees Waaijman puts it:

> The Rule of Carmel embodies three religious concepts: the eremitic way of life, the cenobitic form of life and life as a mendicant brother. The combination of these three concepts is not the product of careful thought but of life lived within a single century: from hermit to cenobite, from cenobite to mendicant. The tensions between these three types of religious life have internally led to conflicts, down to this day. But they have also forced the Carmelites to go below the surface, to a deeper level, to look for the mystical space of contemplation, a level from the perspective of which all forms and concepts are relative.
>
> (Waaijman 1999: 9)

The simplicity and openness of the *Rule* contain a *nostalgie* for the fresh vistas and solitariness of the Holy Mountain of Carmel and it is to this *nostalgie* that later reformers such as Teresa of Avila and John of the Cross would respond in their sixteenth-century 're-formation' of the Order. The 'mitigations' of 1247 included stipulations that brought the order closer to the mendicant life as then envisaged in Europe. Thus, foundations no longer needed to be made in desert places, meals were to be taken in common, the canonical office was recited and abstinence was mitigated. In the words of Joachim Smet: 'the Carmelite Rule of 1247 brought solitude to the town when life in the desert was no longer feasible … and all reforms in Carmel have always been to their contemplative origins' (Smet 1997: 47). For McGreal 'the essence of the Rule (of 1247) is the desire to live a life of allegiance to Jesus Christ, serving him faithfully with a pure heart and a clear conscience' (McGreal 1999: 26). This service of Christ, through prayer and service to one's neighbour, is at the heart of all subsequent Carmelite spirituality.

Entering Carmel

Edith received permission to join the convent on 19 June 1933 and consequently decided not to wait any longer but join on the feast of Our Lady of Mount Carmel, 16 July 1933. She spent the next month, 16 July–15 August, as an extern in the guest quarters of the Cologne Carmel, this being the oldest Carmel in Germany having been founded in 1637. The original site in central Cologne was abandoned in 1802 during the Napoleonic occupation, subsequently becoming a parish church so that the convent Edith actually entered, known as Cologne Linderthal and founded in 1894, was not on the site of the original foundation but some way out of the centre. After the Allied bombing of Linderthal in October 1944, the sisters returned to the site of the original foundation after the war and it is here where their community flourishes today (and where the major Edith Stein archive is located). Accompanying her arrival were six large trunks of books on theology, philosophy and philology which constituted her 'dowry' to the order (many of which are still preserved in Cologne to this day).

Her mother, now eighty-three, was deeply upset by Edith's decision but, as with so much in her life, she finally accepted it with stoicism and gave her a long warm embrace when Edith left, on the day after her forty-second birthday:

> On the first Sunday in September, my mother and I were alone in the house. She was sitting at the window knitting a sock. I sat close by. All of a sudden came the long-expected question: 'What will you do with the Sisters in Cologne?' 'Live with them.' Now there followed a desperate denial. My mother never stopped knitting. Her yarn became tangled; with trembling hands she sought to unravel it, and I helped her as our discussion continued.
>
> (Posselt 2005: 125)

One of the last conversations she records with her mother during this final stay at Breslau concerned the nature of Jesus:

> Now she replied, sounding desperate: 'Why did you have to come to know it? I don't want to say anything against him. He may have been a very good man. But why did he make himself into God?'
>
> (Posselt 2005: 128)

Finally, in a moving passage she describes her mother's final acceptance encapsulating all the stoicism, love and strength of that remarkable woman who had suffered so much in her hard life:

> Then she covered her face with her hands and began to weep. I stood behind her chair and held her silvery head to my breast. Thus we remained for a long while, until she let me persuade her to go to bed. I took her upstairs and helped her to undress, for the first time in my life. Then I sat on the edge of her bed till she herself sent me to bed … I don't think either of us found any rest that night.
>
> (Posselt 2005: 128)

Edith formally entered the convent on the first Vespers of St Teresa of Avila, 14 October 1933 and began her six-month postulancy. She wrote in a letter to her old friend Gertrud von le Fort on 31 January 1935: 'you cannot imagine how embarrassed I am when someone speaks of our life of "sacrifice". I led a life of sacrifice as long as I had to stay outside. Now practically all my burdens have been removed, and I have in fullness what formerly I lacked' (CWES 5: 197/ ESGA 3: 87).

On 15 April 1934, Good Shepherd Sunday, exactly a year after she had had her 'vision', she received the Carmelite habit and took her religious name, which she chose, as we saw earlier, as Teresia Benedicta a Cruce. This occurred at a large ceremony in the Carmel including Abbot Walzer of Beuron, who was the Principal Celebrant of the mass, and old phenomenologist friends such as Hedwig Conrad-Martius (Husserl was not able to be present but sent his best wishes by telegram). In addition to Edith there were three other novices, all twenty years younger than her (Edith at this time being 42).

Writing resumed

Although as a novice sister she had to attend to the ordinary duties of the convent it wasn't long before she was being given permission and, importantly, time to resume her intellectual activities. As we have seen, at this time she worked on editing *Akt und Potenz* which had originally been her *Habilitationsshrift* for presentation at Freiburg University. After revision this would eventually be published as *Finite and Eternal Being* – in many ways the synthesis of so much of her philosophy and one to which we have already made considerable reference in the present volume. However, permission to publish this work was refused by the new Reich's censors in 1936 due to Stein's Jewish origins. Borgmeyer of Breslau promised to print the work if it was published under the name of another sister from Cologne deemed more 'Aryan' by the Reich and a member of the Reich Literary Association (see ESGA 3: 664). Edith also tells us in a letter written at the time that the lead type for the publication of *Finite and Eternal Being* had already been set in Breslau (which the order had paid for) and that she tried to get this printed first in the Low Countries and then the United States, all to no avail.

In addition to *Finite and Eternal Being,* her time in Cologne saw her complete her translation of the *Disputed Questions* of St Thomas Aquinas; *Life in a Jewish Family* and her last completed work, *The Science of the Cross*, a commentary on St John of the Cross for the 400th anniversary of his birth to which we turn shortly. In addition, she completed numerous short articles and occasional pieces on various Carmelites and aspects of Carmelite life.

Her mother's death

Whilst undertaking the renewal of her vows on 14 September 1936 (The Feast of the Exaltation of the Cross), according to two letters written after the event, Edith had a strong sense of her mother's presence (CWES 5: 239 and 262). Later that day she received a telegram from Breslau to say that her mother had passed away from stomach cancer earlier the same day. As she later told Posselt: 'when it was my turn to renew my vows my mother was beside me. I felt her presence quite distinctly' (Posselt 2005: 167). Sadly, with the hostile political climate, it was impossible for the family to continue the business which was subsequently sold and the family scattered, many of them emigrating, as we have seen, to the United States. In summer 1936 *Finite and Eternal Being* was finally completed at the same time as permission was refused to print some articles she had written for *Die Christliche Frau* on the grounds of her Jewish origins. This was also the year, like all German citizens of Jewish origins, that she lost the right to vote in national elections.

Following her mother's death, Edith's sister, Rosa, finally felt free enough to follow Edith in converting to Catholicism which she did at Cologne on 24 December 1936, being baptised at the Cologne Convent whilst staying with the community. As Edith wrote in a letter of 1937: 'she has always accompanied me, interiorly, on my way and suffered for many years because consideration for my mother would not allow her to do more than that' (CWES 5: 231). Having subsequently gone to Belgium to help a distinguished lady establish a convent, which never materialized, Rosa finally turned up at Echt in Holland in1939 where she stayed as a tertiary sister before eventually being deported to the death camps with Edith in 1942.

Edith's final profession was on 21 April 1938, just a week before Husserl died on 27 April. Again the public ceremony to receive her 'black veil' was 'Good Shepherd Sunday' 1938 – 1 May, just six months before the horrific events of

9–10 November 1938 – *Reichskristallnacht* – which included the destruction of her mother's beloved New Synagogue in Breslau.

Having completed her novitiate in Cologne, Stein, after the horrific anti-Semitic riots of November 1938, decided it was in the best interest of the convent and her sister Rosa, if she left Nazi Germany and moved to the convent in Echt in neutral Holland. Her preference had been to go to Palestine and the Carmel at Bethlehem but it was decided that Holland would be the safest option in the short term, from whence she might be able to travel outside Europe or to Switzerland. As she prepared to emigrate to Holland a passport photograph of her was taken in her professed habit which has become one of the most famous final images of her and one that is frequently reproduced.

On 31 December 1938, Edith crossed the border from Germany to the Netherlands whilst Rosa managed to join her in summer 1940 having arrived there via Belgium. The Echt community was a small Carmel of seventeen sisters, all but three of whom were German, the convent itself having been founded from Cologne in 1875 by nuns fleeing Bismarck's anti-Catholic (Falk) laws. In fact German was the language normally spoken at the convent at this time.

Her new prioress, Mother Antonia, asked her to resume writing and in summer 1941 she finished an article on Dionysius the Areopagite that we will discuss shortly. She also started work on the *Science of the Cross* and it is to her relationship with the Spanish Carmelite that we will turn in the next chapter.

6

'Light and death once met' – Stein and St John of the Cross

*'I have to tell you John of the Cross called
Said to remind you light and death once met'*
(EDWIN MORGAN: *SALVADOR DALI: CHRIST OF ST JOHN OF THE CROSS*)[1]

Introduction

Following her entry into the Echt Carmel on 10 May 1940 the German armies invaded Holland and by December 1941 all 'non-Aryan Germans' had to report to the authorities for deportation. At this point the sisters in Echt wrote to the French-speaking Carmel of Le Pâquier in Switzerland asking if Edith might transfer there whilst Rosa found refuge with a religious congregation nearby. Unfortunately, the Swiss Carmels were full at the time and so it was not possible for two foreign sisters to enter together; however, Rosa could enter the third order. Sadly the bureaucratic delays meant that the necessary permissions did not reach Echt in time. As she was preparing to go to Switzerland she was summoned by the Gestapo at Maastricht to make herself known. According to Posselt, as she arrived and was given the '*Heil Hitler*' salute by the Gestapo functionaries she responded with the Carmelite greeting: 'Praised be Jesus Christ!' (*Gelobt sei Jesus Christus*), as she explained to her Mother Superior:

> She had felt driven to behave as she had done, knowing well enough that it was imprudent from a human standpoint, because she saw quite clearly that this was no mere question of politics but was part of the eternal struggle between Jesus and Lucifer.
>
> (Posselt 2005: 197–198)

On seeing her passport the Gestapo were furious for, according to the Nazi laws of 1938–9, she had failed to comply in not having a 'J' stamped on her passport or the middle name 'Sara' added to her name (see Posselt 2015: 177).

As the interminable dealings with the Nazis continued at Maastricht and Amsterdam and no sign appeared of a route out to Switzerland, Edith continued work on her last completed book: *The Science of the Cross*. This work holds a special place in the hearts of those who follow her writings today. First, there is the fact that the unpublished manuscript was left at her desk when the Nazis arrived that fateful afternoon at Echt on 2 August 1942 demanding that she leave with her sister, Rosa, who had become an extern sister at the convent. While this commotion was going on the unfinished manuscript had been left on the desk of her study. After her arrest it passed into the safekeeping of the sisters who, during the bombing of Echt, took it, along with the rest of Edith's manuscripts, to a farm outside the city for safe keeping. The manuscript was first published in 1950 as the first volume of the newly initiated *Edith Steins Werke* and received its first English translation in 2003.

The *Science* is quite unlike Stein's other works. Written to commemorate the 400th anniversary of the birth of St John of the Cross in 1542 for the Carmelite sisters, it is one of Stein's most accessible works and large sections of it consist of unredacted quotations from her German edition of John and Jean Baruzi's influential (and not uncontroversial) study of the saint.[2] However, interspersed with these accounts of the saint, Stein also, perhaps unsurprisingly, weaves her own philosophy and theology – in particular the phenomenological interpretation of the self we have been exploring together in this book. From the point of view of my argument here the *Science* is significant for not only reinforcing some of the anthropological points already made but also introducing new themes and terms, even in this last phase of her truncated writing career. Her conversation with John, just before her cruel death, remains one of the most fruitful of her entire career.

Accordingly, following the format of the rest of the book rather than giving an overview of the whole book (which in many respects is a straightforward overview of the mystical theology of John) I will concentrate on the relevant aspects of Edith's dialogue with John and demonstrate how this throws light on the spiritual anthropology this book seeks to develop. I shall do this by concentrating in particular on John's doctrine of the purgation of the soul, the so-called 'dark night', and how this relates to spiritual 'favours'. Throughout we shall see that John's subtle interaction between the self and the soul will inform and enrich Stein's own interpretation of the same.

John's symbolic night and the *Theologia Mystica*

Like Edith, St John of the Cross (1542–91) is notoriously difficult to categorize. Dean Ralph Inge, writing of him in his *Christian Mysticism* of 1899, said that John 'carried self-abnegation to a fanatical extreme, and presents the life of holiness in a grim and repellant aspect' (Inge 1899: 223). The association of the phrase 'Dark Night of the Soul' with his name has led to many misconstruals of his approach to the spiritual life – usually centred around, as Inge describes it, welcoming 'every kind of suffering' and 'always choosing that which is most painful, difficult and humiliating'.

Perhaps the clearest road into his thought is through the tradition that he himself studied, with great success, at Salamanca and Alcalá universities – the late medieval school of *theologia mystica*/mystical theology.[3] This tradition informs all his spiritual anthropology. This is made clear in the set of documents that appeared with the first complete edition of John's works in Spanish in 1618. These are the *Apuntamientos y Advertencias en Tres Discursos para Más Fácil Inteligencia de Las Frases Místicas y Doctrina de Las Obras Espirituales De Nuestro Padre San Juan de La Cruz/Notes and Remarks to Facilitate the Understanding of the Mystic Phrases and Doctrine of the Spiritual Works of Our Father Saint John of the Cross*[4] written by Diego de Jésus (1570–1621), the first editor of John's works. Just as we are placing Edith in dialogue with John here so the *Apuntamientos* reveal John's own dialogue with the tradition of *theologia mystica* exemplified in the works of Dionysius the Areopagite. The *Remarks* thus show how John's work is grounded in this tradition which, as we have seen, would also prove so fruitful for Edith.

Diego begins his *Remarks* by suggesting that just as each art, faculty and science has its own specific terminology, so too does theology. However, he states, *theologia mystica* has its own terminology distinct from that of scholastic and moral theology. This terminology, moreover, may sometimes appear as *impropiedades y barbarismos* (*improprieties and barbarisms*) to those not acquainted with the purpose of this type of theology:

> This licence to use particular and out of the ordinary terms is especially true in the *mystical theology* as it treats of things very high, sacred and secret and touches on experience more than speculation – on taste (*gusto*) and divine savour *(sabor divino)* rather than knowledge *(saber)*, and this in a high state of supernatural and loving union with God. Which explains the paucity of terms and phrases used in speculative thought, which in these non-material matters are surpassed by the extraordinary experience itself.
> (John of the Cross 1929: I.353)

Diego then proceeds to give examples from St Bernard and St Bonaventure before revealing his direct debt and interpretation of Dionysius:

> The mystic therefore has licence (as long as it is known that in the substance of what they say they do not contradict the truth), in order to encourage and praise, to understand its incomprehensibility and height by the use of terms imperfect, perfect, over-perfect, contradictory and non-contradictory, similar and dissimilar as we have examples in all the Mystical Fathers, especially Saint Dionysius the Areopagite. Who, in Chapter Two of the *Celestial Hierarchy* carries a mystical locution which embraces almost everything we have said, speaking of the excellence of joy (*gozo*) and the quiet that these intellectual substances enjoy.
> (John of the Cross 1929: I.353)

This, 'quiet' Diego tells us is a 'cruel and furious quiet'/*un quietud cruel y furiosa* that distinguishes the 'mystical quiet' from a 'lazy, insipid and cold' quiet of other states. Diego's remarks, then, point to the 'mystical theology' as:

a A particular form of theology to be distinguished from speculative, scholastic or moral theology.

b A form of discourse that subverts other forms of discourse, in particular:

c Destabilizing 'knowing' in a process of 'unknowing' and

d Preferencing experience or 'taste' as a privileged location to engage with the Living God.

e All of this points to the *strangeness* of the mystical as a form of discourse.

Diego's exposition of the 'mystical theology' thus prepares us for what we will encounter in John – another land, as John calls it 'strange islands', where things are done very differently from what we expect. For, as Diego suggests, the gentle stroking of the Spirit is a 'terrible stroking', the 'cruel and furious quiet' (*un quietud cruel y furiosa*) that is received not in pleasant slumbers (the insipid and tepid quiet of the non-spiritual) but in 'the fear and trembling' of the encounter with the living God. As with Dionysius's mystical theology it is also a secret knowledge that can only be disclosed to those who already understand it. Having grasped that the discourse will be unlike any other we are acquainted with, Diego suggests we are now ready to enter John's account of the 'dark night'.

Thus the 'dark night', one of John's most celebrated metaphors, is no 'grim' exercise where, as Inge would have us belief, the spiritual life is taken to extreme, but rather John's beautiful poetic embodiment of the centuries-old teaching of the *theologia mystica*, embellished by the poetic fancy of the Song of Songs. Here it will become *la noche sosegada en par de los levantes de la aurora*: 'the tranquil night at the time of the rising dawn'. For John takes the *sapientia oscura* (literally, 'dark knowledge') of the tradition and fills it with the warmth, poetry and beauty of the Southern night:

> In this spiritual sleep in the bosom of the Beloved, the soul possesses and relishes all the tranquillity, rest, and quietude of the peaceful night; and she receives in God, together with this peace, a fathomless and obscure divine knowledge. As a result she says that her Beloved is a tranquil night to her.
> (*The Spiritual Canticle*, B 14/15: 22 in John of the Cross 1979: 471)

However, he is at pains to stress also that:

> She does not say that the tranquil night is equivalent to a dark night (*oscura noche*), but rather that it is like the night that has reached the time of the rising dawn. This quietude and tranquillity in God is not entirely obscure to the soul as is a dark night; but it is a tranquility and quietude in divine light, in the new knowledge of God, in which the spirit elevated to the divine light is in quiet.
>
> (*The Spiritual Canticle*, B 14/15: 23 in John of the Cross 1979: 471)

This, he says, is the 'morning light' of a new 'supernatural knowledge' that overtakes the previous knowledge. In the true tradition of the *theologia mystica*, having introduced the notion of the 'supernatural knowledge' he will not describe it, but rather, in the authentic Dionysian fashion that we shall return to in the next chapter, he suggests we move from the dialectic to the symbolic as we come across this new place of epistemological revelation.

Having grasped, then, the grounding of John's metaphor in the Dionysian tradition we turn now to the second aspect of his approach, which will have such an impact on Edith. That is, his psychological approach to the doctrine and his analysis of the *anthropology* of the Dark Night. As much as his contemporary Ignatius Loyola (1491–1556), John grasps the psychological dimensions of the ancient tradition and thus acts as a bridge between the medieval symbolic theology and our own contemporary psychological mindset. Edith is able to perceive this in her own writing and is thus able to integrate John's writing into her own anthropological schema to create the final synthesis of the *Science of the Cross*.

John's psychological night and the desert anthropology

Before we turn to Edith's synthesis however, it is worth briefly summarizing how John integrates his account of the Dark Night with his own psychology and anthropology. This is done by him taking the accounts of purification within the overarching metaphor of the Dark Night to produce his understanding of the psychological process of the *theologia mystica* – thus complementing its symbolic 'supernatural knowledge'. John introduces his categories of 'The Dark Night' with the famous poem of that title. It is worth quoting in full:

1. One dark night,
fired with love's urgent longings
- ah, the sheer grace! –
I went out unseen,
my house being now all stilled.

2. In darkness and secure,
by the secret ladder, disguised,
- ah, the sheer grace! –
in darkness and concealment,
my house being now all stilled.

3. On that glad night,
in secret, for no one saw me,
nor did I look at anything,
with no other light or guide
than the one that burned in my heart.

4. This guided me
more surely than the light of noon
to where he was awaiting me
- him I knew so well –
there in a place where no one appeared.

5. O guiding night!
O night more lovely than the dawn!
O night that has united
the Lover with his beloved,
transforming the beloved in her Lover.

6. Upon my flowering breast
which I kept wholly for him alone,
there he lay sleeping,
and I caressing him
there in a breeze from the fanning cedars.

7. When the breeze blew from the turret,
as I parted his hair,
it wounded my neck
with its gentle hand,
suspending all my senses.

8. I abandoned and forgot myself,
laying my face on my Beloved;
all things ceased; I went out from myself,
leaving my cares
forgotten among the lilies.[5]

The first thing to notice about the poem is that John calls it a 'song of the soul's happiness' as the soul passes into 'union with the beloved'. This is no depression or suicidal imagery.[6] This is the ecstatic voice of one who has reached the furthest limits of human existence.

The second notable aspect is John's abundant use of symbol – they tumble from his pen in rich extravagance: the lilies, the ladder, the breeze, the house, the light and over it all the great overarching metaphor, night itself. Yet this is no cold wet Northern night, this is the warm erotic, sensual Southern night full of the smells, sounds and touches of a hot land baked by sun during the day and now at peace and rest in itself.

In his prologue to the commentary on the poem John states that:

> A deeper enlightenment and wider experience than mine is necessary to explain the dark night through which a soul journeys toward that divine light of perfect union with God that is achieved, insofar as possible in this life, through love. The darknesses and trials, spiritual and temporal, that fortunate souls ordinarily undergo on their way to the high state of perfection are so numerous and profound that human science cannot understand them adequately. Nor does experience of them equip one to explain them. Only those who suffer them will know what this experience is like, but they won't be able to describe it.
>
> (*Ascent of Mount Carmel* 1.1 in John of the Cross 1979: 69–70)

From the start, then, John shows that he is concerning himself with a theological perspective rather than what we would broadly call a psychological one. The dark night for John is to be seen as a stage through which the soul journeys 'toward that divine light of perfect union with God which is achieved, insofar as possible in this life, through love'. Yet it would be unfair to say that John has no psychological understanding or perception of the role of psyche as well as spirit.

As with the early Christian desert fathers and mothers,[7] John is keenly aware of the passions and desires of the psyche and if there is one theme that runs through John's writing it is this: the passions and desires are neither good nor bad in themselves. However, they become good when directed towards God and harmful when directed away from Him. In this respect the goal of the spiritual journey is the re-ordering or re-directing of the passions back towards God. Thus, in the first chapters of *The Dark Night of the Soul* John goes through the seven principle passions/vices and assesses their spiritual and psychic behaviour in the journey towards God. The schema he uses, usually referred to rather negatively in the West as 'the Seven Deadly Sins',[8] arose from the ascetic investigations of the early desert fathers and mothers. John takes up this venerable schema and indeed it is difficult to understand his psychology without having some understanding of this 'desert' (and ultimately Carmelite) typology.

As with all the passions, the entrance into the 'Dark Night' is about re-ordering and re-directing. At no time does he state that it is about destroying our human nature, but in true Thomistic style, it is about grace building upon nature:

> When the soul enters the dark night, all these loves are placed in reasonable order. This night strengthens and purifies the love that is of God, and takes away and destroys the other.
> (*The Dark Night of the Soul* 1.4.8 in John of the Cross 2002: 495)

Although John gives priority to the spiritual, like Edith, he does not ignore the importance of the bodily and the sensual.

The purification of the night: Freeing and emptying the self

Having argued that John's 'Night' can be understood from the dual perspectives of the medieval symbolic *theologia mystica* and his reinterpreted desert (Carmelite) psychology we are now in a position to consider just how John describes the purification of the self during the 'Dark Night'.

Throughout his writings John stays with the classic scholastic anthropology (derived ultimately from Augustine, see Tyler 2016) of depicting human personhood in terms of understanding, memory and will. His exposition is thus intimately connected with the 'freeing and emptying' of the 'natural faculties' described in Book Three of the *Ascent of Mount Carmel* to make room for the supernatural in the soul. For, at the bottom of his exposition is the old adage of the *theologia mystica* that we 'must journey by knowing God through what He is not, rather than through what He is' (*Ascent of Mount Carmel* 3.2.3 in John of the Cross 1979: 215). This metaphysical point underlies his anthropology in that that which contributes towards a more distinct and clear image is thus not leading us towards God, whereas the encounter with God is characterized chiefly by 'no form or image comprehensible to the memory' for 'the memory is without form, figure or phantasy when united to God' (*Ascent of Mount Carmel* 3.2.4 in John of the Cross 1979: 215).

I have spent time on this exposition of the metaphysical base of John's anthropology because without it, it is not possible to grasp the heart (and subtlety) of his teaching and Edith's response to it. This is drawn out in Chapter 4 of Book 3 of the *Ascent* where he makes a distinction between the 'formless' experiences of God from the 'form' given them by the distortion of the mind, or as he insists here, by the action of the evil spirit on the self. As he stresses in Chapter 5: 'the soul must go to God by not comprehending rather than by comprehending, and it must exchange the mutable and comprehensible for the Immutable and Incomprehensible' (*Ascent of Mount Carmel* 3.5.3 in John of the Cross 1979: 222–223).

From these general and metaphysical principles derive what is probably one of the most unique and original insights of John and sufficient reason for him to be granted the title 'Doctor of the Church'. This occurs immediately after the discussion above where he moves from the natural phenomena of the memory to the supernatural. In particular, what he classifies as *'visiones, revelacionces, locuciones y sentimientos por via sobrenatural/* visions, revelations, locutions and feelings of a supernatural origin' (*Ascent of Mount Carmel* 3.7.1 in John of the Cross 2002: 413). When these occur in the soul he suggests that although they may leave an *'imagen, forma y figura o noticia impresa/*image, form, figure or notion impressed upon it' the memory should not get attached to them. From this derives the main teaching of this Book:

> I say that the soul, in order to obtain this gift [union with God in pure and complete hope], with regard to the clear and distinct objects which may have passed through it in a supernatural fashion, must never reflect upon them so as to preserve the forms and figures and knowledge of those things. For we must always have before us this principle: the greater importance given by the soul to every apprehension, natural or supernatural, which is distinct and clear then the less capacity and disposition it has to enter into the abyss of faith where all else will be absorbed.
>
> (*Ascent of Mount Carmel* 3.7.2 in John of the Cross 2002: 413)[9]

This important principle of his spiritual teaching thus follows naturally from the metaphysics previously delineated: that is, that all that is clear in our apprehension cannot be, by necessity, God, therefore we must be wary of these aspects of the self as they manifest themselves in our prayer, reflections and meditations. For, as he says, 'every possession is against hope', even, in this case, intellectual 'possessions' which will obstruct the soul's ability to embrace its relationship with the divine as the I seeks possession:

> In the measure that the memory becomes dispossessed of all things, in that measure it will have hope, and the more hope it has the greater will be its union with God
>
> (*Ascent of Mount Carmel* 3.7.2 in John of the Cross 2002: 413)

Here John also references one of the other commonly recurring themes in his writings as he points out that such apprehensions of the memory will also contain *'dulzura y sabor'*, 'sweetness and savour' (see Tyler 2013) which will cause attachment to the I and thus hinder the progress of the soul towards God.

Exposition of John of the Cross by Edith

Throughout her exposition Edith is clear that her own psycho-spiritual structure differs somewhat from John's. She is aware that he approaches the self through the prism of late medieval anthropology whereas her own phenomenological, frankly more psychological, approach will differ from John's. Yet, throughout the exposition she is keen to demonstrate 'whether it is in harmony with his teaching' (CWES 6: 162/ ESW 1: 144) and, indeed, may help to 'clarify his doctrine'. This is certainly how I approach Edith's exposition of John here – we could say she is 'rebooting' John and showing how the essential psycho-spiritual categories expounded above can be translated into a contemporary twentieth-century (and as I do in this book, into a twenty-first century) idiom.

Drawing on John, Edith begins her own exposition of the purification of the self by stressing that: 'this entire realm of enlightenment and graces has been unfolded only to show that one must renounce it' (CWES 6: 81/ ESW 1: 71). For just as John takes Augustinian anthropology as the basis of his exegesis so Edith takes the Mind-Soul-Body-Spirit synthesis that we explored in Part One as the basis for her own approach to John – 'the total construction of the soul-mind being' ('*Gesamtbau des seelisch-geistigen Seins*') (ESW 1: 99) – remembering, with John, that: 'talk of superior and inferior parts is but a spatial image for a being which has nothing spatial about it at all' ('*ein räumliches Bild für etwas, was ganz unräumliches Sein hat*') (ESW 1: 113).

As we explored earlier she retains here the threefold understanding of personhood that she has been developing throughout her writing career. Thus the movements of *Geist*/intellect are dependent upon *Sinn*/sense:

> The spirit (*Geist*) is dependent on the senses (*Sinne*) for its natural activity. It accepts what they offer, keeps what it perceives to be true, recalls it to view on occasion, connects it to other things, changes it, and arrives at judgements and conclusions … this process constitutes the actual function of the intellect (*den eigentlichen Verstandesleistungen*).
>
> (CWES 6: 114–15/ ESW 1: 101)

Geist, through the images presented by the senses, is able to undertake 'acquired contemplation' and a form of self-contemplation (*Betrachtung*), all of which is achieved 'by our freedom and is completed under our own power' (CWES 6: 117). Yet, in this final discourse on St John of the Cross, she suggests that '*Geist*' and '*Sinn*' must be separated – this is the breaking in of the realm of 'mystical theology' with which we began this chapter:

> Therefore we must leave all creatures behind as well as all those powers by which we comprehend and understand creatures in order to raise ourselves in faith to God, the inconceivable and incomprehensible one. For this neither the senses nor the understanding are capable if we understand that capability as thinking in tangible concepts. When we surrender to the incomprehensible God in faith we are pure spirit, freed from all images and concepts.
>
> (CWES 6: 117–118/ ESGA 18: 76)[10]

Geist now has been detached from *Sinn*, so that what is left is 'pure spirit'. At this point she develops the definition of 'soul' presented in *Finite and Eternal Being* so that it too will embrace this notion of 'pure spirit':

> After all, something must remain if union with God and transformation in God is still possible after the suspension of the powers. And this something, beyond the senses and the understanding united with the senses, must first be the *Geist* in its actual sense. John also speaks in this connection of the nature of the soul. The soul is in its nature spirit and is in its most inner nature receptive to everything *geistige*: for God, the pure *Geist* and everything that is created by Him thus possessing his innermost nature, is also *geistige*.
>
> (ESGA 18: 76)[11]

In these final writings the soul seems to have detached itself from all creaturely attributes as it prepares for union with the divine. In this state it is receptive to the divine inflow of graces in what John calls the 'passive', or in Freudian terms, we could call the 'unconscious' night as: 'the powerful meeting of the natural world and the supernatural gifts of grace must be upset by an even mightier reality' (CWES 6: 120/ ESW 1: 106). In Christian terms, this is the 'abandonment to the Cross' which will lead to 'the dark knowledge' of God. The '*Geistes Leben*', 'natural life of the mind', is now superseded as grace, through faith, leads the soul (CWES 6: 121–118/ ESW 1: 107), which in her last theological category is 'the true beginning of eternal life in us' ('*Anfang des ewiges Lebens in uns*') which detaches the soul from all created things. Quoting John she suggests this is the point where: 'the soul walks securely in darkness so that this light or obscure wisdom so absorbs and engulfs it in the dark night of contemplation and brings it near God that it protects and frees it from all that is not God' (*The Dark Night of the Soul* 2.16.10 in John of the Cross 2002: 561).

Thus, as we saw in the previous section, just as John contrasts the 'unknowing' at the heart of the encounter with God with 'particular' experiences (the *dulzuras, sabores* and *gustos* so beloved of Teresa of Avila) so Edith makes a contrast between the particular experiences of the 'mind' and the 'general' sense of the 'soul'. 'Soul' for her, signifies that greater sense of self that is expressed on the symbolic (poetic?) level of the mystical theology. This is the true encounter with the spirit that definitively distinguishes the psychological from the spiritual/theological. John calls it 'the mystical wisdom' ('*sabiduría mistica*') which is 'secret': 'pure contemplation is indescribable and on this account called secret' (*The Dark Night of the Soul* 2.17.6 in John of the Cross 2002: 565). This moment of transition is for John like:

> Being led into the deepest and most remote place set apart from all creatures so that it considers itself to be in the deepest and widest solitude where no other human creature is encountered: it is like an immense desert which has no bounds but which is also the most delightful, delicious and lovely place for it is so deep, remote and solitary.
>
> (*The Dark Night of the Soul* 2.17.6 in John of the Cross 2002: 565)[12]

This vast desert thus leads us 'deep into the views of the wisdom of love' (*de sabiduria al alma*) – the 'science of love' ('*ciencia de amor*') (*The Dark Night of the Soul* 2.17.6 in John of the Cross 2002: 565).

Edith and John are both expounding here a complete epistemological shift. 'Soul' at this point, has 'become spirit' but still 'possesses her own shape' (*sie selbst ist eigentümlich gestaltet*) (CWES 6: 153/ ESW 1: 135). At this point soul is no longer just 'the form that animates the body' or 'the inner of an outer', rather, soul is now 'that which holds in itself the opposites of inner and outer' (*sondern es gibt in ihr selbst den Gegensatz von Innerem und Äußerem*) (ESGA 18: 98).[13] At this point the soul is entirely 'at home' (*eigentlich zu Hause*) at its 'innermost point', its deepest nature or ground (*im Wesen oder tiefsten Grund der Seele*) (ESW 1: 136). In many ways Stein had been working to this point in her earlier writings on the soul, but now, as she herself faced her final journey, she separates the three aspects of the soul she had described in *Finite and Eternal Being* so that, with John, it may make the final journey to the 'dark night'.

Having presented us with this final Steinian conception of the soul as 'pure spirit' on the edge of eternity she brings us back to her lifelong preoccupation with personal anthropology as she asks, 'What then of the large mass of humanity who do not arrive at mystical marriage?' (CWES 6: 162). Her answer illuminates her earlier anthropology as she posits different classes of people who reflect the three aspects of self she delineated in her later works. First, there are the people focused on the '*sinnliche*' element, the sensory; secondly, those who have a strong intellective element who 'seek the truth', living 'principally at the heart of an actively seeking intellect' (*Der Wahrheitsucher lebt vorwiegend im Herzpunkt der forschenden Verstandestätigkeit*) (ESGA 18: 105). To these two categories, which reflect the 'body' and 'spirit' of her earlier anthropology she now coins a new term by describing the third group of people barred from entering the 'realm of the soul' as '*Ichmenschen*' (ESW 1: 145). As a category I find it helpful in contrast to soul, and perhaps to stress this contrast rather than 'I-person' I shall henceforth translate it as 'me-Person' to emphasize the self-centredness she is intimating here:

> That is, the one for whom their own 'I' stands as their middle-point: to the casual observer it may appear that such a person is particularly close to their innermost self – yet, for no other type of person is the way to their innermost so barred.
>
> (ESW 1 145–6)[14]

Thus, for Edith, John's exposition of the purification of the Dark Night is nothing less than the description of the means whereby we move from being a 'me-Person' to a person living from a 'soul' perspective:

> Everyone has within themselves something of the [me-Person], so long as they have not suffered the *Dark Night* to its end.
>
> (ESW 1 146)[15]

Yet, we are not fixed in this position, for all types of person there is the possibility for the *ego* to shift its perspective (*Ichbewegung*) to move from the 'me-centre' to the 'soul-centre'. John's spiritual 'dark night' thus becomes, in Stein's interpretation, a means of reorientating our faculties so that now rather than operating from the 'me' or 'ego' we become 'soul-folk'.

Yet, in Stein's exposition (as in John's) this transformation, this work on the *Reize* ('stimuli' – equivalent to John's 'faculties', c.f. Freud's *Triebe*) is often a long, slow and painful one. The 'old Adam' does not give up its sensual/sensory orientation so easily: 'the words are heard, and perhaps their immediate meaning may be understood, but the area where the real sense of the call would be received is buried in rubble' (CWES 6: 164). Again, we recall here Stein's '*Seelentriebe*' referred to in the previous chapter. Is this an example of such a 'soul-drive' overcoming the sensory/sensual *Reize/Triebe*? Sadly we shall never know as Edith was not given more time to develop these ideas.

For this transformation to occur from a 'me-person' to a 'soul-person' she suggests that there must be a 'change of aspect' such as we shall see in a later chapter when we discuss Wittgenstein:

> [For this to happen] a position must be taken deep in the self: so deep that the crossing appears as a formal transformation of the person which perhaps is not possible by natural means but only can be grounded in an extraordinary *awakening*.
>
> (ESW 1: 147)[16]

Thus the move to becoming a 'soul-person' is a search for the '*innerste*' within[17] – that '*innerste*' is the depth of the soul which is the mystery of God: 'one can never *see through* all this to the innermost part of the self' (*Bei all dem durchschaut er sein Innerstes niemals ganz*), for here lies 'the mystery of God'

(*Geheimnis Gottes*), 'which only God can reveal according to His wishes' (*'das Er allein entschleiern kann, so wet es Ihm gefällt'*). Thus Stein has presented us with a sophisticated anthropology contrasting the *Seele* which overlaps with the mystery of God's being in the '*innerste*' with the day-to-day 'I', or as usually translated into English (following Strachey's English translation of Freud), 'ego':

> The being of the soul – its greater and lesser depth, as well as its innermost – are its natural state and within this space, equally naturally, the 'I' ['ego'] moves, grounded in the possibility of being.
>
> (ESW 1: 145)[18]

Here we have moved far from John, or rather, using the vehicle of Edith's anthropology, John has travelled far into our contemporary world. For Stein is using here the contemporary language of depth psychology – *Ich* and *Seele* – but making it her own. In a rather striking way she is subverting Freud's 'godless' *Ich* – *Es* – *Über-Ich* tripos to present an anthropology fundamentally calibrated (*Wesensmöglichkeit*) by the extent to which it acknowledges its grounding in the mystery of God (the *Seelentriebe*?). This, as we have seen, is something both Freud and Jung never achieved or entertained. We thus have an 'ego/I' – 'soul' polarity with various personalities located upon this spectrum, according to whether our preoccupation is more with the 'me' and 'enjoyment of the sensory world' (*Sinnengenuss*) or the movement away from this towards the pursuit of Truth (*Der Wahrheitsucher*) or the 'developing understanding' (*der forschenden Verstandestätigkeit*) (ESW 1: 145).

In conclusion, she states her assumption which she has found throughout her whole intellectual and spiritual search that:

> A person who, only here and now, seeks what is right and accordingly decides by what he believes he knows, is on the way to God and on the way to himself even when he does not know this.
>
> (CWES 6: 165)

In his last work, *The Philosophical Investigations*, Wittgenstein was at pains to distinguish between 'the continuous seeing' of an aspect and the 'dawning'/*Aufleuchten* of an aspect (Wittgenstein 1958: xi.194e/1993: 1.520) for as he explains 'the expression of a change of aspect is the expression of a <u>new</u> perception and at the same time of the perception's being unchanged' (Wittgenstein 1958: xi.196e/1993: 1.522). For Aspect-seeing/the Dawning of an Aspect is a 'half-visual, half-thought experience' (Wittgenstein 1982: 1.554 '*das Erlebnis des Aspektswechsels/das Aufleuchten des Aspekts scheint halb Seh-, halb Gedankenerlebnis*'). I would interpret this as Wittgenstein suggesting that the dawning of an aspect really goes beyond the logical faculty to a place that is 'half seen/half thought'. Almost against the pull of reason the conditions for the change of aspect reach beyond the bound of Aristotelian logic: 'Aristotelian logic brands a contradiction as a non-sentence, which is to be excluded from language. But this logic only deals with a very small part of the logic of our language' (Wittgenstein 1982: 1.525). For as Wittgenstein beautifully concludes: '*Dem Aspektwechsel wesentlich ist ein Staunen. Und Staunen ist Denken*': 'The Change of Aspect is essentially an *astonishment*. And astonishment is thinking' (Wittgenstein 1982: 1.565). One of the chief characteristics of the Change of Aspect is that it occurs against our will (Wittgenstein 1982: 1.612); it occupies, we could say, adopting the language of mystical theology, the place of unknowing.

Following Stein's analysis and Wittgenstein's description of the 'Change of Aspect', we can conclude by seeing John's 'Dark Night' as the changing of an aspect in our selves. In Steinian terms it is the re-orientation of the self from the 'me-perspective' to the 'soul-perspective'. It is to the implications of this reorientation that we shall turn in the next chapter.

7

'A science of the cross' – Stein's symbolic sense of the self

'A scientia crucis *("science of the cross")* can be gained only when one feels oneself grounded in the Cross.'[1]

Introduction

Following the exposition of Edith's understanding of John of the Cross in the previous chapter I would like in the present chapter to continue this discussion of Stein's 'living philosophy' by examining the practical and pastoral implications of her approach to theology, philosophy and psychology. In the previous chapter we heard how the 'symbolic' became an essential category in this late work of Stein, very much derived, as we have seen, from the medieval writings of Dionysius the Arepagite, upon which she was writing in her final weeks of active intellectual research. Accordingly, as well as exploring the notion of the 'symbolic' that she develops in these final writings I aim to explore the practical implications of her approach by taking a symbolic artwork as an example of this: the poetry of the English Jesuit poet, Gerard Manley Hopkins (1844–99). However, before this is done it is necessary to explore how Stein is using the term 'symbolic' in these late works. To help us in that exposition I shall draw upon the work of the French twentieth-century Dominican theologian and contemporary of Stein's, Jean-Marie Chenu (1895–1990).

Chenu's medieval symbolic

To begin with, then, what do we mean by this weasel word, 'the symbolic'? In his masterful essay on the 'symbolist mentality', Chenu explores in great depth how the 'symbolic mentality' came to characterize the uniquely medieval (or we could say, 'pre-modern') perspective on creation. The term (literally, 'that which brings together' from the Greek *syn-* 'together' and the stem of *ballein* 'to throw') had been associated with Christians since the earliest days. In *c.*250 CE St Cyprian of Carthage commented on its manifestation in the Apostles' Creed remarking that it is the 'mark' that distinguishes Christians from pagans. Following Chenu, the symbolic for the medievals thus became distinguished from the dialectic. It was not considered another form of logic but a different way of 'showing' truth:

> To bring symbolism into play was not to extend or supplement a previous act of the reason; it was to give primary expression to a reality which reason could not attain and which reason, even afterwards, could not conceptualize.
> (Chenu 2013: 124)

In this respect Chenu contrasts the earlier psychologization of Augustine's approach with the non-reducible symbolic of Dionysius, making here a distinction between the 'signs' of Augustine and the 'symbols' of Dionysius, even though both 'streams' would continually interact with each other throughout the medieval period and even into the early modern period (Chenu 2013: 124–5, see also Tyler 2018):

> The symbol was the starting point of knowledge, of 'initiation' and it was no more reducible to analysis than the mystery it made present.
> (Chenu 2013: 126/127)

He characterizes the medieval period as being dominated as much by the 'symbolic' as by the 'dialectic': 'in the whole range of its culture, the medieval period was an era of the symbol, indeed more than, an era of dialectic' (103). 'Nay', he adds further, 'it was through symbolization that reality fulfilled itself' (126). Drawing upon the works of Alan of Lille, the various Arthurian romances, philosophical commentaries, liturgical texts, biblical exegeses and pastoral letters, Chenu presents not only a medieval guide to the symbolic mentality but even a series of 'laws' that guided that mentality. He characterizes it as:

> A permeating influence, of which men were more or less aware, upon their ways and turns of thought; a cast or coloration given to even their commonest notions; a body of assumptions rarely expressed yet accepted everywhere and by all and very difficult to uncover.
> (Chenu 2013: 102)

Accordingly, following Dionysius 'it was not the believer who gave signs their meaning [*pace* Augustine]' but 'it was objective elements themselves which, before everything else and by their very nature, were so many representations, so many "analogies"' (Chenu 2013: 126). The symbol was thus 'the true and proper expression of reality' and through it 'reality revealed itself'.

The medieval laws of symbolism according to Chenu

The 'primary law' of medieval symbolism derived, suggests Chenu, from Dionysius was thus:

> To join two realities within a single symbol was to put the mind into secret contact with transcendent reality, not without a sense of inward exaltation, and certainly with an affective response that inspired poetic creativity.
> (Chenu 2013: 131)

The 'laws' of symbolism must lie secret and hidden. Only through much work and study at the feet of the 'masters' will the 'sacred truths' be revealed – only then will the exaltation of the poetic moment provoke an affective response. One could go further to highlight the role of *eros* (so important to Dionysius) in this response too – the symbolic, no less than the aesthetic moment, may contain within itself an intrinsic trace left by the encounter with the *eros* of God. Such a response 'fixed upon a likeness underlying the contrasting realities and made a leap between them' (Chenu 2013:131). This is Dionysius' 'dissimilar similitude' who states in *The Celestial Hierarchy* 2 'one must be lifted upwards towards the anagogical and symbolic form'.

The second 'law' of Dionysian symbolism is for Chenu intimately connected with the first, namely:

> The crudest symbols are seen as those most capable of signifying the mystery.
>
> (132)

For, 'the more gross the material, the more it induced the anagogic leap, as against the peril of anthropomorphism that was nurtured by symbols too closely resembling the thing they symbolized'. Why should this be so? Chenu supplies the answer: the symbolic value 'emerges only in proportion as the *res* retains its integrity while functioning as *signum*' (Chenu 2013: 133). For if we turn material reality into 'nothing but a figure' are we not dangerously near to a perspective that denies the material world any significance whatsoever?

Chenu thus calls the type of symbolism propounded by Dionysius, Alan of Lille and their followers as a 'realist symbolism' where 'symbolic action is a normal part of the dynamism of a cosmos reaching upward toward God in hierarchical stages' (Chenu 2013: 135). Such realist symbolist would thus come to embrace all actions in a person's life from the most mundane to the most exalted. We shall return to this shortly.

Edith Stein and the symbolic

Appropriately enough, in the light of this discussion, the last academic paper Edith wrote before her death in the Nazi extermination camp of Auschwitz was on the symbolic in Dionysius. In 1940, Professor Marvin Farber, one of Edith's old circle of Göttingen phenomenologists, who had been driven out of German by the anti-semitic policies of the new government, wrote to Stein at her convent in Echt in Holland asking for a contribution to the newly created journal of *Philosophy and Phenomenological Research* (see CWES 8:xii).[2] The result was the article we now know as *Ways to Know God: The 'Symbolic*

Theology' of Dionysius the Areopagite and Its Objective Presupposition (*Wege der Gotteserkenntnis: die Symbolische Theologie des Areopagiten und ihre sachlichen Voraussetzungen*) published in ESGA17/ CWES 8.

Stein begins her discussion in this article by noting that part of our problem with accepting the symbolic perspective lies in the ambiguity hidden within the term 'theology'. She interprets Dionysius, on whom her article is based, as not seeing theology as 'a science or systematic doctrine about God', but rather as 'Holy Scripture – God's word' (CWES 8: 87) and those who speak this word, 'the sacred writers', are the *theologians*. That is, people who 'speak of God because God has taken hold of them' – in this respect then Christ becomes the highest of the theologians, the first theologian – '*der Ur-Theologe*'. Thus, different theologies become 'different manners of speaking about God or manners of knowing God' (CWES 8: 87).

Accordingly, what we are speaking of here is thus on the threshold of the deepest mysteries of human existence for, as Edith writes, 'the higher the knowledge, the darker and more mysterious it is, the less it can be put into words' (CWES 8: 87). The symbol, then, is a *Bild*, a picture that holds all together – light and dark, evil and holiness, love and hate – here Stein takes her lead from the original Greek meaning of the term 'symbol': 'a throwing-together' (CWES 8: 96). This Christian 'symbol' will appear as words, things named, events narrated or actions 'by which the prophets often graphically illustrate what they were to preach, as Christ, too revealed divine truth not only by word but also by deed, and as the church through her liturgical acts gives us matters to understand' (CWES 8: 96). The believer, the 'theologian' thus speaks the word of God through speech, action and deed (and having done unto). *They become themselves a symbol in its deepest sense*:

> What the prophet hears and sees is as it were the great school of symbolic theology where images and words become available to the sacred writer so that the unsayable may be said and the invisible made visible.
>
> (ESGA 17: 49)

Taking this view, which accords with Chenu's analysis with which we began, God himself is the 'Primal Theologian' who takes the material of creation to express His symbolic meaning (CWES 8: 100).

Stein's thoughts here accord with the views on 'the science of the cross' we explored in the previous chapter – especially the notion that as the soul comes closer to this 'creating *Geist*' it too becomes a 'creating *Geist*' itself. Accordingly, I would like to suggest that the 'symbolic mentality' is at the heart of Stein's final view of the world. This is not as Chenu called it 'a psychological game played by an esthete' (Chenu 1957: 99, even though, he adds, 'literary elegance – *elegans pictura* – is also involved'). Rather than an escape from reality, from suffering, the symbolic mode is one that draws us to the ground of being: 'the profound truth that lies hidden within the dense substance of things and is revealed by these means' (Chenu 1957: 99).

Both Stein and Chenu emphasize the importance of the creative faculty in this perception of the symbolic. The discerning eyes and ears of poets, artists and creators may employ 'the use of poetic fiction to express intellectual truth', where poetry is put 'in the service of wisdom – of philosophical and theological wisdom' (Chenu 100).

The shorthand for this symbolic form is, of course, 'the Cross'. The Cross, for the Christian, straddles these two realities of existential despair and eschatological fulfilment. The Christian, as Stein suggested, thus becomes the symbol as they face the Cross in an act of faith, or as Chenu put it:

> To join two realities within a single symbol was to put the mind into secret contact with transcendent reality ... the result was a double resonance within the single grasp of a 'dissimilar similitude'
> (Chenu 1957: 131, c.f., Dionysius, *The Celestial Hierarchy*: 2)

As we have contemplated Edith Stein's 'Passion' in this book (or our own responses to the numerous adversities of our own lives) we are thus asked, following Stein and Chenu, to part company with simplistic, materialist notions of the self and enter the symbolic world as described by medieval theologians such as Dionysius. In this respect the adversity itself becomes a symbol in the rich sense delineated by Stein in her 'Science of the Cross':

> The Crucified One demands from the artist more than a mere portrayal of the picture. He demands that the artist, just as every other person, follows him: that they themselves become the picture of the Cross-Bearer and Crucified One and allow themselves to be so transformed.[3]

Therefore, we can suggest, the symbolic perspective turns the theologian, artist (or, indeed, philosopher) *into* a symbol of God's action in the world: whether it is Stein during the last months of her life on earth or any person suffering the tragic consequences of the seeming brutality or indifference of a dark world. These, following Stein, must all be ways to know God, especially God at the foot of the Cross, which are expressed *symbolically*. In this respect the artists, poets, musicians and liturgists are the 'keepers of the mystery' for in their symbolic language the outward sign of God's action in the world is made manifest. Thus, in her life and eventual horrendous death, Edith *becomes the symbol* that she so prophetically described in her last published essay.

Hopkins' symbol

To summarize my argument so far, I have used Chenu and Stein, both drawing upon Dionysius, to argue for a symbolic Christian modality that ushers us into the mystery of human life on earth, especially, following Chenu's second law of the symbolic, into the brutal suffering at the heart of human existence. Such a modality, in common with its Latin medieval origins, attempts to hold together the transcendent and immanent poles of human existence, often, following Chenu, drawing attention to the crudest and darkest aspects of human existence. In Stein's essay we saw her suggesting how a Christian would ultimately *become the symbol* expressed in this symbolic modality as they entered into the Passion and Death of the High Symbol of all existence – Jesus Christ.

To conclude this chapter I would like to once again put Stein into dialogue with another interlocutor. This time the English poet and priest: Gerard Manley Hopkins. In particular, I would like to use one of his greatest poems, *The Wreck of the Deutschland,* to illustrate Stein's symbolic mode as presented above.

The circumstances surrounding the writing of the poem, probably one of the greatest pieces of nineteenth-century English literature, are almost too well known to be reiterated. Yet, as with the beginnings of St John of the Cross' poetic career in the dungeons of Toledo or St Teresa of Avila's whilst recovering from a life-threatening illness, it is worth recalling these circumstances so as to give us an insight into the underlying themes of the work.

Hopkins was lucky enough to have studied in Oxford in the 1860s with and under some of the greatest philosophical and aesthetic minds that venerable institution has ever produced: John Henry Newman, Coventry Patmore, Robert Bridges and Benjamin Jowett could all be listed as, amongst others, his confidantes, advisors and mentors. At this time he himself showed great promise as a poet and literary scholar. But, after his conversion to Roman Catholicism in 1866 and subsequent entrance into the Society of Jesus ('The Jesuits') in 1868, he abruptly decided to burn all his early poetry in an oblation he called 'the slaughter of the innocents' in his diary. For the following seven years he placed himself under the spiritual discipline of the sons of Ignatius Loyola inwardly determining only to write again should his gifts be required for the 'greater glory of God'. In 1875 whilst at the Jesuit theologate at St Beuno's on 'a pastoral forehead of Wales' he finally received the permission he had been waiting for to write again. The Jesuit community read with shock the lurid accounts in the newspapers of the drowning of sixty passengers on the German ship, *The Deutschland*, as she foundered off the Kent coast during a horrific storm between the 6th and 7th of December 1875.

Amongst the passengers were five Franciscan tertiaries, driven from Germany by the Falk laws, all of whom drowned: Mothers Barbara Hultenschmidt, Norberta Reinkober, Aurea Badziura, Brigitta Damhorst and Henrica Fassbänder. One of them, 'the tall nun', was heard to cry before she perished: '*Mein Gott! Mach es schnell mit uns!*' – 'My God! Come quickly to us!' (Martin 1991: 247). Poignantly, for Hopkins, they were finally laid to rest near his childhood home at St Patrick's Cemetery, Leytonstone. Whilst discussing the incident with his rector at St Beuno's, Fr Jones, the priest opined that he 'wished someone would write a poem on the subject' (Martin 1991: 247). This was all Hopkins needed to rekindle his writing career and within a few weeks he had produced the great ode of thirty-five verses – what Bridges would later call in his first edition of Hopkins' poetry 'the great dragon guarding the entrance to his work'.

Unique, untranslatable and possibly one of the most misunderstood religious poems in the English language, *The Wreck of the Deutschland* can thus be seen as illustrative of the main theme this chapter is exploring in reference to Stein's writing. That is, the role of the *symbolic* as we enter the deepest suffering that can be faced within human existence, whether that is by the nuns depicted in Hopkins' poem or in Stein's final months leading to her death in Auschwitz-Birkenau. My contention here being that by interpreting the poetic artefact through the symbolic 'key' provided by Stein we are able to face such suffering, at a personal or even cosmic level, by living and acting through the symbolic mode. Not, as some aesthetic diversion from the suffering facing us, but rather as an insight into the reality, or as Hopkins puts it, 'the granite of being' that lies at the heart of human life on earth. In this respect, an appreciation of the symbolic sense of self, derived from Dionysius, remains one of the key contributions Stein makes to developing a 'philosophy of life'.

The pitch of existence

What is striking in Hopkins's poem is that the first third of the poem is not given over to a narrative of the *Deutschland's* destruction (this only begins in 'Part the Second' at verse 11). Rather, the first ten verses, 'Part the First', beginning with the opening verse, are given over to a sort of 'examination of conscience' as Hopkins explores his own Christian perspective on the events he is about to narrate. He is, as it were, preparing himself and us his readers for the events we are about to witness. This begins with a '*fiat*' rather like Mary's at the Annunciation when Hopkins first says 'Yes' to the reordering of his life around Christ's pattern or *Bild*:

> I did say yes
>   O at lightning and lashed rod;
> Thou heardst me truer than tongue confess
>   Thy terror, O Christ, O God;
> Thou knowest the walls, altar and hour and night:
> The swoon of a heart that the sweep and the hurl of thee trod
>   Hard down with a horror of height:
> And the midriff astrain with leaning of, laced with fire of stress.
>   (Hopkins 1918: 56)[4]

'Laced with fire of stress'. In this second verse Hopkins introduces one of his personal *leitmotiven* – the 'stress', 'pitch' or as he famously calls it 'instress' of being. In an early undergraduate essay on Parmenides he had linked the 'instress' of creation with being itself:

> It [Parmenides' notion of being] means all things are upheld by *instress* and are meaningless objects without it ... the feeling for instress, for the flush and foredrawn, and for inscape is most striking.
>
> (*Essay on Parmenides* in House1959: 71–72)

As Abraham comments:

> Instress then in its ultimate sense is being or the final principle in virtue of which all things are unified and upheld and by reason of which the mind can make univocal and particular judgements and can say 'Yes' and 'is' and can conform itself to reality.
>
> (Abraham 1959: 262)

By being aware of the 'pitch' of existence the individual can conform themselves to the reality of Christ's presence in all things as the one who 'plays in ten thousand places'. This cosmic being, this divine 'inscape' and indwelling was one of the chief insights Hopkins derived from the British medieval theologian, Duns Scotus, whom he described as: 'of realty the rarest-veinèd unraveller' (*Duns Scotus's Oxford*). What is exceptional, and shown exceptionally in the First Part of the *Wreck*, is how Hopkins takes this cosmic sense of Christ's presence and personalizes it into our own 'pitched' 'taste' of realty/reality. As he put it in his commentary on Ignatius' *Spiritual Exercises*:

> For human nature, being more highly pitched, selved, and distinctive than anything in the world, can have been developed, evolved, condensed from the vastness of the world not anyhow or by the working of common powers but only by such finer or higher pitch and determination than itself.
>
> (Hopkins 1985: 147)

For:

> Nothing else in nature comes near this unspeakable stress of pitch, distinctiveness and selving, this selfbeing of my own. Nothing explains it or resembles it.
>
> (Hopkins 1985: 148)

Indeed, later on in the commentary, this 'pitch' or 'stress' will explicitly be linked by Hopkins with Scotus' *haeccitas* or thisness:

> Is this pitch or whatever we call it then the same as Scotus's *ecceitas*?
>
> (House 1959: 328)

From this pitch, this insight into Christ's presence in reality, comes the *fiat* to that same creative force: 'I did say Yes'. A typical Hopkinsian move – the shift of the pronoun from the third-person plural of the nuns, and even the third-person singular of Mary at Nazareth to the 'I', the pitched selving of individual existence with its own taste 'more distinctive than the taste of ale or alum, more distinctive that the smell of walnutleaf or camphor' (*Notes on the Exercises*, Hopkins 1985: 145). From this *fiat*, my personal Yes, flows everything else as we are pitched with the nuns into the dark and distressing destruction of the winter storm off the Kent coast:

> I kiss my hand
> To the stars, lovely-asunder
> Starlight, wafting him out of it; and
> Glow, glory in thunder;
> Kiss my hand to the dappled-with-damson west:
> Since, tho' he is under the world's splendour and wonder,
> His mystery must be instressed, stressed;
> For I greet him the days I meet him, and bless when I understand.
>
> Not out of his bliss
> Springs the stress felt
> Nor first from heaven (and few know this)
> Swings the stroke dealt—
> Stroke and a stress that stars and storms deliver,
> That guilt is hushed by, hearts are flushed by and melt—
> But it rides time like riding a river
> (And here the faithful waver, the faithless fable and miss).
> (Hopkins 1918: 57)

'The faithless fable and miss'. The symbolic presence of Christ is the key, not only to the believer's existence but to all that happens in the world, including its grossest and coarsest destruction as depicted in the poem. For the symbolic interpretation of these events comes through knowing Christ:

> It dates from day
> Of his going in Galilee;
> Warm-laid grave of a womb-life grey;
> Manger, maiden's knee;
> The dense and the driven Passion, and frightful sweat;
> Thence the discharge of it, there its swelling to be,
> Though felt before, though in high flood yet—
> What none would have known of it, only the heart, being hard
> at bay.
>
> (Hopkins 1918: 57)

From this symbolic perspective, even the ghastly events off the Kent coast begin to make sense.[5] The poetic representation of the symbolic thus presents something of the structure of the universe, and God's saving (and loving) plan for suffering creation. In this respect the winter storms that destroy the *Deutschland* become the *symbolic* signifiers for Hopkins' vision of the Creator's plan for his creation – the nuns' suffering off the Kent coast becomes the means for their instantiation of the grace of God:

> Surf, snow, river and earth
> Gnashed: but thou art above, thou Orion of light;
> Thy unchancelling poising palms were weighing the worth,
> Thou martyr-master:in thy sight
> Storm flakes were scroll-leaved flowers, lily showers – sweet
> heaven was astrew in them.
>
> (Hopkins 1918: 62)

The nuns' suffering thus becomes an insight into the profound truth that lies hidden within our selves and our world. Or as Hopkins calls it, the 'ground of being, and granite of it,' which is:

> throned behind
> Death with a sovereignty that heeds but hides, bodes but abides;

> With a mercy that outrides
> The all of water, an ark
> For the listener; for the lingerer with a love glides
> Lower than death and the dark.
>
> (Hopkins 1918: 62)

The deepest disasters, including death, are thus transformed, from the symbolic perspective, into the entrance to the 'double-naturèd name', 'the heaven-flung, heart-fleshed, maiden-furled, Miracle-in-Mary-of-flame, Mid-numbered he in three of the thunder-throne!' Following this argument, entering into the symbolic – Stein's 'science of the cross' – is thus an invitation to let Christ 'easter in us' so that ultimately He becomes for us, as Hopkins concludes his epic poem:

> A dayspring to the dimness of us, be
>   a crimson-cresseted east…
>   Pride, rose, prince, hero of us, high-priest,
> Our hearts' charity's hearth's fire, our thoughts' chivalry's throng's
>   Lord.
>
> (Hopkins 1918: 67)

The darkness of this time: The transcendent perspective

Wittgenstein, writing during the middle of the twentieth century, once referred to it as 'the darkness of this time' (Wittgenstein 1958: viii). Following several years of lock-down and worldwide pandemic, and now upheavals in Europe, there is no doubt that for many in our world today, especially the young and for those less well off, there is a palpable sense of darkness as we embark upon the third decade of this young century. It is hard to look at the political, economic and social turmoil of the past decade and declare that it would have no impact on the souls of our fellow citizens. Across the world, psychologists have begun to look outside the traditional post-Freudian bounds of the psyche to areas as diverse as well-being, mindfulness and spirituality to seek answers to our ever-pressing problems. From Stein's perspective, such a 'science of the soul' must have a transcendent perspective. Indeed, writing in the 1930s on her fellow

German, St Elizabeth of Thuringia, Stein characterized the chief malaises of her own time as arising from the lack of, and hunger, for the transcendent:

> We are a spiritually impoverished generation; we search in all the places the Spirit ever flowed in the hope of finding water. And that is a valid impulse. For if the Spirit is living and never dies, he must still be present wherever he once was active forming human life and the work of human hands. Not in a trail of monuments, however, but in secret being (*ein geheimnisvolles Dasein*) – like a small but carefully tended spark, ready to flare, glow and burst into flame the moment a life-giving breath strokes it.
>
> (ESGA 19: 31)

As stated already, for Edith the transcendent is a *sine qua non* for the human soul. *Pace* Freud and most contemporary psychology, Stein's understanding of personhood is essentially, as said, that of a *homo transcendens*. Further, as we saw in Part One of this book, the receptive soul is also a *creative* soul. The 'breath' of the Holy Spirit she describes here will inflame the individual soul 'within which it is enkindled, turning it into a creating force that overcomes and shapes contemporary life' (ESGA 19: 31).

If we follow Stein's argument, then, the contemporary human thirst for the transcendent is actually a mirror of the ground of the human soul in its relation to the infinite. Or, as Gerard Manley Hopkins, put it, the 'ground of being, and the granite of it' (Hopkins 1985: 23). To crush the transcendent desire is to court disaster, or at the very least maim the soul. Yet, as sufferers such as Stein reveal, to open the self to the possibility of the transcendent revivifies and redirects the vital energy of the self to its home in the forgotten transcendent.

Conclusion: The science of the cross

In the long hot summer of 1942 as Nazi deportations and persecutions of the Jews in Holland continued unabated, the Dutch churches composed a joint pastoral letter for their respective congregations opposing the vile acts. The Bishop of Utrecht had it read in all Catholic parishes in his diocese on 26 July 1942:

Dear Brethren,

> When Jesus drew near to Jerusalem and saw the city before him, he wept over it and said, 'Oh! If even today you understood the things that make for peace! But now they are concealed from your sight.' ... Dear brethren, let us begin by examining ourselves in a spirit of profound humility and sorrow. Are we not partly to blame for the calamities which we are suffering? Have we always sought first for God's Kingdom and his righteousness? Have we always fulfilled the demands of justice and charity towards our neighbours?'
>
> (*Pastoral Letter of the Dutch Catholic Bishops*, 20th July 1942 in Herbstrith 1992: 178)

As we saw in the last chapter, Stein at this point was working on her last published book – *The Science of the Cross*. Here, as we have seen, she wrote of how the symbolism of the sixteenth-century master embodied the theology of the man. As with her earlier exposition of the term 'theology' in her article on Dionysius, again she explained her meaning of the term 'science' (*Wissenschaft*):

> When we speak of a *science of the cross*, this is not to be understood in the usual meaning of *science*: it is not mere theory, that is, not a pure juxtaposition of – real or presumed – true propositions. Neither are we dealing with a structure built of ideas laid out in reasoned steps. It is well-recognised truth – a theology of the cross – but a living, real and effective truth: a seed-corn buried deep in the soul which takes root there and grows, giving the soul a distinct impression or shape (*Gepräge*) and determining what it does and omits.
>
> (ESW 1: 3)

St John, Stein emphasized in her prelude, was first and foremost an artist, and as an artist he was able to hold the symbolic value of all that he experienced in his own suffering resilience. The pictures he presented (*Bilde*) were, for Stein 'simultaneously picture (*Bild*) in which something manifests itself (*zur Darstellung kommt*) and pattern (*Gebilde*) as something formed into a complete and all-encompassing little world of its own' (ESW 1: 6).[6] For as she states, reiterating her previous essay, 'every genuine work of art is in addition a symbol (*Sinnbild*) whether or not it is the creator's intention.' But, the master, 'the Crucified One', 'demands from the artist more than a mere portrayal of the picture. He demands that the artist, just as every other person, follows him: that they themselves become the picture of the Cross-Bearer and Crucified One and allow themselves to be so transformed' (ESW 1: 6).[7] As Stein wrote these words did she know that shortly she would be asked to walk this very same 'way of the Cross' and become a 'Cross-bearer' herself and so become the symbol she had so passionately advocated?

In the early evening of 2 August 1942 the evening hour of silent meditation had begun, as usual, at 5 pm. Sister Teresia Benedicta read out the points for meditation and in the silence that followed the S.S. troops arrived, pounding on the convent door for admittance. Mother Posselt takes up the story in her biography:

> One of them, the spokesman, ordered Sr. Benedicta to leave the monastery within five minutes. She replied, 'I can't do that. We are strictly cloistered.' 'Get this out of the way [he meant the iron grille] and come out.' 'You must show me how to do it first.' 'Call your superior.' Having heard it all myself I made a slight detour to go to the speakroom while Sr. Benedicta returned to the Choir.
>
> She knelt reverently in front of the Blessed Sacrament and then left the Choir with the whispered words, 'Please pray, Sisters!' She signalled to Sister Pia who hurried after her and asked anxiously, 'Where to, Sr. Benedicta?' 'I must leave the house in ten minutes.' 'But where to?' 'He didn't say.'
>
> (Posselt 2005: 207)

In the shock and surprise, the whole neighbourhood came out to protest at this indecent act. In the crowd and confusion Rosa, her sister, became alarmed and upset. In this distress and confusion Edith gently took her hand and said: 'come, Rosa. We're going for our people'.[8]

In conclusion, it seems that psychological resilience required to endure such hardship as Edith underwent during her final years lies upon a paradox: on the one hand the grim reality within which we must make sense of suffering, on the other the promise of a 'positive outcome' – of a better way of being, loving and happening. My argument here, following Stein, is that it is possible to envisage an anthropology, reflecting the immanent and transcendent nature of the human being, that invites us to enter into the symbol of suffering which will be made manifest by what we nowadays often term 'resilience'. The shorthand for this symbol in Christian terms is 'the Cross'. The Cross, for the Christian, straddles these two realities of existential despair and eschatological fulfilment. The Christian, as Stein suggested, thus becomes the symbol as they face the Cross in an act of 'resilience'. What then are the implications of this 'science of the Cross' for the living out of resilience in the contemporary situation?

My argument in this chapter has been that the resilient response of someone such as Edith Stein to the most extreme adversity is not a random happening, rather it is based on a spiritual anthropology that allows her unique perspective to alter our relationship to adversity. An anthropology that balances the transcendent perspective with the material will mean that resilience for someone such as Stein is not reduced to 'simplistic "input-output" mechanics limited by assumptions of naturalistic scientific materialism' (White and Cook 2020: 3). Rather, contemplating Stein's (or the Franciscan nuns') response to adversity, we are asked to part company with straightforward materialist notions of the self and enter the symbolic world as described by medieval theologians such as Dionysius. In this respect the crisis itself becomes a symbol in the rich sense delineated by Stein. In practical terms this will have implications in treating patients displaying negative responses to adversity. For the 'symptom' now becomes a 'symbol' rather than an adversity to battle. Writing in 1975 in *Revisioning Psychology*, James Hillman stated:

> Today we have rather lost this difference that most cultures, even tribal ones, know and live in terms of. Our distinctions are Cartesian: between outer tangible reality and inner states of mind, or between body and a fuzzy conglomerate of mind, psyche and spirit. We have lost the third, middle position which earlier in our tradition and in others too, was the place of soul: a world of imagination, passion, fantasy, reflection, that is neither physical and material on the one hand, nor spiritual and abstract on the other, yet bound to them both.
>
> (Hillman 1975: 67–68)

Hillman waged a lifelong war against what he termed the 'nominalism' of medical terminology applied to psychic states (or what he would refer to as 'soul-states', see *inter alia*, Hillman 1983: 40–3). The choreography of labelling the 'sickness' of 'depression', 'anxiety', 'paranoia', etc., possesses, he argued, its own sickness:

> The 'real' sickness is probably less in the style – paranoid, depressed – and more in the fixedness, the literalism with which the style is taken by the patient and the doctor.
>
> (Hillman 1983: 42)

Rather, he encouraged the counsellor/psychologist/therapist to work with the symptoms, to 'befriend' and explore them, to enable them to do the work they have to do for the person at that time in their life. This is what he called 'staying with the mess' (1975: 74): 'we try to follow the soul wherever it leads, trying to learn what the imagination is doing in its madness. By staying with the mess, the morbid, the fantastic, we do not abandon method itself, only its medical model. Instead we adopt the method of the imagination' (Hillman 1975: 74).

This chapter has necessarily dealt with the darkest extremes of human experience, yet the truths revealed by Stein hold too, I would contend, for the most mundane situations encountered in a day-to-day clinical or social setting. The explorations of this chapter, and indeed this book, remind us that philosophy and psychology are situated between science, art and religion. Often, when all else fails, only by unleashing the imagination – the symbolic quality of the psyche, can the necessary healing conditions of the mind be initiated. From Stein's perspective such a healing will also, as we have seen, contain a necessary transcendent function. In this spirit I leave the last words with Hopkins:

> Thou mastering me
> God! giver of breath and bread;
> World's strand, sway of the sea;
> Lord of living and dead;
> Thou hast bound bones and veins in me, fastened me flesh,
> And after it almost unmade, what with dread,
> Thy doing: and dost thou touch me afresh?
> Over again I feel thy finger and find thee.
>
> (Hopkins 1918: 55)

8

The duty of the philosopher: Stein and Wittgenstein

Immediately before, and for a good while after my conversion, I was of the opinion that to lead a religious life meant one had to give up all that was secular and to live totally immersed in thoughts of the Divine. But gradually I realized that something else is asked of us in this world and that, even in the contemplative life, one may not sever the connection with the world. I even believe that the deeper one is drawn into God, the more one must 'go out of oneself'; that is, one must go to the world in order to carry the divine life into it.
(LETTER TO SR CALLISTA KOPF, 12TH FEBRUARY 1928, CWES 5: 54)

Introduction

In this last chapter, before we walk with Edith on the final steps of her path in this world, we conclude our conversations with her by examining the last and possibly most important issue her thought raises, namely, what is the *duty* of the philosopher in the contemporary world – or rather – what *role* does the philosopher play in the context of the *polis*, especially in a world guided by darkness, violence and mistrust?

To engage with this topic we shall explore her interaction with the social and political issues of her own, and our, time. In so doing we shall investigate her views on the role of women in society and the relationship of Judaism and culture. This will be set against her historical encounter with the totalitarian oppression of the Third Reich. As we explore her responses we shall trace the similar answers arrived at by her fellow traveller through the Nazi realms, Ludwig Wittgenstein. Out of this arise some preliminary conclusions as to 'the philosopher's duty' in response to the times they live in, and perhaps some indications towards the philosopher's duty in our own equally troubled times.

Why Wittgenstein?

As with some of the other interlocutors I have introduced in this book it may at first seem surprising that I am initiating a dialogue between Stein and her contemporary Ludwig Wittgenstein (and, as far as I know, this is the first time this has been done). To my knowledge, neither knew of the works of the other and as they moved in quite different philosophical, and cultural, circles this is unsurprising. As we shall see shortly Wittgenstein, through the Vienna Circle, was acquainted with the work of Husserl, but it seems unlikely he had any familiarity with Edith and her work.

As stated earlier, Ludwig was almost an exact contemporary of Edith's having been born two years earlier than her in April 1889. However, their birth circumstances were somewhat different. The Wittgensteins were one of the grand late nineteenth-century Austrian dynasties who shaped the culture of *fin de siècle* Vienna. The famous photograph of his parent's silver wedding anniversary depicts the High Summer of the family in 1898 when Ludwig was nine years old (see Monk 1990: 126–7). The little boy, wearing the fetching sailor suit typical of children of the era, seems strangely detached from serried ranks of Wittgensteins, cousins and well-wishers arranged above him. Yet even in this sunny picture there were clouds. Within a few years his artistic brothers Hans and Rudi, seen standing with elegant sophistication in the photograph, had both committed suicide. The family's wealth arose from the business acumen of the dynasty's patriarch, Ludwig's father Karl Wittgenstein, whose steel empire made the family enormously wealthy after the economic collapse following the First World War. Ludwig was expected to follow in the family enterprise and, after the death of his two brothers, the pressure to succeed here became stronger. To this end he was sent to study at the Technische Hochschule in Charlottenburg, Berlin, and then on to Manchester in England to develop skills in engineering and aeronautics. However, the attempt to groom the young Ludwig for his role in the family firm failed as he increasingly fell under the spell of philosophy, especially the philosophy of mathematics and logic then being pursued by Bertrand Russell (1872–1970) at Cambridge. Having left his engineering studies he moved to Cambridge to work with Russell on the development of formal and symbolic logic.

Thus, like Stein, Wittgenstein found in philosophy the medium to express his own 'outsider status' in the world. Both were born from Jewish families; however, whereas the Steins continued to be practising Jews the Wittgensteins had drifted from their ancestral Judaism to Catholicism. This was blended with their sponsorship and patronage of some of the greatest artistic names of the Viennese Golden Age including, amongst others, Johannes Brahms, Gustav Mahler and Gustav Klimt.

As we have seen, both Wittgenstein's studies in Cambridge and Stein's in Göttingen were severely disrupted by the outbreak of the Great War in summer 1914. As we heard earlier Edith used this time to work as a nurse in Czechia where she encountered a group and class of people she had not previously met. Wittgenstein, on the other hand, in an attempt to find 'the nearness to death which will bring light into life' (Wittgenstein 1984: 4.5.16) enlisted in the Imperial and Royal Austria-Hungarian army on 7 August 1914 shortly after Austria-Hungary declared war against Russia. The initial stages of the war were seemingly quiet and much of Ludwig's time was spent on the battleship *Goplana* on the Vistula river, captured from the Russians early on in the war, and working in military workshops around Krakow and Lemberg. On 21 April 1916, however, he found himself in battle for the first time and at this time he remained in solitary duty on the observation post. On 4 June the Austrian offensive was followed by an equally severe Russian offensive. Wittgenstein clearly acquitted himself well during this hellish time and was awarded a silver *Tapferkeitsmedaille* Second Class on 6 October. His decoration commendation stated:

Ignoring the heavy artillery fire on the casement and the exploding mortar bombs he observed the discharge of the mortars and located them ... On the Battery Observation Post, Hill 417, he observed without intermission in the drumfire, although I several times shouted to him to take cover. By this distinctive behaviour he exercised a very calming effect on his comrades.

(McGuinness 1988: 242)

As equally distressing, for the sensitive son of a *hochbürgerlich* Austrian family, was the time he had to spend in close proximity to the 'great unwashed' of the Austria-Hungary army. Ordinary folk, whom he had first met at the *Realschule* at Linz (including, notoriously, Adolf Hitler), were as stressful to him as the Russian enemy. As he wrote in his diary:

The people I am with are not so much nasty as *terribly* limited. This makes relations with them almost impossible as they almost always misunderstand me. They are not stupid, but limited. Within their circles they are clever enough. But they lack character and with that a breadth of understanding. 'The right-believing heart understands everything.'

(Wittgenstein 2000: 103.10v, 8.5.1916)[1]

By the time Wittgenstein was withdrawn from the front line in August 1916 he had been continuously in the firing line for five months. Of the notes made at this time McGuinness comments: 'they testify to a change in his thinking as great as that which he himself saw in his countenance ... It was as if he had bridged – or was about to bridge – some gap between his philosophy and his inner life' (McGuinness 1988: 245). From this point onwards there is no separation between the remarks on logical form and those on religion and ethics in his private diaries: 'yes my work has broadened out from the foundations of logic to the essence of the world' (Wittgenstein 1984: 2.8.16).

Both of his biographers, Monk and McGuinness, suggest that at this point in his life, having pushed himself hard on the logical boundaries of language both in Cambridge with Russell and on his own in his retreat in Norway before the outbreak of the First World War, it was as though he 'sought embodiment' and needed the experiences of the trenches to bridge gaps between how he experienced his thought and how he experienced his life. In this respect his experiences on the Eastern Front in 1916 are central for understanding the move in his philosophy from the disembodied exploration of logical form to the embodied researches of the later (or perhaps better 'post-1916') Wittgenstein. This all bore fruit in the final version of the sole published philosophical work of Wittgenstein's life: *The Tractatus Logico-Philosophicus* – a logical tract ending, notoriously, with Wittgenstein's comments on aesthetics, the mystical and ethics (Wittgenstein 1961).

So, just as Edith's war experiences opened new worlds to her, so likewise, Wittgenstein's war transformed the philosopher to such an extent that when he was demobbed in 1918 he was a changed man: no longer the young logician who had studied the foundations of mathematics with Russell in Cambridge. Rather he now sought a form of knowledge that was not just 'head knowledge' but embodied knowledge – search for wisdom rather than intellectual curiosity, or, as we have called it here, a 'living philosophy'. As his fellow soldier and lifelong friend Paul Engelmann would later observe: 'what prompted him was an overpowering – and no doubt long-suppressed – urge to cast off all encumbrances that imposed an insupportable burden on his attitude to the outside world: his fortune as well as his necktie' (Wittgenstein 1967: 78).

As with Stein, in the events that led to her conversion in 1922, deep philosophical questions were put on one side as Wittgenstein now struggled with the articulation of faith and what it meant to him. Also, as with Stein, this new transcendental (or soul) perspective complemented rather than erased his pre-war searches. For both Stein and Wittgenstein the question now, aside from the metaphysical implications of their new perspective, became, what does the philosopher *do* in society – How should one respond to the demands of the times?

Wittgenstein, Husserl and phenomenology

Despite the parallels in their philosophical development, as stated, it is highly unlikely that Edith and Ludwig knew each other in their lifetimes. If we compare their philosophical approaches there are also marked differences. They were both philosophers of consciousness yet their approach to the subject was, to paraphrase the words of the eminent Steinian scholar Mary Baseheart, 'the anti-thesis of the Enlightenment tendency to conceive consciousness as pure thought and the subject as merely a thinking self, sufficient to itself' (Baseheart 1997: x). It could be, and has been, argued that both were in a sense 'phenomenologists' in that they wanted to bring 'thought' and 'philosophy' into the heart of the everyday 'stream of life' (and vice versa).

Towards the end of his life, in conversation with his pupil Maurice Drury, Wittgenstein once remarked: 'you could say of my work that it is "phenomenology"' (Rhees 1987: 116) and throughout his life, as with Edith, there is a continued fascination with the nature of immediate experience and how it relates to thought. However, despite the similarities in their approaches to philosophical problems Wittgenstein was clear that he was 'no phenomenologist' even though he admitted that 'there *are* phenomenological problems' (Wittgenstein 1977: 3. 248). We shall explore some of those differences shortly.

Husserl, on the other hand, was aware of the work of the logical positivists, with whom Wittgenstein was associated in Vienna in the 1920s (although Ludwig always kept a sceptical distance from the work of the Vienna Circle, see Tyler 2016: 149–68). In his reaction to the Vienna Circle Manifesto of 1929 Husserl was scathing in a letter to Roman Ingarden, for although he saw it is as a 'bulwark against irrationalistic skepticism' he felt that ultimately it will not 'help for long since people will ultimately discover that it is a sham philosophy and not a true philosophy'(Husserl 1970: xxvi). He went further in his *Krisis* to say that by denying legitimacy to philosophical questions on, for example, 'the absolute, meaning, the metaphysical and the eternal' positivism 'in a manner of speaking, decapitates philosophy' (Husserl 1970: 9). Even if both philosophers shared a common subject matter their approaches to the language in which this speculation was expressed differed substantially. Wittgenstein favoured 'ordinary language' and his objection to 'the phenomenologists' was partly based on a suspicion of their need to create new technical terms to describe the phenomena they were scrutinizing. In December 1929 Moritz Schlick (1882–1936), Professor of Natural Philosophy and one of the key founders of the Vienna Circle, asked Wittgenstein for his views on Husserl and phenomenology, his answer is revealing:

I used to believe that there was the everyday language that we all usually spoke and a primary language that expressed what we really knew, namely phenomena. I also spoke of a first system and a second system. Now I wish to explain why I do not adhere to that conception any more. I think that essentially we have only one language, and that is our everyday language. We need not invent a new language or construct a new symbolism, but our everyday language already is the language, provided we rid it of the obscurities that lie hidden in it.

(Waismann 1979: 45, 22.12.1929)

How far Wittgenstein explicitly embraced a 'phenomenological' approach, and for how long, is a moot point. Commentators such as Hintikka (see Hintikka 1986) see it as an important, if ultimately abandoned phase, in his development summed up in the oft-quoted remark from his later notebooks: 'phenomenology is grammar' (Wittgenstein 1977: 2,16). As one of the early advocates of a 'phenomenological Wittgenstein', Hintikka, remarks: 'it is Wittgenstein's rejection of phenomenological language as an independent basis language, combined with his continued interest in phenomenological problems (problems concerning "the given" or immediate experience) that lends the characteristic flavour to his later use of the terms "phenomenology" and "phenomenological"' (Hintikka 1986: 151). However, later commentators urge caution, for example, Ometita who stresses in his 2015 doctoral thesis that:

Despite Wittgenstein's referring to phenomenological language as a past goal (*Ziel*), this language was never a goal in itself or for its own sake. As a method of clarification of ordinary language and of describing immediate experience, phenomenological language was in fact envisaged as a means to dispel philosophical puzzles by grasping the logical structure of language and its relation to reality.

(Ometita 2015: 98)[2]

Notwithstanding, as a 'philosopher of consciousness' there *are* parallels in the philosophical approaches of Wittgenstein and Stein, especially, as I have said, with regard to the nature of thought and the thinking processes, not least in both their attitudes to psychology and the twentieth-century 'psychological turn' and it is to Wittgenstein's views on that we turn next.

The nature of psychology

The influence of science and 'scientism' over the emerging discipline of psychology was the subject of Wittgenstein's final set of lectures given in Cambridge from autumn 1946 to summer 1947.³ Jackson gives a good overview of the nature and scope of the lectures in his record of Wittgenstein's introduction to them:

> These lectures are on the philosophy of psychology. And it may seem odd that we should be going to discuss matters arising out of, and occurring in, a science, seeing that we are not going to do the science of psychology, and we have no particular information about the sorts of thing that are found when the science is done. But there are questions, puzzles that naturally suggest themselves when we look at what psychologists may say, and at what non-psychologists (and we) say.

Which then continued:

> Psychology is often defined as the science of mental phenomena. This may seem misleading, as we shall see. Contrast it with physics as the science of physical phenomena. It is the word 'phenomena' which may mislead. We get the idea: on the one hand you have phenomena of one kind which do certain things, on the other, phenomena of another kind which do other things; so how do the two sorts of thing they do compare? But perhaps it makes no sense to say that each does all the sorts of thing the other does.
>
> (Wittgenstein 1988: 235)

The problem, then, for Wittgenstein, like Stein, lies in the term 'psychological phenomena'. He pointed out how our language seems to draw a parallel between physical 'entities' and mental 'entities'. The latter, presumably, following the behaviour of the former, this would include 'processes' such as thinking, feeling, perceiving, etc. For Wittgenstein the problem therefore arises right at the beginning in defining these 'entities' as 'phenomena':

> We are in difficulty right at the beginning, as soon as we use the term 'psychological phenomena'. The psychologist in his laboratory is investigating psychological phenomena. What does he observe? The answer is not at all obvious.
>
> (Wittgenstein 1988: 172)

Is the clinical psychologist 'observing' mental phenomena as such or rather is she 'observing my face, listening to what I say and watching how I react'? Therefore, for Wittgenstein, the term 'psychological phenomena' is 'ambiguous': 'psychological phenomena are phenomena in a different sense' (Wittgenstein 1988: 172). He suggests that the psychological 'fog' this presents us cannot be resolved by new data, no matter how sophisticated, but, better, by a philosophical analysis of the *roots* of our psychological *Weltanschauung*. Accordingly, Wittgenstein is proposing in these last final years, like Stein and Husserl, a new approach to psychology that doesn't seek either more empirical data or more introspection. The conceptual confusion of psychology, he suggests on the last page of the *Investigations*, is often attributed to the fact that it is a 'young science' (Wittgenstein 1958: ii: 232, as indeed Stein had done). Surely, then, if this were the case, given another 100 years these problems could be sorted? Wittgenstein disputes this and sees the confusion arising from a 'scientistic' approach to the subject which would like to compare it with, say, the discipline of physics (Wittgenstein 1958: ii: 232). Rather, the 'fog' will be pierced by conceptual investigation of the use of terms such as 'intention', 'willing', 'hoping', 'thinking', etc. This is the content of these last Cambridge lectures and conversations, much of which will find its way into the version of the *Philosophical Investigations* published after his death (especially the second part).

His views on psychology here dovetail into his reflections on 'mental processes' themselves. In the *Philosophical Investigations*, in sentences written in 1945–6 in Cambridge and Swansea, he asserts his fundamental position that they are 'not a something, but not a nothing either' (Wittgenstein 1958: 304), going further to say: 'the conclusion was only that a nothing would serve just as well as a something about which nothing could be said.' The ambiguity of his statement is well chosen here. For it places him neither as a 'realist' with regard to mental phenomena nor, in contra-distinction to many of his Vienna

Circle colleagues at the time, as a behaviourist. This is important and central to his argument. Just like children fooled by a conjuror, he suggests, as we embark upon our 'psychological investigations' we miss the first sleight of hand that holds up the whole illusion. That is to say:

> The first step is the one that altogether escapes notice. We talk of processes and states and leave their nature undecided. Sometimes perhaps we shall know more about them – we think. But this is just what commits us to a particular way of looking at the matter. For we have a definite concept of what it means to learn to know a process better. (the decisive movement in the conjuring trick has been made, and it was the very one that we thought quite innocent).
>
> (Wittgenstein 1958: 308)

The nature of inwardness

Having resisted the siren voices of neo-empirical psychology, Wittgenstein in these last writings turns his guns on what he sees as the other chief distraction in creating the 'bewitchment of psychology', that is, what I have called elsewhere, 'the lure of inwardness'. As he warns: 'do not try to analyse the experience in your self!' (Wittgenstein 1958: 204e/1993: 537/1982: 1.548).[4] The notion of 'inner pictures' (*Inneren Bilden*) when talking psychologically is, he suggests, misleading 'for this concept uses the "*outer* picture" as a model; yet the uses of the words for these concepts are no more like one another than the uses of "numeral" and "number". (And if one chose to call numbers "ideal numerals", one might produce a similar confusion)' (Wittgenstein 1958: ii.196e/1993: 523).[5] A characteristic of Wittgenstein's style, which may surprise the unwary reader, is his use of 'shock tactics' to force his reader to think for themselves. As I wrote in *The Return to the Mystical* (Tyler 2011), Wittgenstein 'prods and pokes' his reader to allow each of us trapped flies to escape our own personal 'fly-bottles'. Like two strong influences on his writing, Karl Kraus (1874–1936) and Søren Kierkegaard (1813–55), he frequently uses irony, exaggeration, paradox and humour to move the fly through the fly-bottle. Wittgenstein's later writings are peppered with many examples of all of these strategies and one of these appears in his critique of the inner:

> I can know what someone else is thinking, not what I am thinking.
>
> It is correct to say 'I know what you are thinking', and wrong to say 'I know what I am thinking'
>
> (A whole cloud of philosophy condensed into a drop of grammar).
> (Wittgenstein 1958: ii.222e/1993: 565)

The grammar in question is our use of first- and third-person verbs in referring to psychological events. In the Cambridge lectures of 1946 he clarifies this gnomic 'anti-philosophical' statement further, as he puts it there:

> One characteristic of psychological facts, mirrored in psychological concepts, is the privacy of an experience. I cannot know what you experience.
> (Wittgenstein 1988: 154)

Commenting on this he suggests the muddle arises from the following:

> Oddly enough 'I cannot know' is a muddle. Really there is no sense in saying 'I know'. Or else: 'Rubbish! I *know* he has pain.' And I *do not know* I have pain, I *have* pain. Once again this is about the concept.
> (Wittgenstein 1988: 154)

The grammar of the word 'know' introduces, he suggests, an extra category, or veil even, between the experience and our *perception* of it. By analysing the concept thus we remove one of the conjuror's veils. 'The queer relation of first and third person', so typical he suggests of 'psychological' grammar defines the boundaries of how these experiences are expressed. From this separation of 'know' and the 'experience' arises, he suggests, from the 'muddle' between first- and third-person grammar in the employment of psychological concepts. From this muddle arises 'the fact that what the first person expresses is a state of affairs *within* [my emphasis] myself, which I alone can directly see' (Wittgenstein 1988: 155). This he challenges for 'there is no question of knowing indirectly, because there is no question of knowing directly.'

We are certainly inclined to rebel against this conclusion which seems so contrary to our 'common sense'. 'Surely', we say, 'I am so near to myself that I see it' (Wittgenstein 1988: 227). But, Wittgenstein replies, 'this will not do – it is an incredible picture.' The notion that I am 'inside myself', like a Cartesian homunculus observing the phenomena within, 'that is, in predicting my behaviour, I will have to draw a conclusion, from my inner state', this, he says, 'is exactly what I am not doing.'[6] Which leads, inevitably, to the famous principle of the 'Other Minds' argument:

> It is said that we not know other minds, and we know our own. But in a sort of way – it is rubbish. But why do people say it? It is based on a queer sort of misunderstanding.
>
> (Wittgenstein 1988: 276)

In summary, returning to his initial analysis of psychological grammar, that is the 'asymmetry' between the first and third persons in psychological accounts, we can suggest that this asymmetry leads to the 'muddle' that 'the first person expresses a state of affairs inside me which only I can know and the third person tells only about someone's behaviour' (Wittgenstein 1988: 34). The conjuror, in the first sleight of hand between knowing and experiencing, has allowed this muddle of the 'state of affairs' within 'my head' to arise:

> It is absurd to call the third person an expression of indirect knowledge, because there is no question of direct knowledge. It isn't like rain, which I can either see or infer from the noise, the wet wall etc.
>
> (Wittgenstein 1988: 34)

The illusion of equating 'psychological' grammar with 'physical' grammar (e.g. a description of rain showers) gives us the illusion of 'physicalist entities' 'in the mind'.

These remarks reveal, then, the meaning behind his gnomic statement that 'phenomenology is grammar'. Rather than grasping after 'entities' of thinking – a muddle as far as Wittgenstein is concerned – we need to ask ourselves grammatical questions of usage, such as 'why do we group together the heterogenous first and third persons of psychological verbs?' (Wittgenstein 1988: 49). As the last writings and remarks reveal, we may not necessarily come to any definite answers on this but at least we can begin to let 'the fly out the conceptual fly-bottle' as we seek to iron out some of the muddles our psychological grammar leads us towards. As he put it in the 1946 lectures:

> I have been trying to change the point of view. Everything is of the form 'Look at it this way'; 'Compare it to this and not to that'. The question 'What is thinking?' vanishes when we cease to compare the phenomena concerned with phenomena happening inside things and hidden from us.
>
> (Wittgenstein 1988: 285)

In this respect, as so often in the later Wittgenstein, the role (duty?) of the philosopher is thus to 'change our point of view' rather than create metaphysical castles. As he would finally summarize it in the *Investigations*:

> Try not to think of understanding as a 'mental process' at all. – For *that* is the expression that confuses you. But ask yourself: in what sort of case, in what kind of circumstances, do we say, 'Now, I know how to go on'.
>
> (Wittgenstein 1958: 154)

As with Stein, then, the philosophical process cannot be divorced from our 'life in the world'. The duty of the philosopher is to bring the clarity of thought to bear not just on the phenomenological processes within which we exist as human beings but also the wider realities of society and our place in society.

Stein, Wittgenstein and Husserl were unfortunately forced to face these questions against the backdrop of some of the most challenging years of modern Western history. As all three were of Jewish descent this task was made especially fraught. Yet, for all three this connection between clarity of thought and social responsibility was paramount. As Husserl put it:

> If [the philosopher] is to be one who thinks for themselves (*selbstdenker*), an autonomous philosopher with the will to liberate themselves from all prejudices, they must have the insight that all the things they take for granted are prejudices, that all prejudices are obscurities arising out of a sedimentation of tradition ('*das alle Vorurteile Unklarheiten aus einer traditionalen Sedimentierung sind*')
>
> (Husserl 1954: 72/1970: 73)

It is to this 'philosophical duty' in troubled and troubling times that we shall turn for the remainder of this chapter concentrating on Stein's reactions to the social and cultural maelstrom within which she found herself before drawing some conclusions.

The duty of the philosopher: On Women

We have already had occasion to remark on how the fact of Edith's gender affected not just her philosophical career but also her philosophical approach. After her conversion to Catholicism in 1922 and before entry into religious life in 1933 she developed, as we have heard, an 'intellectual apostolate' as a Catholic, laywoman. As well as her duties in Speyer, and later at Münster, she would travel around the German-speaking countries giving lectures, especially on the role and vocation of contemporary women. As the Nazis came into power these talks became more and more urgent as she responded to the growing ugliness in civil and social discourse. These lectures and reflections are collected in Volume 13 of the ESGA (*Die Frau*) and Vol. 2, of CWES (*Essays on Women*). They began in April 1928 with a lecture at Ludwigshafen which is published in CWES 2 as *The Significance of Woman's Intrinsic Value in National Life* and continued throughout the late 1920s and early 1930s in Salzburg, Switzerland and Vienna, amongst other influential centres of Catholic education. By examining them we see a good example of how Stein's own philosophical and anthropological investigations translated into a spirited response to the darkness of the times she lived in.

Her interest in the role of women in society, however, was nothing new. Since her early enrolment at Breslau University (as we have said, one of the first women to be admitted to university in Europe, let alone Germany) she had held the cause of women's rights and liberation close to her heart. At this time she joined the Prussian Society for Women's Right to Vote for, as she later wrote in *Life in a Jewish Family*:

> We were all passionately moved by the women's rights movement …. We often discussed the issue of a double career. Erna and our two girl friends had many misgivings, wondering whether one ought not to give up a career

for the sake of marriage. I was alone in maintaining always that I would not sacrifice my profession on any account. If one could have predicted the future for us then! The other three married but, nevertheless, continued in their careers. I alone did not marry, but I alone have assumed an obligation for which, joyfully, I would willingly sacrifice any other career.

(CWES 1: 123)

And as part of this campaign for women's equality she challenged the decision of the Prussian ministry of education not to allow women university posts. A circumstance, as we have seen, that directly affected her own intellectual development and career.

Before we turn to look at Edith's writing on women it is important to bear in mind the comments of the Steinian scholar Linda Lopez McAlister in her 2006 essay on the subject. She points out that to date there has not been a widespread interest in Stein's writing on women from feminist scholars. This she attributes to a 'matter of timing':

Stein's work on women appeared in English at a singularly inauspicious time. As a phenomenologist she is a philosopher engaged in the search for essences, yet her *Essays on Women (Die Frau)* appeared exactly at the time when anti-essentialism was reaching its peak among English-speaking feminist philosophers.

(Lopez McAlister 2006: 201)

At the time of writing this debate between 'essentialism' and 'anti-essentialism' remains as controversial as it was a decade ago, if not more so. Accordingly, in the future reception of Edith's writing on the subject in the coming decades it is to be expected that this aspect of her thought will receive increasing scrutiny. Yet, as we have seen throughout this book, by adopting her consistently fruitful phenomenological approach to the subject of women and their role in society, Edith still has much to contribute to the present debate. In addition, as we saw earlier in the book, Edith is consistently flexible in her approach to the phenomenology of the self and adapts it to the circumstances within which she finds it. Her notions of 'core' and 'soul' *do* have essentialist elements, but, as we have seen, she is wary of being too rigid in the deployment of these terms.

In his analysis of her use of the terms, Colagno emphasizes, as we have done here, the importance of 'depth' for her descriptions of the human person, as he puts it:

> Depth will become a specifically human and personal way to describe the relationships that exist between self and self, self and others, and ultimately self and God. Depth becomes not only a way of describing the nature of certain relationships, in that depth is viewed as a *quale* of the soul, a quality of the nature of its existence, but also a place – and a place of poignant encounter. The soul also becomes depth, an infinite space where the human person can encounter the divine persons.
>
> (Calcagno 2006: 262)

Thus, in four talks she gave to the Katholische Frauenorganisation in Zurich in 1932 (published as *Christliches Frauenleben* in ESGA 13 and *Spirituality of the Christian Woman* in CWES 2) she states that:

> The human soul as such is not a complete, resting Being. Its being is to become, in which its powers, brought into the world within itself as a seed contains its development, should unfold – this unfolding only happens however through activity.[7]
>
> (ESGA 13: 68)

As before we see in her 'structure of the soul' this subtle notion of a mediating element between material sensing and spirit (*Sinnlichkeit* and *Geist*) that holds the 'form' of an individual in an Aristoteleian-Thomist sense:

> The soul is housed in a body on whose vigour and health its own vigour and health depend – even if not exclusively nor simply. On the other hand, the body receives its nature as body – life, motion, form, *gestalt*, and intellective (*geistigen*) significance – through the soul. Grounded in the sensory, as much bodily as concerned with the soul, it is a *geistiges* Being, which as a knowing capability, discloses a world; as will intervenes in this world in creative and shaping form and as feeling inwardly engages with this world and so explains it.
>
> (ESGA 13: 68/CWES 2: 94–95)[8]

Yet, despite this common ground between all human beings she would like to differentiate differing tendencies in the souls of men and women:

> Woman's soul is present and lives more intensely in all parts of the body, and it is inwardly affected by that which happens to the body; whereas, with men, the body has more pronouncedly the character of an instrument which serves them in their work and which is accompanied by a certain detachment.
>
> (CWES 2: 95)

Again, following the exposition of her spiritual anthropology in Part One of the present book, we would not expect a gross or superficial understanding of gender difference to be expressed by her. And this is just what we find in passages such as those above. This is confirmed in a letter to her friend Sr Callista Kopf from August 1931 where she discusses her recent Salzburg lectures on women (published in *On Women* as *Ethos of Women*). Here she stresses that as a young woman she was a 'radical advocate of women's rights' and then lost interest in the whole question. Now, having to revisit her ideas on the subject (and presumably following the post-conversion philosophical synthesis she had undertaken over the past decade) she realizes that the best approach to the matter is to 'seek purely objective solutions'. Accordingly, from this standpoint:

> The insistence that the sexual differences are 'stipulated by the body alone' is questionable from various points of view. 1) if *anima = forma corporis*, then bodily differentiation constitutes an index of differentiation in the soul (*seelischer*). 2) Matter serves form, not the reverse. That strongly suggests that the difference in the soul (*seelischer*) is the primary one. Thorough consideration must be given, of course, to the question: 'to what extent can and should growth into the supernatural be a growing beyond differences endowed by nature?'
>
> (CWES 5: 99)[9]

For as she says in the 1932 lecture *The Problem of Women's Education* she sees the human species as having two aspects: 'man' and 'woman' and that the essence of humanity is characterized by this duality.

> There is a difference, not only in body structure and in particular physiological functions, but also in the entire corporeal life. The relationship of soul and body is different in man and woman; and within the life of the soul, the relationship between *Geist* and senses, as indeed amongst the 'spiritual faculties' (*geistigen Kräfte*) themselves. The feminine species expresses a unity and wholeness of the total body-soul (*leiblich-seelischen*) personality and a harmonious unfolding of faculties. The masculine species strives to enhance individual abilities in order that they may attain their highest achievements.
>
> (CWES 2: 187–8/ ESGA 13: 130)[10]

So the 'needs' of each gender, socially and culturally, will, she suggests, be subtly different but complementary. From these phenomenological observations about the degree of expression of the 'life of the soul' in men and women, Edith follows through by investigating the systematic implications that derive from these observations.

Then, as now, these observations, could not take place in indifference to the political events that were unfolding around her. When she gave her first talk in Ludwigshafen in 1928 she steered a middle way between the traditionalist view that refused women any role in society but, on the other hand, she did not want to take the other position which she regarded as equally extreme: that men and women are exactly alike. This much is evident from her phenomenology which respects the differences in a 'soul' that is so intimately connected with a body that is differentiated according to gender.

By the time of her final lectures in the early 1930s the situation had become even more alarming as the 'traditionalist' views reasserted themselves in the guise of Nazi ideology. As she piquantly remarked:

> Curiously, this romantic view is connected to that brutal attitude which considers woman merely from the biological point of view; indeed, this is the attitude which characterizes the political group now in power. Gains won during the last decades are being wiped out because of this romanticist ideology, the use of women to bear babies of Aryan stock.
>
> (CWES 2: 57)

Faced, as Wittgenstein was, with this growing threat she concludes in her lecture, *The Significance of Woman's Intrinsic Value in National Life*, that in the present time women face three tasks/challenges:

1   To become a complete person oneself; i.e., a person all of whose faculties are developed and coexist in harmony;
2   To help others to become complete human beings;
3   In all contact with other persons, to respect the complete human being. (CWES 2: 37)

Thus, by following this 'vocation':

> Certain maladies of modern culture such as the dehumanization of the person, fragmentation, and the one-sided development of certain faculties leading to the atrophy of others may be cured through recourse to the intrinsic value of woman.
>
> (CWES 2: 39)

In this respect women, because of their unique physical-soul constitution, are particularly well suited to holding this role in protecting society from its dehumanization and brutalization: 'such a woman is like a seminal spore bringing new life to the national body. At the same time, she is protected naturally against the poison infecting the body of our society' (CWES 2: 39). This will happen not only through the traditional role of mother and educator but also in many other professions such as medical workers, where 'the woman doctor is equipped to give the patient the needed human sympathy while preserving the objectivity required for diagnosis and therapy of the whole psychosomatic system' (CWES 2: 39). Though advocating this wider professional role for women in society she also wants to remind her readers of a danger that 'lies in changing over to the hyper-masculine type of abstract objectivity and in suppressing the drive towards total humanity' (CWES 2: 39).

For Edith, as with Wittgenstein, the necessary stand for the philosopher (or indeed sincere human being) against the prevailing dehumanizing and politicized totalitarianism of contemporary culture, thus lies in the return to becoming 'complete human beings', which of course for her will embrace our physical, psychological, intellective *and* spiritual dimensions. By doing so, she argues, this dehumanizing and brutalizing culture can be held at bay. The alternative is the abyss.

The duty of the philosopher: A Jew

Like Wittgenstein, Edith was aware of 'the darkness of the times' she lived in. And like Wittgenstein she was aware of the particular resonance for herself as a woman and a Jew. Yet, as we have seen throughout this book, she approached this darkness with the clear insights her philosophy had gifted her with. For the manifestations of this darkness, whether as anti-Semitism or misogyny, were results of that underlying brutality that the modern world had unleashed.[11] Thus in her Ludwigshafen address of 1928 she noted:

> What is, then, the great sickness of our time and of our people? There is an inner disunion, a complete deficiency of set convictions and strong principles, an aimless drifting. Therefore, the great mass of humanity seeks for an anesthetic in ever new, ever more refined delights. Those who wish to maintain a sober level of life, in order to protect themselves from contemporary turmoil, frequently annihilate this level by one-sided professional work; but even they cannot do anything to escape the turmoil. Only whole human beings as we have described them are immune to the contemporary sickness: such beings are steadfast on eternal first principles, unperturbed in their views and in their actions by the changing modes of thoughts, follies, and depravities surrounding them.
>
> (CWES 2: 259–60)

As the situation darkened in the early 1930s Edith took it upon herself to undertake two actions that continue to provoke controversy and comment today. We can see both as arising out of her 'life philosophy' from the need to affirm the wholeness of human personhood. In this respect her reactions to the challenges of the times she lived in begin to make sense. Her philosophy, as we stated at the outset of this book, does not arise from someone who 'lived in a box' and therefore her reactions to the anti-Semitic climate within which she found herself cannot either be 'boxed off' into those of a 'Catholic martyr', 'Jewish freedom-fighter' or, even, 'disinterested philosopher'.

The first of these reactions was that she felt the moral responsibility as a Christian with Jewish heritage to draw the darkening situation in Germany to the attention of the reigning Pope Pius XI. She had wanted to undertake a pilgrimage to Rome to tell the pontiff herself but the 'Holy Year' of 1933 (the anniversary of Christ's death and resurrection) meant that the pope himself would be unable to receive her. Consequently, she took it upon herself to express her feelings in the manner most suited to her – a well-poised and well-argued letter that alerted the Vatican not just to the danger to the Jews, but to the whole of modern culture that was thus being undermined by their persecution. As she wrote there:

> Everything that happened and continues to happen on a daily basis originates with a government that calls itself 'Christian.' For weeks not only Jews but also thousands of faithful Catholics in Germany, and, I believe, all over the world, have been waiting and hoping for the Church of Christ to raise its voice to put a stop to this abuse of Christ's name. Is not this idolization of race and governmental power that is being pounded into the public consciousness by the radio open heresy? Isn't the effort to destroy Jewish blood an abuse of the holiest humanity of our Savior, of the most blessed Virgin and the apostles? Is not all this diametrically opposed to the conduct of our Lord and Savior, who, even on the Cross, still prayed for his persecutors? And isn't this a black mark on the record of this Holy Year that was intended to be a year of peace and reconciliation?
>
> (12 April 1933 in Posselt 2005: 239)

Yet, despite her 'direct action' by writing to the Pope, Edith's responses to the Holocaust have been mired in controversy. Two books that appeared at the time of her canonization in 1998 exposed the variety of reactions to a supposed Catholic 'take over' of Edith's Judaism: Susanne Batzdorff's *Aunt Edith: The Jewish Heritage of a Catholic Saint* (Batzdorff 1998) and Waltraud Herbstrith's *Never Forget: Christian and Jewish Perspectives on Edith Stein* (Herbstrith 1998). The reaction of her nephew, Ernst Biberstein, to the canonization is indicative of a view held by many in her family:

To others in the family, such as her nephew Ernst Ludwig Biberstein, to speak of Edith being martyred 'on behalf of' her people is to imply she died for their atonement and salvation. 'In that case, I could not allow myself to take part in this ceremony. That would be an almost blasphemous debasement of the sacrifice of the millions who, for the sake of their faith … went, like her, to a bestial death.'

(Batzdorff 1998: 204–5)

As throughout this book it is again evidence of the legacy of the mysterious woman 'sealed with seven seals'. On the one hand she was a clear activist against the Nazi regime, as evidenced in her pleas to the sisters in Cologne not to vote for the Hitler regime in 1938: 'repeatedly she implored the Sisters not to vote for Hitler no matter what the consequences to individuals or to the community might be. He was an enemy of God and would drag Germany into perdition with himself' (Posselt 2005: 182). Yet, on the other hand, she seemed to have a mystical identification with the fate of her people and referred repeatedly to her offering herself as a '*holocaustum*' for the sake of her persecuted people. As she wrote to Sr. Adelgundis (Amelia Jaegerschmid) in 1930:

> After every encounter in which I am made aware how powerless we are to exercise direct influence, I have a deeper sense of the urgency of my own '*holocaustum*'. And this awareness culminates increasingly in a 'hic Rhodus, hic salta!'[12]
>
> (CWES 5: 60)

Culminating in her letter of offering sent to Mother Ottilia Thannisch on Passion Sunday 1939:

> Dear Mother: please, will [Your Reverence] allow me to offer myself to the heart of Jesus as a sacrifice of atonement (*als Sühnopfer*) for true peace, that the dominion of the Antichrist may collapse, if possible, without a new world war, and that a new order may be established? I would like [my request] granted this very day because it is the twelfth hour. I know that I am a nothing, but Jesus desires it, and surely he will call many others to do likewise in these days.
>
> (CWES 5: 305, 26.3.39)

It is difficult for us to read these words today. Calcagno talked of her description of the soul as a 'place of poignant encounter'. As we read these most intimate words, knowing now where Edith would be led, we are indeed brought to the place of 'poignant encounter'. That, as we have seen, can be a place of anger, fear, confusion and rage – as well as astonishment, awe and reverence. I would like to finish this chapter by suggesting that if Edith's writing, continually and perpetually challenging, has brought us, its readers, to that place, then she has succeeded. 'Never again', as Herbstrith wrote, can we face the threats and lies of brutal and brutalizing socio-political regimes without hearing the fragile but determined words of this most remarkable woman who, as we said at the beginning of this book, took the full force of the European unconscious upon her and transformed it into an enduring and radical 'living philosophy'.

Epilogue: The author addresses the subject

Transit Ad Orientum – final days

After her arrest we have fragmentary accounts of what happened to Edith next including reports from Westerbork, the Nazi holding camp in Holland for all deported Jews (where the other great Jewish mystic, Etty Hillesum, would also be held) and from guards and functionaries as her train moved slowly East to the killing fields of Auschwitz. One account, from the Dutch official Mr Wielek at Westerbork, will suffice to give a sense of Edith's last days on earth at Westerbork from 4 to 6 August 1942:

> The one sister who impressed me immediately, whose warm, glowing smile has never been erased from my memory, despite the disgusting incidents I was forced to witness, is the one whom I think the Vatican may one day canonize. From the moment I met her in the camp at Westerbork ... I knew: here is someone truly great. For a couple of days she lived in that hellhole, walking, talking and praying ... like a saint. And she really was one. That is the only fitting way to describe this middle-aged woman who struck everyone as so young, who was so whole and honest and genuine.
>
> (Herbstrith 1992:186)

Strangely enough, when she was finally put on a cattle train to Auschwitz the train route recapitulated her life spent in Germany. First the line went South to Cologne where she first entered Carmel. From here, following the testimony of Valentin Fouquet, station master of Schifferstadt station, the train stopped at Schifferstadt, not far from Speyer where she had taught with the Dominicans. He wrote to the investigators for the cause of her canonization in the 1960s:

A woman in dark clothing hailed him from inside the compartment and asked him whether he knew the family of Dean Schwind. When he answered that he and the dean had been classmates and that the dean himself had been on the platform just a few minutes before, the woman asked him to convey Edith Stein's greetings to the dean and his family, and let them know she was on her way to the east.

(*Kölner Selig- und Heiligsprechungsprozess der Dienerin Gottes Sr Teresia Benedicta a Cruce – Edith Stein* in Herbstrith 1992: 189)

Here she 'peered out, called to three different people on the platform, and dropped a note onto the tracks, which a priest picked up and gave to two teachers from St Magdalena's: "Greetings from Sister Teresia Benedicta a Cruce. En route for the East"' (Feldes 1998: 74).

The last account of Edith on earth comes from Johannes Wieners, a postal employee in the Cologne branch of the Reich Postal Service which he published in August 1982. Conscripted to form a mobile postal unit with seventeen other men he had set off to the East in a large mobile postal train in summer 1942. On 7 August he was waiting with the group for the train to be re-signalled at Breslau, then, as now, an important terminus for all trains travelling to Southern Poland, another train pulled up alongside theirs. His account continues:

> When the guard opened one of the sliding doors, we could see people all penned up, listlessly squatting on the floor. There was a horrible stench coming from the car. A woman dressed like a nun appeared at the door, and I guess because I looked sympathetic to her, she said to me, 'It's terrible. We don't even have containers to relieve ourselves.' After that, she looked into the distance at Breslau and said, 'This is my home; I'll never see it again.' I stared at her, wondering what she was talking about. She paused for a minute, then said, 'We are going to our death.' That really shook me. I remember that I asked her, 'Do the other prisoners know this?' She answered very slowly, 'It's better for them not to know.'

(J. Wieners *Meine begegnung mit Edith Stein* in *Kölnische Rundschau*, 9th August 1982, reproduced in Herbstrith 1992: 192/3)

As the conversation proceeded Wieners had become increasingly disturbed and sought at this point, despite the jeers of his fellow postal workers, to organize some food and drink for the prisoners. However, when they put their suggestion to her she replied: 'No, thank you. We won't take anything.' These are the last recorded words that we have of Edith Stein: philosopher, women's rights activist, Jew, Catholic, Carmelite and saint.

Long after the war was finished final confirmation of her fate was officially recorded by the Bureau of Information of the Netherlands Red Cross in June 1950:

> Chief of the Settlement Bureau for Jewish Affairs of the Netherlands Red Cross Bureau of Information confirms hereby that according to the papers kept in our archives Edith Teresa Hedwig Stein, born on 12th October 1891 in Breslau, last residence: Monastery of the Carmelite Nuns, Bovenstestraat 48, Echt (Holland), for reasons of race, and specifically because of Jewish descent, on 2nd August 1942, arrested in Echt, via K.L. [Concentration Camp] Amersfoort (Holland), on 5th August 1942, handed over in K.L. Westerbork and on 7th August 1942, deported from K.L. Westerbork to K.L. Auschwitz. The above named person is to be considered as having died on 9th August 1942 in Auschwitz. Notice to this effect is given on 15th February 1950 in Echt.
>
> (CWES 1: 434)

A last conversation with Edith

After all the time we have spent together it is sad to have to say goodbye. Studying your philosophy and reading the accounts of your life have affected me more profoundly than I had anticipated. You have taken your secret with you and we cannot know what that was. But you have left us two legacies: your life and your teaching. I have tried in this book to be faithful to both, realizing that, as with Ludwig Wittgenstein, it is almost impossible to separate the two, and if that is done irreparable damage is done to both, they are indeed a seamless garment. My wish is that this book will lead readers who have been inspired by your life to try to read more of your philosophy, and lead philosophical enquirers to ponder on your life choices which for you were never separate from your philosophy. You are the great enigma Edith, even your family never fathomed you, 'a secret bound by seven seals' they said. But now, as we approach you again in the light of what we have discovered over the past decades since your death, let us do so in the spirit you yourself cultivated: one of humility, joy and thanksgiving for the miracle of being that unites us all, whatever our race, creed, colour or religion.

Notes

Prologue

1 Words ascribed to Thomas Aquinas by Edith Stein in an imaginary dialogue, CWES 8: 7/8.

2 A recurrent theme in this book will be the ambiguity both of Edith Stein and her place in philosophy, theology, psychology and history. Part of the narrative we shall address in this volume will be the moves by different groups to appropriate the woman and her heritage. This begins with her name. After her entry into Carmelite life in 1934, Edith Stein (1891–1942) took the religious name Sr Teresia Benedicta a Cruce. The name itself is deliberately ambiguous suggesting various English translations including Sr Teresa Benedict of the Cross, Sr Teresa Blessed by the Cross and Sr Teresa Benedicta at the Cross. Throughout this volume I shall refer to her usually with the name 'Edith Stein', either addressing her as Edith or Stein according to context. I shall discuss the multivalent nuances of her name in religion later.

3 Saying of Edith Stein attributed by her first biographer in Posselt 1957: 55, my translation.

4 Tyler 2016: *The Pursuit of the Soul: Psychoanalysis, Soul-making and the Christian Tradition* (T & T Clark).

5 See bibliographical note at the end of this chapter.

6 "*Mi Amado, las montañas, los valles solitarios nemorosos, las insulas extrañas, los ríos sonorosos, el silbo de los aires amorosos.*" *The Spiritual Canticle*, CA: 13 in John of the Cross 2002: 606.

7 ESGA 3: 285. Letter to Sr Adelgundis Jaegerschmid 23.3.38.

8 Attributed to an unnamed school friend in Posselt 1957: 14–15.

Chapter 1

1 Inaugural Dissertation, *On the Problem of Empathy*, Halle 1917: 133, quoted in CWES 1:15.

2 For an authoritative account of the city in English see Norman Davies' *Microcosm: Portrait of a Central European City* (Davies 2003). As he points out, there

is still a great deal of political freight in the choice of name for Edith's home town. He preferences the mediaeval 'Vratislava' which neatly sidesteps the twentieth century controversies connected to the city. Here, where referring to the city's name in Edith's lifetime I shall usually use, as she did, Breslau. Outside of that context I shall use its present name, Wroclaw, wherever possible. Silesia, as an administrative district, largely remains intact as it always has – today, of course, mostly lying in Poland rather than neighbouring Germany or Czechia.

3   The German edition of *Life in a Jewish Family* referred to is in ESGA 1 and the English edition in CWES 1, further details in the bibliography.

4   For more on this complicated history, see the account by her niece, Susanne Batzdorff, in Batzdorff 1998.

5   Although as the editors of the most recent editions acknowledge, a number of pages were lost in this tortuous journey which probably will never be recovered.

6   Following the First World War, Lublinitz was ceded to Poland after a plebiscite, despite the majority in the town preferring to stay part of Germany. This was too much for the Courants who sold up and left. Most of the family subsequently moved to German speaking parts of Silesia or Berlin.

7   "… *Ist sie kein Kulturmensch, sondern ganz schlichte und starke Natur.*"

8   The description of these events in the *Life* would later become one of the contested passages by her surviving family members when publication was sought after her death.

9   "*Von früher Kindheit an wurde ich in der ganzen großen Verwandtschaft hauptsächlich durch zwei Eigenschaften charakterisiert: Man warf mir Ehrgeiz vor (sehr mit Recht), und man nannte mich mit Nachdruck die »kluge« Edith. Beides schmerzte mich sehr.*"

10 The equivalent to a British Secondary School or American High School.

11 Hans Biberstein (1889–1965) would eventually marry Edith's sister Erna. The couple escaped to the United States during the Nazi persecution and would later become, with their daughter Susanne, important guardians of Edith's heritage.

12 In her 8 August 1931 letter to Sr Callista Kopf, Edith says that as a student she had been a '*radikale Frauenrechtlerin*' (ESGA 2: 169). In CWES 5: 100 this is translated as a 'radical feminist'. Following helpful comments on this from Fr John Sullivan OCD I have stayed with the original description. We shall return to Edith's views on women's rights in the penultimate chapter.

13 An early experimental school of psychology centred around Oswald Külpe 1862–1915, Karl Marbe 1869–1953 and Karl Bühler 1879–1963, see Hoffmann and Stock 2010.

14 "*Entzückte mich darum so sehr, weil sie ganz eigentlich in solcher Klärungsarbeit bestand und weil man sich hier das gedankliche Rüstzeug, das man braucht, von Anfang an selbst schmiedete.*"

15 "*Aber sie erschloß mir einen Bereich von 'Phänomenen', an denen ich nun nicht mehr blind vorbeigehen konnte. Nicht umsonst wurde uns beständig eingeschärft, daß wir alle*

Dinge vorurteilsfrei ins Auge fassen, alle 'Scheuklappen' abwerfen sollten. Die Schranken der rationalistischen Vorurteile, in denen ich aufgewachsen war, ohne es zu wissen, fielen, und die Welt des Glaubens stand plötzlich vor mir" (ESGA 1: 160).

16 "*Andererseits hatte ich Bedenken, ob das nicht eine egoistische Regung sei*" (ESGA 1: 227).

17 Posselt's biography exists in several German and English versions. I have chosen to cite the 1957 German version and the most recent English version of 2005, see bibliography for details.

18 Initially a Protestant convert, Pauline had become a Catholic in 1922 at the Carmelite church of the Trinity in Munich, having been received into the church by Cardinal Pacelli (later to become Pope Pius XII). She moved finally to Ermeton, Belgium, where she later died.

19 As the most recent English edition of Posselt's biography (2005) states: 'The alternative explanation was asserted as early on as 1952 by Elisabeth de Mirabel, *Edith Stein, 1891–1942* (Paris: Eds. du Seuil, 1952), 60. More recently, Joachim Feldes supplies greater detail still in "Diesen lieben Blick vergesse ich nie": *Edith Stein und der Liebfrauenberg* (private publication, 2000), 9–12. Feldes concurs with Neyer on the details of eventual return of the book to the town where it made such a significant difference in Edith's life. Cf. Uwe Müller and Maria Amata Neyer, *Edith Stein: Das Leben einer ungewöhnlichen Frau* (Zürich/Düsseldorf: Benziger, 1998), 149–50, n. 12.' (Posselt 2005: 239, fn. 3).

20 "*Seine Seelenführung war ruhig, sicher und besonnen, auf weise Menschenkenntnis und die Erfahrung jahrzehntelanger Seelsorgearbeit gestützt, doch zugleich voll heiliger Ehrfurcht vor dem Wirken Gottes in der Seele und da ebenso zart wie kühn.*"

21 I have introduced my own translation of the final paragraph from ESGA 2: Letter 45: "*Wie das geschehen ist, darüber lassen Sie mich heute schweigen. Ich habe keine Scheu, davon zu sprechen, und werde es sicherlich zu gegebener Stunde auch Ihnen gegenüber tun, aber das muß sich 'ergeben', ich kann nicht darüber 'berichten'.*"

22 Remembering, as her former student, Gertrud Koebner, reported: 'with her, Latin was like German' (in Herbstrith 1992: 71).

23 See also ESGA 2: Letter 150.

Chapter 2

1 Although there are earlier drafts, the final version we have today was begun about 1934, and worked upon until 1937 when Husserl succumbed to the terminal illness that would lead to his death on 27 April 1938. I shall draw upon the German edition in Husserl's collected works: Husserl, E. (1954) *Die Krisis der Europäischen Wissenschaften und die Transzendentale Phänomenologie* edited by Walter Biemel and the English translation of David Carr in Husserl, E. (1970) *The Crisis of European Sciences and Transcendental Phenomenology.* Hereon *Krisis*.

2   For the Influence of *Krisis* on the development of Merleau-Ponty's work (which he had read in draft at the Husserl archive in Louvain in 1939) see Husserl 1970: xxx/xxxi and Carman and Hansen 2005.

3   *"Wissenschaft von Weltall, von der Alleinheit alles Seienden."*

4   At this point Husserl stresses that this 'universalizing science' also arose in diverse cultures such as Chinese and Indian cultures, but that he will concentrate on the particular instance of Greece and the arising of European universalizing thought.

5   As he puts it in the *Abhandlung* of 'before 1930', the 'naturalistic viewpoint' sees 'the world as the universe of realities in the form of mutual exteriority. Nature as the realm of the pure *res extensae*. Everything real is a body or has a body, but only the body has actual and true *coextension*, understood at once temporally and spatially' (Husserl 1970: 315/1954: 294).

6   In a perceptive essay Charles Taylor refers to this as the 'representational attitude' or 'inside-outside picture' (Taylor 2005).

7   *"Die naturwissenschaftliche Methode muss auch die Geistesgeheimnisse erschliessen"* (Husserl 1954: 341).

8   *"Blosse Tatsachenwissenshaften machen blosse Tatsachenmenschen"* (Husserl 1954: 4).

9   *"Ist Vernunft und Seiendes zu trennen, wo erkennende Vernunft bestimmt, was Seiendes ist?"* (Husserl 1954: 9).

10 *Geist* is yet another German term that is a minefield for the translator: 'spirit', 'mind', 'intellect' or 'wit' could all be equally used as equivalent English translations. Accordingly, to emphasize the ambiguity of the original German term at points I shall leave it untranslated. We shall return to this issue in the following chapter.

11 *"Das alle Vorurteile Unklarheiten aus einer traditionalen Sedimentierung sind"* (Husserl 1954: 73).

12 *"Wie soll da das Seelenleben, das ganz und gar Bewusstseinsleben ist, intentionales Leben des Ich, das Gegenständlichkeiten als ihm bewusst hat, mit ihnen erkennend, wertend usw. beschäftigt ist, wie soll es bei einem Übersehen der Intentionalität ernstlich erforscht, wie können da Vernuftprobleme überhaupt angregriffen werden?"* (Husserl 1954: 88).

13 Throughout the present work I have translated the German *Ich* as the English 'I'. In doing so I am aware that a number of English translators opt for various options such as 'ego', 'i' or 'self'. I believe that staying with consistency here helps to clarify where German authors want to contrast 'I' with, for example, 'self' or 'soul'. We shall return to this in a later chapter.

14 *"Liegen nicht am Ende hinter den psychologisch-erkenntnistheoretischen Problemen die von Descartes berührten, aber nicht erfassten Probleme des 'ego' jener Cartesianischen Epoché?"* (Husserl 1954: 88). In the original text Husserl seems to make a clear

distinction between the 'I' as existing in its full intentional self (notated as 'Ich') and the non-intentional move made in Descartes' 'cogito'. The latter he refers to in inverted commas as the 'ego'. By translating both terms as 'ego' I think Carr (whose translation is otherwise excellent) blurs this distinction so I have restored it to the modified English translation. Perhaps Husserl's use of 'ego' and 'I' is not as indiscriminate as at times Carr seems to imply (e.g. see fn 1 in Husserl 1970: 77).

15 We shall return to the nature of *Seele*/soul throughout this book, for now I refer the reader to the discussions in the following chapter.

16 *"Durch ihren Objektivismus kann die Psychologie gar nicht die Seele, das ist doch das Ich, das tut und leidet, in seinem eigenwesentlichen Sinn ins Thema bekommen"* (Husserl 1954: 343/4).

17 *"Das ständige Fundament seiner doch subjective Denkarbeit die Lebensumwelt ist"* (Husserl 1954: 342).

18 Husserl called this 'clarification of the transcendental problem' the opera that would follow the 'overture' of the historical overview which we have already presented, as such it was meant by him to be the main section of the work of *Krisis* (Husserl 1970: 102).

19 *"Wir sind andererseits Subjekte für diese Welt, nämlich als die sie erfahrenden, bedenkenden, bewertenden, zwecktätig auf sie bezogenen Ichsubjekte."*

20 *"Das Objekt, in der Seinsgeltung des Modus 'selbst gegenwärtig'"* (Husserl 1954: 107). Hence Husserl's famous and constant refrain throughout his philosophical career: 'to the objects themselves!'.

21 *"Wahrnehmung ist der Urmodus der Anschauung, sie stellt in Uroriginalität, das ist im Modus der Selbstgegenwart dar"* (Husserl 1954: 107).

22 In many ways, as I shall argue later in this book, Hopkins can be seen as a 'proto-phenomenologist'.

23 *"Einer konsquent reflexiven Einstellung auf das Wie der subjektiven Gegebenheitsweise der Lebenswelt und der lebensweltlichen Objekte"* (Husserl 1954: 146).

24 *"Nur am Eingangstor des nie betretenen Reiches der 'Mütter der Erkenntnis' stehen"* Husserl 1954: 156, c.f. *Faust* 2: 6216 in Goethe 1959: 77: 'Loth am I now high mystery to unfold: Goddesses dwell, in solitude, sublime, Enthroned beyond the world of place or time; Even to speak of them dismays the bold. These are The Mothers.'

Chapter 3

1 *Zum Problem der Einfühlung*, hereafter *Empathy*. Unfortunately the other parts of the thesis have been lost. I shall refer largely to ESGA 5 and CWES 3.

2 *"Allem Streit über die Einfühlung liegt die still schweigende Voraussetzung zugrunde: es sind uns fremde Subjekte und ihr Erleben gegeben"* (ESGA 5:11).

3 *"Die gesamte uns umgebende Welt, die physische wie die psychophysische, die Körper wie die Menschen- und Tierseelen (einschließlich der psychophysischen Person des Forschers selbst"* (ESGA 5: 11).

4 *"Die Welt, in der ich lebe, ist nicht nur eine Welt physischer Körper, es gibt darin auch außer mir erlebende Subjekte, und ich weiß von diesem Erleben"* (ESGA 5: 12).

5 As argued in my earlier *The Pursuit of the Soul* (Tyler 2016) there is a clear, and perhaps understandable, antipathy in present-day Anglo-American discourse to the term 'soul' when referring to the phenomena of the psyche. I will not rehearse the arguments again here but refer the interested reader to the earlier work. Suffice it to say that for Stein, as for her contemporaries Husserl, Freud and Jung, the German *Seele* holds a rich freight which the English term 'mind' (or in this case 'psychic life') scatters. By pursuing the meaning of key Steinian terms such as *Seele* in the present volume I do not aim to criticize present English versions of her work but rather, consonant with the picture presented in the Prologue, I want to suggest that we are now in the second phase of Anglophone Steinian studies where we need to carefully weigh up the English equivalents of her terminology, some of which present difficulties to an Anglophone readership that may be unacquainted with the nuances of the twentieth-century German psycho-philosophical discourse within which Stein's works still have much to contribute. The present work aims to contribute to, and initiate, those conversations mindful of the fact that future work must be built on the foundations of the last half century of Steinian scholarship.

6 *"So erfaßt der Mensch das Seelenleben seines Mitmenschen, so erfaßt er aber auch als Gläubiger die Liebe, den Zorn, das Gebot seines Gottes, und nicht anders vermag Gott sein Leben zu erfassen."*

7 *"Und soll Einfühlung den von uns streng definierten Sinn: Erfahrung von fremdem Bewußtsein haben, dann ist nur das nicht-originäre Erlebnis, das ein originäres bekundet, Einfühlung, das originäre aber wie das »angenommene« nicht."*

8 *"Diese Erlebnisse rückwärts durchlaufend gelange ich von Schritt zu Schritt immer wieder zu einem Erlebnis, in dem dies jetzt lebende Ich einst gelebt hat, auch dann, wenn ich jenes Erlebnis nicht mehr direkt greifen kann, sondern es mir durch erinnernde Vergegenwärtigung zu Gesicht bringen muß"* (ESGA 5: 38).

9 *"Der Bewußtseinsstrom, der als 'er selbst und kein anderer' und als eigentümlich beschaffener charakterisiert ist, ergibt einen ganz bestimmt umgrenzten und guten Sinn von Individualität"* (ESGA 5: 38).

10 *"In unseren Erlebnissen… gibt sich uns ein ihnen zugrunde Liegendes, das sich und seine beharrlichen Eigenschaften in ihnen bekundet, als ihr identischer 'Träger': das ist die substanzielle Seele"* (ESGA 5: 39).

11 In common with many English translations, the CWES translation alternates between 'psychic' and 'soul' for 'Seele'. Thus, in the passage immediately after the one that introduces the 'substantial soul' we read in English: 'We have already become acquainted with single such psychic attributes too' (CWES 3: 40), whereas the German states: *"Wir haben auch schon einzelne solcher seelischen Eigenschaften kennen gelernt"*

(ESGA 5: 39). From now on, for the reasons stated above, I shall retain the '*seelische*' in English as the 'soul-like' or 'of the soul', thus rendering this passage: 'we have also already encountered such individual properties of the soul'.

12 "*Eine substanzielle Einheit, die sich – ganz analog dem physischen Ding – aufbaut aus kategorialen Elementen, und die Reihe der Kategorien.*"

13 "*Die eigentümliche Struktur der seelischen Einheit hängt von dem eigentümlichen Gehalt des Erlebnisstroms ab und umgekehrt... der Gehalt des Erlebnisstroms hängt von der Struktur der Seele.*"

14 "*Diese substanzielle Einheit ist 'meine' Seele, wenn die Erlebnisse, in denen sie sich bekundet, 'meine' Erlebnisse sind, Akte, in denen mein reines Ich lebt.*"

15 "*Diese Abhängigkeit der Erlebnisse von Einflüssen des Leibes ist ein wesentliches Charakteristikum des Seelischen.*"

16 "*Die Trennung, die wir vorgenommen haben, war eine künstliche, denn Seele ist uns gegeben als Seele in einem Leibe.*"

17 "*Diese Abhängigkeit der Erlebnisse von Einflüssen des Leibes*", the CWES translation reverts from 'soul' to 'psychic' at this point.

18 "*Die Seele als die sich in den einzelnen psychischen Erlebnissen bekundende substanzielle Einheit ist – wie das geschilderte Phänomen der 'psychophysischen Kausalität' und das Wesen der Empfindungen zeigt – auf Leib fundiert, bildet mit ihm das 'psychophysische Individuum'.*"

19 This, of course, is quite contrary to many common usages of the English word 'soul' which, if considered at all, is usually regarded as 'that which is not body'. In this respect the reluctance of some translators to opt for 'soul' in translation of '*seelisch*' is understandable, if perhaps a little confusing. Stein herself at this stage sometimes interchanges '*seelisch*' for '*psychisch*' which doesn't help clarity in some places.

20 "*Die Bezeichnung lehrt uns, daß man sie als außerwesentlich psychisch, als nicht leibgebunden betrachtet (wenn auch die betreffenden Psychologen sich nicht zu dieser Konsequenz bekennen mögen).*"

21 "*Ein einheitliches Objekt, in dem die Bewußtseinseinheit eines Ichs und ein physischer Körper sich untrennbar zusammenschießen, wobei jedes von ihnen einen neuen Charakter annimmt, der Körper als Leib, das Bewußtsein als Seele des einheitlichen Individuums auftritt.*"

22 "*Ist der fremde Leib als Leib 'gesehen'. Wir sind dieser Art der Gegebenheit, die wir 'Konoriginarität' nennen wollen, bei der Dingwahrnehmung begegnet.*"

23 "*Auch das Mitsehen der fremden Empfindungsfelder impliziert Tendenzen, aber ihre originäre Erfüllung ist hier prinzipiell ausgeschlossen, weder in fortschreitender äußerer Wahrnehmung noch im Übergang zur Leibwahrnehmung kann ich sie mir zu originärer Gegebenheit bringen. Die einzige Erfüllung, die hier möglich ist, ist die einfühlende Vergegenwärtigung.*"

24 *"Die Welt, die ich phantasierend erblicke, ist kraft ihres Widerstreits zu meiner originären Orientierung nichtseiende Welt (ohne daß ich mir, in der Phantasie lebend, diese Nicht-Existenz zur Gegebenheit zu bringen brauche); die Welt, die ich einfühlend erblicke, ist existierende Welt, als seiend gesetzt wie die originär wahrgenommene."*

25 *"Die im Ich entstehenden Strebungen und Widerstrebungen – so führt er aus – haben in diesem Ich doch nicht die gleiche Lage. Dieses Ich besitzt nämlich eine eigenartige Struktur: das eigentliche Ichzentrum oder der Ichkern ist umgeben von dem Ichleib. Und die Strebungen können nun zwar im Ich, aber außerhalb des Ichzentrums im Ichleib entstehen, also in diesem Sinne als exzentrische Strebungen erlebt werden."*

26 *"Natürlich werden auch die personalen Eigenschaften – die Güte, die Opferwilligkeit, die Tatkraft, die ich in meinen Handlungen erlebe – zu seelischen, wenn sie an einem psychophysischen Individuum wahrgenommen werden."*

27 *"Nicht nur, daß die kategoriale Struktur der Seele als Seele erhalten bleiben muß, auch innerhalb ihrer individuellen Gestalt treffen wir auf einen unwandelbaren Kern: die personale Struktur."*

28 *"So kann die psychophysische empirische Person eine mehr oder weniger vollkommene Realisation der geistigen sein."*

Chapter 4

1 Nietzsche 1908: 126. *"Hat man mich verstanden? – Dionysos gegen den Gekreuzigten..."*,

2 Most of what came after under Nietzsche's name was heavily redacted by his sister Elizabeth, often driven by her proto-Nazi ideology.

3 As we saw when examining Husserl's work, 'the Greeks' had become a cipher not only for Nietzsche but for most of his contemporary cultural critics for a state of mind that precedes and underpins our modern culture. However, what Nietzsche, Jung, Stein or Martin Heidegger for that matter, understood as early Attic culture and what actually occurred in pre-Common Era Greece may not necessarily be the same thing. Our aim here is to see how Nietzsche, Jung and Stein worked with this cipher to develop their own analyses of the modern self/soul.

4 The Dionysian/Apollonian trope is a common feature of early twentieth-century culture. As well as the examples cited we can reference E. M. Forster's 1902 short story, *The Story of a Panic* and Karol Szymanowski's 1918 opera *King Roger*.

5 Mann describes Aschenbach's encounter with the denizens of the 'Stranger God' thus: 'they laughed, they howled, they thrust their pointed staves into each other's flesh and licked the blood as it ran down. But now the dreamer was in them and of them, the stranger god was his own. Yes it was he who was flinging himself upon the animals, who bit and tore and swallowed smoking gobbets of flesh ... and in his very soul he tasted the bestial degradation of his fall' (Mann 1955: 74–6).

6. We can contrast Nietzsche's conclusions here with those of Husserl we saw earlier.

7. "*Nicht nur die Symbolik des Mundes, des Gesichts, des Wortes, sondern die volle, alle Glieder rhythmisch bewegende Tanzgebärde*" (Nietzsche 1990: 24/25).

8. As he famously put it in the late 1886 Preface to *The Gay Science*: 'Oh, those Greeks! They knew how to live: what is needed for that is to stop bravely at the surface, the fold, the skin; to worship appearance, to believe in shapes, tones, words – in the whole Olympus of appearance! Those Greeks were superficial – out of profundity! And is not this precisely what we are coming back to, we daredevils of the spirit who have climbed the highest and most dangerous peak of current thought and looked around from up there, looked down from up there? Are we not just in this respect – Greeks? Worshippers of shapes, tones, words? And therefore – artists?' (Nietzsche 2001: 8/9).

9. See, too the passage from *The Gay Science* 11 where Nietzsche calls the 'Kern'/Core of human self not 'consciousness' (as he calls it here *Bewusstheit*) but the 'instincts' (*instinkiv*). This, as we saw earlier and shall return to in the next chapter, is in marked contrast to Edith's own view of the nature of the *Kern*.

10. It is worth contrasting Jung's view here with that of the post-Freudian, Julia Kristeva. In *This Incredible Need to Believe* (Kristeva 2009: 84) she contrasts Nietzsche's 'Dionysius's drunkenness' with the suffering 'God-man' of Christianity. She preferences the latter.

11. "*Die Welt ist nicht nur entgöttert, sondern auch etwas entseelt.*"

12. "*(Die Libido) ist unser Unsterbliches, indem sie jenes Band darstellt, durch welches wir uns als nie erlöschend, in der Rasse fühlen. Sie ist Leben vom Leben der Menschheit. Ihre aus den Tiefen des Unbewussten emporströmenden Quellen kommen, wie unser Leben überhaupt, aus dem Stamme der ganzen Menschheit, indem wir ja nur ein von der Mutter abgebrochener und verpflanzer Zweig sind.*"

13. "*In dieser Tiefe dunkle Gewalten am Werk sind.*"

14. Interestingly enough, a similar critique of psycho-analysis was presented by Edith's contemporary – the Viennese man of letters, Karl Kraus (1874–1936). I hope to return to this parallel in a later work.

15. "*Die grosse Frage der Metaphysik ist die Frage nach dem Sein.*"

16. "*Der Mensch ist nur durch Gott, und ist, was er ist, durch Gott. Weil er Geist ist und weil er als Geist mit dem Licht der Vernunft, d.h. mit dem Abbild des göttlichen Logos, ausgerüstet ist, kann er erkennen.*" Here Stein cites her work on the translation of Aquinas's *Disputed Questions* and how he too was influenced by Augustine in this respect (ESGA 14: 9–10).

17. Stein will later develop these ideas in *Endliches und Ewiges Sein* to which we will return in the next chapter.

18. "*Der Mensch hat keine Macht über die Gewalten der Tiefe und kann von sich aus den Weg zur Höhe nicht finden.*"

19 *"Das natürliche Licht seines Verstandes ist gestärkt durch das Gnadenlicht und ist besser geschützt gegen Irrtümer, wenn auch nicht dagegen versichert, vor allem ist sein geistiges Auge geöffnet für alles, was in deiser Welt uns von einer andern Welt Kunde gibt."*

20 *"Im Innern des Menschen wohnt die Wahrheit."*

21 *"Das ist die Wahrheit, auf die man stösst, wenn man im eigenen Innern bis auf den Grund geht. Erkennt die Seele sich selbst, so erkennt sie Gott in sich."*

22 *"Er ist ein Mikrokosmos, der alle Reiche der geschaffenen Welt in sich vereinigt."*

23 Written shortly after completion of her doctorate it can be found in ESGA 6 and CWES 7.

24 *"Der Strom ist einer, weil er einem Ich erströmt. Denn was aus der Vergangenheit in die Zukunft hineinlebt, in jedem Moment neues Leben aus sich hervorspringen fühlt und den ganzen Schweif des vergangenen mit sich trägt – das ist das Ich."*

25 We noted earlier (footnote 9) that Nietzsche in the *Gay Science* (11) makes a similar distinction between '*Bewusstheit*' and the '*instinctiv*'.

26 *"Das Ich, das im Besitz dieser realen Eigenschaft ist, darf natürlich nicht verwechselt warden mit dem reinen Ich, dem als Ausstrahlungspunkt der reinen Erlebnisse ursprünglich erlebten."*

27 In their 2000 translation of *the Beiträge* for the ICS edition of Stein's works, Sawicki and Baseheart at this point introduce a footnote to explain their use of 'sentient' as a translation of 'psychische': 'unfortunately, in English "psychic" has another meaning that is inappropriate here; "sensate" and "sentient" are closer to Stein's meaning' (CWES 7: 23 fn 36). For reasons given earlier in this book which will be reiterated in the next chapter, I will retain the German *psychische* where necessary translating it sometimes as *psychical* or 'of the psyche'. I shall retain 'soul' as a translation for *Seele*.

28 *"Diese Struktur der Psyche, wie wir sie bisher geschildert haben, hat einen letzten Kern noch unberücksichtigt gelassen."*

29 The subsequent history of the unsavoury antics of the 'master's' successors on the 'Green Hill' seems to confirm Nietzsche's initial impression. See, for example, Nietzsche 1967: 283–9.

30 For more on this genealogy see Tyler 2016.

31 On this see, for example, Hamann 2005.

Chapter 5

1 See, for example, Beckmann-Zöller 2008, Betschart 2016, Ales Bello 2008.

2 We have already noted in previous footnotes the problems with translation of the German terms *Seele*, *Geist* and *Ich*. Commentators on Stein and her translators over

the past half century since her death have adopted various strategies to get around these issues. Thus, for example, Sawicki in her influential 1997 text refers to *Ich* throughout as 'i', whilst in many translations commentators alternate between 'I', 'self' and the Freudian 'ego'. I have set out my own rationale for my translation choices as I have gone along trying throughout to be true to the sense of the original whilst retaining consistency in English use.

3 Strachey's 24 Volume 'Standard Edition of the Complete Psychological Works of Sigmund Freud' appeared between 1953 and 1974 published by the Hogarth Press and now published by Penguin. Most of Strachey's editorial choices were taken up by later editors and created the climate by which Freud's works were, and still are, discussed in the English-speaking world.

4 Perhaps this may no longer be the case with psychoanalytic training but it is sadly all too apparent still amongst university graduates wanting to apply post-Freudian concepts to academic arguments, often without recourse to personal analysis or experience of the terms explored by Freud.

5 "*Einem Stand von weltlichen Seelsorgern, die Ärzte nicht zu sein brache und Priesten nicht sein dürfen.*"

6 "*Der Seele Grenzen wirst du nie ausfinden, und ob auch jegliche Strasse abschrittest: so tiefen Grund hat sie*" (Husserl 1954: 173). Husserl here substitutes Heraclitus's original 'sense' with 'ground' in his rendition of Fragment 45.

7 Translated Ales Bello and Calcagno in Ales Bello 2008: 149.

8 The former, as noted above, is referred to in the English edition of the *Collected Works* as 'Sentient Causality'. For the reasons given earlier, I preference the title 'Psychic Causality' here.

9 "*Die Seele wird als der innerste Teil des gesamten psychophysische Individuums verstanden.*"

10 "*Was dieses geheimnisvolle Etwas – die Seele – ist, dem müssen wir näherzukommen suchen. Nach Hedwig Conrad-Martius" "Gespräch von der Seele' ist die Eigentümlichkeit der Wesen, die eine Seele haben – im Gegensatz etwa zu den Elementargeistern, zu deren Idee es gehört, nur leiblich-geistige Figuration zu besitzen, – eine Beschwertheit und Fixiertheit in sich selbst. Während jene Geistwesen von dem Geist der Sphäre, der sie zugehören, getragen werden, lebt der Mensch aus seiner Seele heraus, die das Zentrum seines Seins ist.*"

11 If a seasoned phenomenologist such as Ales Bello is 'bowled over' by Stein's terminology here this does not bode well for the rest of us. One of the most sophisticated and finely argued analyses of Stein's shifting use of *Seele* is presently found in Betschart's doctoral dissertation published in 2014 (Betschart 2014) which has been of immense help in formulating my analysis here. Throughout this chapter, so important for the whole book, I have tried to stay close to Stein's finely argued phenomenology (which in many ways is a development of Husserl's formulation of the self presented in Chapter 3 above) whilst keeping her in dialogue with present-day

understandings of the self, especially from a psycho-analytic perspective. In so doing I would argue that we can talk of a 'Steinian' approach to the self and therapy which is as sophisticated and revolutionary as, for example, the Freudian or Jungian view of the self.

12 "*Damit wäre ich bei meiner Wenigkeit angelangt und will Ihnen zwecks Wiederherstellung der abgerissenen Fäden noch einen detaillierten Bericht über mein Befinden geben: körperlich wie immer ausgezeichnet; geistig bei genügendem Energieaufwand ganz leidlich; seelisch äußerst schwankend, aber nie ganz schlecht; psychisch (was Sie sich aus meiner Terminologie in die gewöhnliche Redeweise mit »Nerven« übersetzen können) dauernd miserabel*" (ESGA 4: 86).

13 "*Diese Zentralstellung bedeutet aber nicht, daß von der Seele her die Ichtotalität, die sich in Seele, Leib und Geist entfaltet, gestaltet und durchbestimmt wird. Vielmehr wächst die Seele aus einer Wurzel hervor, die das gesamte Sein des individuellen Seelenwesens in allen seinen Dimensionen bestimmt. Wenn wir diese Wurzel oder diesen 'Kern' als das Formende ansehen, aus dem heraus sich das Sein des Individuums gestaltet, so müssen wir uns doch darüber klar sein, daß nicht alles leibliche und nicht alles psychische Sein und Geschehen 'kernhaft', vom Kern her gestaltet ist. Es gibt psychische wie physische Vorgänge, die für die einheitliche Gestalt, für die 'Persönlichkeit' gleichgültig sind und nicht ihren Stempel tragen. Das gilt nicht für die Seele. Alles Seelische wurzelt im Kern.*"

14 Betschart suggests that as her argument develops she will gradually move in her terminology from *Wesen* to *Sein*, see Betschart 2014: 100/101. We can translate *Wesen* as 'nature', *Sein* as 'being'.

15 "*Mit dem Geist nehmen wir die Welt schlicht entgegen, die Seele aber nimmt die Welt in sich selbst auf, in ihr 'schlägt sie zusammen', und in jeder individuellen Seele auf besondere Weise.*"

16 "*Was die Seele ist, die individuelle Seele – so sagten wir – das lässt sich nicht in angebbaren Eigenschaften ausdrücken.*"

17 "*Ihr Sein ist wie der Kern, in dem es wurzelt, ein schlechthin Individuelles, Unauflösliches und Unnennbares.*"

18 "*Unter der Decke der psychischen Entwicklung reift die Seele heran und drückt dieser Entwicklung ihren Sempel auf, ohne selbst durch sie bestimmt zu warden.*"

19 "*Der ganze Reichtum der Seele ergiesst sich in die Lebensaktualität und tritt an ihr zutagen, das Leben wird jetzt 'seelenvoll'.*"

20 "*1. Ist der Kern der Person etwas Aktuelles oder Potentielles? 2. Ist er etwas Einfaches oder etwas Teilbares? 3. Ist er etwas Wandelbares oder Unwandelbares? 4. Ist das aktuelle Leben der Person ganz oder nur teilweise im Kern verankert, oder kann es gar ganz ohne Beteiligung des Kerns – 'unpersönlich' – verlaufen?*"

21 "*Thomas unterscheidet scharf zwischen dem gesamten potentiellen, habituellen und aktuellen Bestand der Seele und ihrem 'Wesen', das wir als ihr inneres Formprinzip in Anspruch zu nehmen haben: Potenz und Wesen der Seele können unmöglich identisch*

sein, weil das Wesen einfach ist, die Potenzen aber mannigfach, entsprechend den Akten. Sie sind nicht das Wesen selbst, sondern die natürlichen Eigenschaften, die im Wesen begründet sind."

22 "*Die Entfaltung der Seele, die Zunahme ihres inneren Reichtums, wirkt sich in der nachfolgenden Lebensaktualität und habituellen Prägung (also in der Entwicklung) aus. Die volle Entfaltung ist als Telos in der Entelechie, dem ursprünglichen Kern der Person, vorgezeichnet.*"

23 Communication with the author.

24 "*Gott schuf den Menschen nach Seinem Bilde.*"

25 "*Sondern geht in ihrer Geistestätigkeit in persönlicher Freiheit aus sich heraus*" (ESGA 11/12: 387).

26 "*Die Seele ist 'Geist' (= spiritus) ihrem innersten Wesen nach, das der Ausbildung aller ihrer 'Kräfte' zugrunde liegt*" (ESGA 11/12: 388).

27 "*Ist ein persönlich-geistiges Gebilde, darum ist ihr Innerstes und Eigentlichstes, ihr Wesen, aus dem ihre Kräfte und das Wechselspiel ihres Lebens entspringen, nicht nu rein unbekanntes X, das wir zur Erklärung der erfahrbaren seelischen Tatsachen annehmen, sondern etwas, was uns aufleuchten und spürbar werden kann, wenn es auch immer geheimnisvoll bleibt*" (ESGA 11/12: 524).

28 "*Zunächst sei darauf hingewiesen, daß auch das menschliche Geistesleben als ein dreifaltiges und dreieiniges zu betrachten ist. Die bahnbrechenden Versuche in dieser Richtung verdanken wir dem hl. Augustinus. Wir finden bei ihm einen mehrfachen Ansatz: die Liebe als solche, ferner Geist, Liebe und Erkenntnis bezeichnet er als drei und eins, sodann Gedächtnis, Verstand und Willen*" (ESGA 11/12: 377).

29 "*Es verbinden und durchdringen sich hier die naturhafte Bindung an den Leib, die die Seele zur Seele macht, und die – noch über alle persönliche Freiheit der geschaffenen Geister erhabene – Herrschermacht der göttlichen Person.*"

30 "*Die Menschenseele nicht nur ein Mittleres zwischen Geist und Stoff, sondern ein geistiges Geschöpf, nicht nur Gebilde des Geistes, sonder bildender Geist.*"

31 The text is to be found as an appendix to ESGA 11/12. Sadly it is presently missing in CWES 9 although I understand a new translation is being prepared at the time of writing.

32 "*Die Kennzeichnung der Seele als der Mitte des ganzen leiblich-seelisch-geistigen Gebildes, das wir 'Mensch' nennen.*"

33 "*Gotteserkenntnis und Selbsterkenntnis stützen sich gegenseitig. Durch die Selbsterkenntnis nähern wir uns Gott.*"

34 "*Trieb der Seele nach Selbstauszeugung, der im Wesen der Seele begründet ist.*"

35 "*Sie ist aber wesentlich Geschöpf und nicht der Schöpfer ihrer selbst. Sie erzeugt nicht sich selbst, sondern sie kann sich selbst nur auszeugen. Im tiefsten Punkt ihrer selbst ist*

sie nach rückwärts verbunden mit dem dauernd schöpferischen Grund ihrer selbst. Sie kann sich selbst daher nur voll auszeugen, indem sie dauernd in Kontakt bleibt mit dem dauernd schöpferischen Grund."

36 *"Das Ich, das sich selbst wahrnimmt, beobachtet und bearbeitet gleich einem äußeren Ding, sitzt offenbar nicht im Inneren. Es scheint fast, als hätte es die Burg verlassen, um sie von außen zu betrachten. Das ist nun freilich nicht möglich; denn das Betrachten seiner selbst ist 'Ichleben', und das Ich hat kein Leben, das nicht Leben der Seele wäre; ohne Zusammenhang mit ihr wäre es nichts."*

Part Two

1 See also her letter of 23.7.34 to Petra Brüning: 'He adopted me and gave me the rights of home in his Order, even though I was not even an Oblate since I always had the Mount of Carmel before my eyes' (CWES 5: 182).

2 P. Florencio's book written before the troubles in the Holy Land in the middle of the twentieth century gives some fascinating details about the mutual respect between the 'dervish and sufi' communities of the Holy Mountain and the Carmelite Order.

3 Bernard Oller in the late fourteenth century wrote that 'good faith and prescription were sufficient for them' (Smet 1988: 1:18). A manuscript that comes closest to the form of the original is that preserved in the collection of Carmelite writings edited by the Catalan provincial, Philip Ribot (d.1391). Although many scholars dismiss the reliability of Ribot, Waaijman, whose account of the *Rule* I draw heavily on here, is happy that his manuscript gives us a close perspective on the original rule (Waaijman 1999: 18).

4 Just to complicate scholarship, the original text of this Bull is also lost. A copy of the original is however still in the Vatican (see Waaijman 1999: 19).

Chapter 6

1 Morgan 2007: 79.

2 For a good recent account in English of the relationship between Baruzi and John see Murphy 2018.

3 For an extended treatment of this category see Tyler 2011.

4 To be found in John of the Cross 1929: Vol. 1.

5 John of the Cross 1979: 711–12:
1 *En una noche oscura,*

con ansias, en amores inflamada,
¡oh dichosa ventura!,
salí sin ser notada
estando ya mi casa sosegada.

2. A oscuras y segura,
por la secreta escala, disfrazada,
¡oh dichosa ventura!,
a oscuras y en celada,
estando ya mi casa sosegada.

3. En la noche dichosa,
en secreto, que nadie me veía,
ni yo miraba cosa,
sin otra luz y guía
sino la que en el corazón ardía.

4. Aquésta me guiaba
más cierto que la luz del mediodía,
adonde me esperaba
quien yo bien me sabía,
en parte donde nadie parecía.

5. ¡Oh noche que guiaste!
¡Oh noche amable más que la alborada!
¡Oh noche que juntaste
Amado con amada,
amada en el Amado transformada!

6. En mi pecho florido,
que entero para él solo se guardaba,
allí quedó dormido,
y yo le regalaba,
y el ventalle de cedros aire daba.

7. El aire de la almena,
cuando yo sus cabellos esparcía,
con su mano serena
en mi cuello hería y todos mis sentidos suspendía.

8. Quedéme y olvidéme,
el rostro recliné sobre el Amado,
cesó todo y dejéme,
dejando mi cuidado
entre las azucenas olvidado.

6 For an interesting essay on the relationship between 'depression' and 'dark night' see Cook in Howells and Tyler, Forthcoming.

7 See Ward 2012 for a good introduction to this tradition.

8   John himself prefers the term 'capital vices' (see *Dark Night* 1.1.3), I am grateful to Prof. Iain Matthew O.C.D. for drawing my attention to this.

9   "*Y digo que el alma, para conseguir este bien, nunca sobre las cosas claras y distintas que por ella hayan pasado pro vía sobrenatural ha de hacer reflexión para conserver en sí las formas y figures y noticias de aquellas cosas, porque siempre habemos de llevar este presupuesto: que cuanto el alma más presa hace en alguna apprehension natural o sobrenatural distinta y clara, menos capacidad y disposición tiene en sí para entrar en abismo de la fe, donde todo lo demás se absorbe.*"

10 "*Darum müssen wir alle Geschöpfe hinter uns lassen und alle unsere Kräfte, mit denen wir die Geschöpfe fassen und begreifen, um uns im Glauben zu Gott, dem Unfaßlichen und Unbegreiflichen, zu erheben. Dazu sind weder die Sinne fähig noch der Verstand, wenn wir darunter die Fähigkeit zu begrifflichem Denken verstehen. In der gläubigen Hingabe an den unbegreiflichen Gott sind wir reiner Geist, gelöst von allen Bildern und Begriffen.*"

11 "*Es muß ja etwas bleiben, wenn erst nach der Aufhebung der Kräfte die Vereinigung mit Gott und die Umformung in Gott möglich sein soll. Und dieses Etwas jenseits von Sinnlichkeit und sinnlich-gebundenem Verstand muß erst der Geist im eigentlichen Sinne sein. Johannes spricht in diesem Zusammenhang auch vom Wesen der Seele. Die Seele ist ihrem Wesen nach Geist und ist ihrem innersten Wesen nach empfänglich für alles Geistige: für Gott, den reinen Geist, und alles, was er geschaffen hat und was seinem innersten Wesen nach auch geistig ist.*" The CWES English version here introduces the definition of pure *Geist* as 'beyond being' but this phrase is neither in ESGA nor ESW.

12 "*Un abismo secreto ... un immenso desierto que por ninguna parte ... fue, tanto más deleitoso, sabroso y amoroso, cuanto más profundo, ancho y solo.*"

13 Here Stein helpfully reminds us that we are using spatial images to refer to that which is beyond space, c.f. *The Living Flame of Love* 1.5.3: 'the soul has no parts and there is no distinction here between inner and outer' (ESW 1: 136).

14 "*D.h. den für den das eigene Ich im Mittelpunkt steht; es mag dem oberflächlichen Blick scheinen, als sei ein solcher Mensch seinem Innersten besonders nahe, und doch ist vielleicht für keinen andern Typus der Weg dorthin so verbaut wie für diesen.*"

15 "*Etwas davon hat jeder Mensch in sich, solange er nicht die* Dunkle Nacht *bis ans* Ende *durchlitten hat.*"

16 "*Dazu muss er aber sehr tief in sich selbst Stellung nehmen: so tief, dass der Übergang einer förmlichen Umwandlung des Menschen gleichkommt und vielleicht natürlicherweise gar nicht müglich ist, sondern nur auf Grund einer ausserordentlichen Erweckung.*"

17 Stein states at this point in the *Science of the Cross*: "*Der Mensch ist dazu berufen, in seinem Innerten zu leben und sich selbst so in die Hand zu nehmen*" (ESW 1: 143) which

is translated in CWES 6: 160 as 'Human beings are called upon to live in their inmost region and to have themselves as much in hand as is possible only from that center-point'. Unfortunately Stein does not use the terms *Zentrum* or *Zentrumpunkt* here which is found in the English translation, for as we have seen, she consistently seeks to retain a central unknowing instability in the 'space of the soul'.

18 "*Der Wesensbau der Seele – ihre grössere und geringere Tiefe, auch das Innerste – besteht von Natur aus, und in ihm ist, gleichfalls natürlicherweise, die Bewegung des Ich in diesem Raum als Wesensmöglichkeit begründet.*"

Chapter 7

1 "*Eine 'scientia crucis' (Kreuzeswissenschaft) kann man nur gewinnen, wenn man das Kreuz gründlich zu spüren bekommt*", Letter to Mother Ambrosia Antonia Engelmann, the Prioress of Echt Convent, December 1941, nine months before Edith Stein's deportation to and death at Auschwitz Concentration Camp (ESGA 3: 500).

2 Whilst Farber and his colleagues discussed the academic merit of Stein's essay she had been arrested and transported to the concentration camps. After much discussion following her death the article eventually appeared in the July 1946 edition of *The Thomist* in an English translation by Rudolf Allers (CWES 8: xii–xvii).

3 "*Aber der Gekreuzigte verlangt auch vom Künstler mehr als ein solches Bild. Er fordert von ihm wie von jedem Menschen die Nachfolge: dass er sich selbst zum Bild des Kreuztragenden und Gekreuzigten gestalte und gestalten lasse*" (ESW 1: 6).

4 Quotations from *The Wreck of the Deutschland* are taken from the First Edition *Poems of Gerard Manley Hopkins*, edited by his friend and confidant, Robert Bridges (Hopkins 1918).

5 As I write this, twenty-eight refugees fleeing persecution drown off the Kent coast during a winter storm. The parallels are chilling.

6 "*Es ist zugleich Bild, in dem etwas zur Darstellung kommt, und Gebilde als ein Gebildetes und in sich Geschlossenes, zu einer eigenen kleinen Welt gerundetes.*" In this passage Stein once again plays on the ambiguity of the terms *Bild* and *Gebilde* as she does in the passage quoted earlier from *Endliches und Ewiges Sein*. Unfortunately this doesn't translate well into English but the sense she is trying to convey is the formed and forming aspect of the human soul as it reflects the 'impression' received upon it by the Creator Spirit itself. As before this reflects her Augustinian belief in the human soul being made in the 'image and likeness' of a Triune God that continues to act in and through the human person.

7 "*Aber der Gekreuzigte verlangt auch vom Künstler mehr als ein solches Bild. Er fordert von ihm wie von jedem Menschen die Nachfolge: dass er sich selbst zum Bild des*

Kreuztragenden und Gekreuzigten gestalte und gestalten lasse."

8   From the *Kölner Selig- und Heiligsprechungsprozess der Dienerin Gottes Sr. Teresia Benedicta a Cruce – Edith Stein* quoted in Herbstrith 1992:180.

Chapter 8

1   This quote is taken from his personal diaries in the Bergen Electronic Edition of Wittgenstein's *Nachlass* with my own translation: "*Die Leute, mit denen ich beisammen bin, sind nicht so sehr gemein, als ungeheuer beschränkt. Das macht den Verkehr mit ihnen fast unmöglich, weil sie einen ewig missverstehen. Die Leute sind nicht dumm, aber beschränkt. Sie sind in ihrem Kreise klug genug. Aber es fehlt ihnen der Charakter und damit die Ausdehnung. 'Alles versteht das rechtgläubige Herz'.*"

2   Ometita's thesis is an excellent summary of the problems that have beset the 'phenomenological' approaches to Wittgenstein this past half century. However, by returning to Wittgenstein's original notebooks I think he presents a convincing case for the limits that Wittgenstein set for a separate 'phenomenological language' to 'ordinary language'. As Wittgenstein put it in a notebook entry of November 1922, at the time he was conducting his interviews with Schlick: 'the assumption that a phenomenological language was possible and that it would adequately first say what we in philosophy want to say is – I believe – absurd. We must manage with our ordinary language and only understand it correctly, that is, we may not let ourselves be tempted by it to speak nonsense' (Ms 107: 176, 22.11.1929, translated Ometita 2015: 96).

3   'Lecture' is probably too grand a title for the discussions that Wittgenstein initiated in his classes. He had a well-known abhorrence towards the lecture hall and the grandstanding 'theatrical' of the set lecture. Here I am relying on the accounts of the lectures from three of his students at the time: Peter Geach (husband of his other pupil Elizabeth Anscombe and later Professor of Logic at Leeds University), K.J. Shah and Andrew Jackson. Their accounts are supplemented by concomitant material from the notes on the philosophy of psychology and the *Investigations* which Wittgenstein was working on at that time.

4   The German reads here: "*Versuche nicht, in dir selbst das Erlebnis zu analysieren!*" with the official translation given as: 'Do not try to analyse your own inner experience'.

5   See also Wittgenstein 1982: 'the "inner" is a delusion. That is: the whole complex of ideas alluded to by this word is like a painted curtain drawn in front of the scene of the actual word use' (2:84e).

6   Again, we return to the disputed area of Cartesian epistemology that we discussed with respect to Husserl's interpretation in Chapter 2 above.

7   "*Die Menschenseele als solche ist kein fertiges, ruhendes Seiendes. Ihr Sein ist Werden, in dem ihre Kräfte, die sie als keimhafte Anlagen mit zur Welt bringt, zur Entfaltung*

kommen sollen; sie kommen aber nur zur Entfaltung durch Betätigung", c.f. CWES 2: 98: 'it is not inanimate material which must be entirely developed or formed in an exterior way, as is clay by the artist's hand or stone by the weather's elemental forces; it is rather a living formative root which possesses within itself the driving power (inner form) toward development in a particular direction; the seed must grow and ripen into the perfect gestalt, *perfect creation*'.

8 "*Die Seele eingesenkt in einen Leib, von dessen Kraft und Gesundheit ihre eigene Kraft und Gesundheit – wenn auch nicht allein und schlechthin – abhängt, der andererseits durch sie sein Sein als Leib – Leben, Bewegung, Form und Gestalt und geistigen Sinn – bekommt; auf dem Grunde der Sinnlichkeit, die ebenso sehr leibliches wie seelisches Sein ist, ein geistiges Sein, das als Verstandestätigkeit sich erkennend eine Welt erschließt, als Wille schaffend und gestaltend in diese Welt eingreift, als Gemüt diese Welt innerlich entgegennimmt und sich damit auseinandersetzt.*"

9 The English version translates the consistent term *seelischer* with two different phrases: 'spirit' and 'psyche'. As maintained throughout the present book I have tried here to preserve her terminological consistency.

10 "*Es ist nicht nur der Körper verschieden gebaut, es sind nicht nur einzelne physiologische Funktionen verschieden, sondern das ganze Leibesleben ist ein anderes, das Verhältnis von Seele und Leib ist ein anderes und innerhalb des Seelischen das Verhältnis von Geist und Sinnlichkeit, ebenso das Verhältnis der geistigen Kräfte zueinander. Der weiblichen Species entspricht Einheit und Geschlossenheit der gesamten leiblich-seelischen Persönlichkeit, harmonische Entfaltung der Kräfte; der männlichen Species Steigerung einzelner Kräfte zu Höchstleistungen.*"

11 Here again there are resonances with Husserl's final writings on the 'Crisis of Civilisation' that we explored earlier in the book.

12 'Here is Rhodes, Jump here!' A quote from the Aesop Fables where a boastful athlete is challenged to enact the feat he claims.

Bibliography

Edith Stein primary sources

The collected works of Edith Stein (CWES)

12 Volumes, ed L. Gelber and M. Linssen, 1987 – present, Washington, DC: Institute of Carmelite Studies

Volume 1: *Life in a Jewish Family, 1891–1916, an Autobiography,* trans. J. Koeppel, 1987.
Volume 2: *Essays on Woman*, trans. F. Oben, 1987/1996/2017.
Volume 3: *On the Problem of Empathy*, trans. W. Stein, 1989.
Volume 4: *The Hidden Life: Essays, Meditations, Spiritual Texts*, trans. W. Stein, 1992.
Volume 5: *Self Portrait in Letters, 1916–1942*, trans. J. Koeppel, 1993.
Volume 6: *The Science of the Cross*, trans. J. Koeppel, 2002.
Volume 7: *Philosophy of Psychology and the Humanities*, trans. M. Baseheart and M. Sawicki, 2000.
Volume 8: *Knowledge and Faith*, trans. W. Redmond, 2000.
Volume 9: *Finite and Eternal Being*, trans. K. Reinhardt, 2002.
Volume 10: *An Investigation Concerning the State*, trans. M. Sawicki, 2006.
Volume 11: *Potency and Act. Studies toward a Philosophy of Being*, trans. W. Redmond, 2009.
Volume 12: *Letters to Roman Ingarden*, trans. H. Candler Hunt, 2014.

Edith Stein Gesamtausgabe (ESGA)

28 Volumes, ed H-B. Gerl-Falkovitz, 2000–2020, Freiburg: Herder:

Volume 1: *Aus dem Leben einer Jüdischen Familie und Weitere Autobiographische Beiträge*, ed M. Amata Neyer, 2010.
Volume 2: *Selbstbildnis in Briefen. Teil 1: 1916–1944*, ed M. Amata Neyer, 2000/ 2010.
Volume 3: *Selbstbildnis in Briefen, Teil 2: 1933–1942*, ed M. Amata Neyer, 2000/2006/2015.
Volume 4: *Selbstbildnis in Briefen, Teil 3: Briefe an Roman Ingarden*, ed M. Amata Neyer, 2001/2005/2015.
Volume 5: *Zum Problem der Einfühlung*, ed M. Sondermann, 2008/2010.
Volume 6: *Beiträge zur Philosophischen Begründung der Psychologie und der Geisteswissenschaften*, ed B. Beckmann-Zöller, 2010.

Volume 7: *Eine Untersuchung über den Staat,* ed I. Riedel-Spangenberger, 2006.
Volume 8: *Einführung in die Philosophie,* ed C. Mariéle Wulf, 2004/2010.
Volume 9: *'Freiheit und Gnade' und weitere Beiträge zu Phänomenologie und Ontologie (1917 bis 1937),* ed B. Beckmann-Zöller and H. Rainer Sepp, 2014.
Volume 10: *Potenz und Akt. Studien zu einer Philosophie des Seins.* ed H. Rainer Sepp. 2005.
Volume 11/12: *Endliches und Ewiges Sein: Versuch eines Aufstiegs zum Sinn des Seins. Anhang: Martin Heideggers Existenzphilosophie. Die Seelenburg,* ed A. Uwe Müller, 2006/2013/2016.
Volume 13: *Die Frau. Fragestellungen und Reflexionen,* ed M. Amata Neyer, 2000/2010.
Volume 14: *Der Aufbau der Menschlichen Person: Vorlesung zur philosophischen Anthropologie,* ed B. Beckmann-Zöller, 2004/2010/2015.
Volume 15: *Was ist der Mensch? Theologische Anthropologie,* ed B. Beckmann-Zöller, 2005.
Volume 16: *Bildung und Entfaltung der Individualität. Beiträge zum christlichen Erziehungsauftrag,* ed M. Amata Neyer and B. Beckmann-Zöller, 2001/2014.
Volume 17: *Wege der Gotteserkenntnis: Studie zu Dionysius Areopagita und Übersetzung seiner Werke,* ed B. Beckmann-Zöller and V. Ranff, 2003/2007/2013.
Volume 18: *Kreuzeswissenschaft: Studie über Johannes vom Kreuz,* ed U. Dobhan, 2003/2004/2007/2013.
Volume 19: *Geistliche Texte I,* ed U. Dobhan, 2009/2014.
Volume 20: *Geistliche Texte II,* ed S. Binggeli, 2007/2015.
Volume 21: *Übersetzung von John Henry Newman, Die Idee der Universität,* ed H-B. Gerl-Falkovitz, 2004/2010.
Volume 22: *Übersetzung von John Henry Newman, Briefe und Texte zur ersten Lebenshälfte (1801–1846),* ed H-B. Gerl-Falkovitz, 2002/2009.
Volume 23: *Übersetzung: Des Hl. Thomas von Aquino Untersuchung über die Wahrheit, 'Quaestiones disputatae de veritate', Teil 1,* ed A. Speer and F. Valerio Tommasi, 2008.
Volume 24: *Übersetzung: Des Hl. Thomas von Aquino Untersuchung über die Wahrheit, 'Quaestiones disputatae de veritate' Teil 2,* ed A. Speer and F. Valerio Tommasi, 2008.
Volume 25: *Übersetzung von Alexandre Koyré, Descartes und die Scholastik (Edith Stein mit Hedwig Conrad-Martius),* ed H-B. Gerl-Falkovitz, 2005.
Volume 26: *Übersetzung: Thomas von Aquin, Über das Seiende und das Wesen, 'De ente et essentia' mit den Roland-Gosselin-Exzerpten,* ed A. Speer and F. Valerio Tommasi, 2010.
Volume 27: *Miscellanea thomistica. Übersetzungen – Abbreviationen – Exzerpte aus Werken des Thomas von Aquin und der Forschungsliteratur.* ed A. Speer and F. Valerio Tommasi, 2013.
Volume 28: *Neuaufgefundene Texte und Übersetzungen VII: Texte zu Philosophie, Politik, Pädagogik; Übersetzungen: Bonaventura, Karmel-Geschichte, 'Judenfrage'. Neu aufgefundene Briefe und Dokumente.* ed B. Beckmann-Zöller, U. Dobhan and H-B. Gerl-Falkovitz, 2020.

Edith Steins Werke (ESW)

18 Volumes, ed L. Gelber, R. Leuven and M. Lissen, 1950 – present, Louvain/Freiburg: Nauwelaerts/Herder/Druten:

Volume 1: *Kreuzeswissenschaft: Studie über Joannes a Cruce*, ed L. Gelber, 1950.
Volume 2: *Endliches und Ewiges Sein: Versuch eines Aufsteigs zum Sinn des Seins*, ed L. Gelber and R. Leuven, 1950/1986.
Volume 3: *Des hl. Thomas Aquino Untersuchungen über die Wahrheit I. Quaestio 1–13*, ed L. Gelber and R. Leuven, 1952.
Volume 4: *Des hl. Thomas von Aquino Untersuchungen über die Wahrheit II. Quaestio 14–29*, ed L. Gelber and R. Leuven, 1955.
Volume 5: *Die Frau. Ihre Aufgabe nach Natur und Gnade*, ed L. Gelber and R. Leuven, 1959.
Volume 6: *Welt und Person: Beitrag zum christlichen Wahrheitsstrebe*, ed L. Gelber and M. Linssen, 1962.
Volume 7: *Aus dem Leben einer jüdischen Familie. Das Leben Edith Steins: Kindheit und Jugend*, ed L. Gelber, 1965.
Volume 8: *Selbstbildnis in Briefen. Teil 1: 1916–1934*, ed L. Gelber and R. Leuven, 1976.
Volume 9: *Selbstbildnis in Briefen. Teil 2: 1934–1942*, ed L. Gelber and R. Leuven, 1977.
Volume 10: *Heil im Unheil. Das Leben Edith Steins. Reife und Vollendung*, ed R. Leuven, 1983.
Volume 11: *Verborgenes Leben. Hagiographische Essays, Meditationen, Geistliche Texte*, ed L. Gelber and M. Linssen, 1987.
Volume 12: *Ganzheitliches Leben,* ed L. Gelber and M. Linssen, 1990.
Volume 13: *Einführung in die Philosophie.* ed L. Gelber and M. Linssen, 1991.
Volume 14: *Briefe an Roman Ingarden,* ed L. Gelber and M. Linssen, 1991.
Volume 15: *Erkenntnis und Glaube,* ed L. Gelber and M. Linssen, 1993.
Volume 16: *Der Aufbau der menschlichen Person,* ed L. Gelber and M. Linssen, 1994.
Volume 17: *Was ist der Mensch? Eine theologische Anthropologie,* ed L. Gelber and M. Linssen, 1994.
Volume 18: *Potenz und Akt. Studien zu einer Philosophie des Seins*, ed H. Rainer Sepp, 1998.

Other Steinian sources

Sacra Congregatio pro causis sanctorum, Canonisationis servae Dei Teresiae Benedictae a Cruce, Rome, 1983.

General bibliography

Abraham, J. (1959) *Hopkins and Scotus: An Analogy between Inscape and Individuation.* PhD Thesis. University of Wisconsin.
Badiou, A. and B. Bosteels (2011) *Wittgenstein's Anti-Philosophy.* London: Verso.
Ales Bello, A. (2008) 'Edmund Husserl and Edith Stein: The Question of the Human Subject' in *American Catholic Philosophical Quarterly*, Vol. 82, No. 1, pp. 143–160.
Baseheart, M. (1997) *Person in the World: Introduction to the Philosophy of Edith Stein.* London: Kluwer Academic.

Batzdorff, S. (1998) *Aunt Edith: The Jewish Heritage of a Catholic Saint*. Springfield, IL: Templegate.
Beckmann-Zöller, B. (2008) 'Edith Stein's Theory of the Person in Her Münster Years (1932–1933)' in *American Catholic Philosophical Quarterly*, Vol. 82: 1, pp. 47–70.
Berkman, J., ed. (2006) *Contemplating Edith Stein*. Notre Dame, IN: University of Notre Dame Press.
Betschart, C. (2014) *Unwiederholbares Gottessiegel: Personale Individualität nach Edith Stein*. Basel: Friedrich Reinhardt Verlag.
Betschart, C. (2016) 'The Individuality of the Human Person in the Phenomenological Works of Edith Stein' in *Edith Stein: Women, Social-Political Philosophy, Theology, Metaphysics and Public History: New Approaches and Applications*, ed A. Calcagno, pp. 73–86. New York: Springer.
Bettelheim, B. (1982) *Freud and Man's Soul*. London: Pimlico.
Bishop, P. (1995) *The Dionysian Self: C. G. Jung's Reception of Friedrich Nietzsche*. Berlin: Walter de Gruyter.
Calcagno, A. (2006) 'Assistant and/or Collaborator? Edith Stein's Relationship to Edmund Husserl's *Ideen II*' in *Contemplating Edith Stein*, ed J. Berkman, pp. 243–270. Notre Dame, IN: University of Notre Dame Press.
Calcagno, A. (2007) *The Philosophy of Edith Stein*. Pittsburgh: Duquesne University Press.
Carman, T. and M. Hansen (2005) *The Cambridge Companion to Merleau-Ponty*. Cambridge: Cambridge University Press.
Chenu, M.-D. (1957/2013) *Nature, Man and Society in the Twelfth Century*. Trans. J. Taylor and L. Little. Toronto: University of Toronto Press.
Conrad-Martius, H. (1921) *Metaphysische Gespräche*. Halle: Max Niemeyer.
Cook, C. and N. White (2021) *Biblical and Theological Visions of Resilience: Pastoral and Clinical Insights*. London: Routledge.
Davies, N. and R. Moorhouse (2003) *Microcosm: Portrait of a Central European City*. London: Pimlico.
Deleuze, G. (1986) *Nietzsche and Philosophy*. Trans. H. Tomlinson. London: Continuum.
Dionysius the Areopagite (1987) *Pseudo-Dionysius: The Complete Works*. Trans. C. Luibheid and P. Rorem. New York: Paulist.
Feldes, J. (1998) *Edith Stein und Schifferstadt*. Schifferstadt: Geier.
Florencio del Niño Jesús (1924) *El Monte Carmelo: Tradiciones e Historia de La Santa Montaña, de la Virgen del Carmen y De La Orden Carmelitana y la Luz do Los Monumentos y Documentos*. Madrid: Mensajero de Santa Teresa.
Freud, S. (1963) *Sigmund Freud, Oskar Pfister: Briefe 1909–1939*. Frankfurt am Main: Fischer Verlag.
Fuentes, P. (2016) 'The Inseparability of Consciousness from Embodiment in the Phenomenology of Edith Stein' in *Edith Stein: Women, Social-Political Philosophy, Theology, Metaphysics and Public History: New Approaches and Applications*, ed A. Calcagno, pp. 87–92. New York: Springer.
Giordano, S. (1995) *Carmel in the Holy Land: From Its Beginnings to the Present Day*. Arenzano: Il Messaggero di Gesu Bambino.
Goethe, J. W. (1949) *Faust: Part One*. Trans. P. Wayne. London: Penguin.
Goethe, J. W. (1959) *Faust: Part Two*. Trans. P. Wayne. London: Penguin.

Goethe, J. W. (1971) *Faust, Der Tragödie: Erster Teil*. Ed L. Scheithauer. Stuttgart: Philipp Reclam.
Goethe, J. W. (1986) *Faust, Der Tragödie: Zweite Teil*. Ed L. Scheithauer. Stuttgart: Philipp Reclam.
Hamann, B. (2005) *Winifred Wagner: A Life at the Heart of Hitler's Bayreuth*. London: Granta.
Herbstrith, W. (1992) *Edith Stein: The Untold Story of the Philosopher and Mystic Who Lost Her Life in the Death Camps of Auschwitz*. Trans. B. Bonowitz. San Francisco: Ignatius.
Herbstrith, W. (1998) *Never Forget: Christian and Jewish Perspectives on Edith Stein*. Trans. S. Batzdorff. Washington, DC: ICS.
Hillman, J. (1975) *Re-Visioning Psychology*. New York: Harper.
Hillman, J. (1983) *Inter Views: Conversations with Laura Pozzo on Psychotherapy, Biography, Love, Soul, the Gods, Animals, Dreams, Imagination, Work, Cities and the State of Culture*. Dallas, TX: Spring Publications.
Hintikka, M. J. (1986) *Investigating Wittgenstein*. Oxford: Blackwell.
Hoffmann, J. and A. Stock (2010) *The Würzburg School*. Würzburg: Universität Würzburg.
Hopkins, G. M. (1918) *Poems of Gerard Manley Hopkins*. Ed R.Bridges. Oxford: Oxford University Press.
Hopkins, G. M. (1985) *Gerard Manley Hopkins: Poems and Prose*. Ed W. H. Gardner. London: Penguin.
House, H., ed. (1959) *The Journals and Papers of Gerard Manley Hopkins*. Oxford: Oxford University Press.
Howells, E. and P. M. Tyler (forthcoming) *St John of the Cross: Desire, Transformation and Carmel*. London: Routledge.
Husserl, E. (1954) *Die Krisis der Europäischen Wissenschaften und die Transzendentale Phänomenologie*. Volume VI, *Husserliana: Edmund Husserl, Gesammelte Werke*. Ed W. Biemel. The Hague: Martinus Nijhoff.
Husserl, E. (1960) *Cartesian Meditations: An Introduction to Phenomenology*. Trans. D. Cairns. The Hague: Martinus Nijhoff.
Husserl, E. (1970) *The Crisis of European Sciences and Transcendental Phenomenology*. Trans. D. Carr. Evanston: Northwestern University Press.
Inge, R. (1899) *Christian Mysticism*. London: Methuen.
John of the Cross (1929–1931) *Obras de San Juan de La Cruz, Doctor de la Iglesia*. Ed P. Silverio de Santa Teresa. Burgos: Biblioteca Mistica Carmelitana (5 Vols).
John of the Cross (1979) *The Collected Works of St John of the Cross*. Trans. K. Kavanaugh and O. Rodriguez. Washington: Institute of Carmelite Studies.
John of the Cross (2002) *San Juan de La Cruz: Obras Completas*. Ed L. Ruano de la Iglesia. Madrid: Biblioteca de Autores Cristianos.
Jung, C. G. (1912/1925) *Wandlungen und Symbole der Libido*. Vienna: Franz Deuticke.
Jung, C. G. (1971/1999) *The Collected Works of C.G. Jung*. Trans. R. Hull and H. Baynes. London: Routledge.
Jung, C. G. and S. Freud (1974) *Briefwechsel*. Ed W. McGuire and W. Sauerländer. Frankfurt am Main: Fischer.
Jung, C. G. and S. Freud (1988) *The Freud/Jung Letters: The Correspondence between Sigmund Freud and C. G. Jung*. Trans. R. Manheim and R. Hull. Cambridge, MA: Harvard University Press.

Jung, C. G. (2009) *The Red Book: Liber Novus*. Ed S. Shamdasani. London: Norton & Co.
Klueting and Klueting eds (2021) *Edith Stein's Itinerary: Phenomenology, Christian Philosophy and Carmelite Spirituality*. Münster: Aschendorff.
Kristeva, J. (2009) *This Incredible Need to Believe*. Trans. B. Bie Brahic. New York: Columbia University Press.
Lebech, M. (2015) *The Philosophy of Edith Stein: From Phenomenology to Metaphysics*. Oxford: Peter Lang.
Lopez Mcalister, L. (2006) 'Edith Stein: Essential Differences' in *Contemplating Edith Stein*, ed J. Berkman, pp. 201–12. Notre Dame, IN: University of Notre Dame Press.
Malcolm, N. (2001) *Ludwig Wittgenstein: A Memoir*. Oxford: Clarendon.
Mann, T. (1955) *Death in Venice, Tristan, Tonio Kröger*. Trans. H. Lowe-Porter. London: Penguin.
Mann, T. (1973) 'Nietzsche's Philosophy in the Light of Contemporary Events' in *Nietzsche: A Collection of Critical Essays*, ed R. Solomon, pp. 358–370. New York: Anchor.
MacIntyre, A. (2006) *Edith Stein: A Philosophical Prologue*. London: Continuum.
Martin, R. B. (1991) *Gerard Manley Hopkins: A Very Private Life*. London: HarperCollins.
McGreal, W. (1999) *At the Fountain of Elijah: The Carmelite Tradition*. London: Darton, Longman and Todd.
McGuinness, B. (1988) *Wittgenstein: A Life. The Young Ludwig (1889–1921)*. London: Penguin.
Monk, R. (1990) *Ludwig Wittgenstein – The Duty of Genius*. London: Jonathan Cape.
Morgan, E. (2007) *A Book of Lives*. Manchester: Carcanet.
Mosley, J. (2006) *Edith Stein: Modern Saint and Martyr*. New York: Paulist Press.
Murphy, M. (2018) *The Direction of Desire: John of the Cross, Jacques Lacan and the Contemporary Understanding of Spiritual Direction*. PhD thesis, University of Surrey.
Neyer, M. (1999) *Edith Stein: Her Life in Photos and Documents*. Washington, DC: ICS.
Nietzsche, F. (1908) *Ecce Homo*. Leipzig: Insel Verlag.
Nietzsche, F. (1967) *On the Genealogy of Morals and Ecce Homo*. Trans. W. Kaufmann and R. Hollingdale. New York: Random House.
Nietzsche, F. (1990) *Friedrich Nietzsche Werke in Zwei Bänden*. Munich: Carl Hanser Verlag.
Nietzsche, F. (1993) *The Birth of Tragedy out of the Spirit of Music*. Trans. S. Whiteside. London: Penguin.
Nietzsche, F. (2001) *The Gay Science*. Trans. J. Nauckhoff. Cambridge: Cambridge University Press.
O'Meara, T. (2002) *Erich Przywara, S.J.: His Theology and His World*. Notre Dame, IN: University of Notre Dame Press.
Ometita, M. (2015) *Wittgenstein and the Problem of Phenomenology*. PhD thesis, University of East Anglia.
Pfänder, A. (1933) *Die Seele des Menschen: Versuch einer Verstehenden Psychologie*. Halle: Max Niemeyer Verlag.
Posselt, T. R. (Sr Teresia Renata de Spiritu Sancto) (1957) *Edith Stein: Schwester Teresia Benedicta a Cruce, Philosophin und Karmelitin, ein Lebensbild, Gewonnen aus Erinnerungen und Briefen*. Freiburg: Herder.

Posselt, T. R. (Sr Teresia Renata de Spiritu Sancto) (2005) *Edith Stein: The Life of a Philosopher and Carmelite*. Ed S. Batzdorff, J. Koeppel, J. Sullivan and M. A. Neyer. Washington, DC: ICS.
Przywara, E. (1955) *In und Gegen: Stellungnahmen zur Zeit*. Nuremberg: Glock and Lutz.
Rhees, R., ed. (1987) *Recollections of Wittgenstein*. Oxford: Oxford Paperback.
Sawicki, M. (1997) *Body, Text, and Science: The Literacy of Investigative Practices and the Phenomenology of Edith Stein*. London: Kluwer Academic.
Schutz, A. (1940) 'Phenomenology and Social Sciences' in *Philosophical Essays in Memory of Edmund Husserl*, ed M. Farber. Cambridge, MA: Harvard University Press.
Smet, J. (1988) *The Carmelites: A History of the Brothers of Our Lady of Mount Carmel* (3 Vols). Illinois: Carmelite Spiritual Center.
Smet, J. (1997) 'The Carmelite Rule after 750 Years' in *Carmelus*, Vol. 44, p. 1.
Szasz, T. (1976) *Karl Kraus and the Soul-Doctors*. Baton Rouge: Louisiana State University Press.
Sullivan, J. (1998) 'Liturgical Creativity from Edith Stein' in *Teresianum*, Vol. 49, p. 165.
Taylor, C. (2005) 'Merleau-Ponty and the Epistemological Picture' in *The Cambridge Companion to Merleau-Ponty*, ed T. Carman and M. Hansen. Cambridge: Cambridge University Press.
Tomlinson, H. (1988) 'Nietzsche on the Edge of Town: Deleuze and Reflexivity' in *Exceedingly Nietzsche*, ed D. Farrell Krell and D. Wood, pp. 150–63. London: Routledge.
Tyler, P. M. (2011) *The Return to the Mystical: Ludwig Wittgenstein, Teresa of Avila and the Christian Mystical Tradition*. London: Continuum.
Tyler, P. M. (2013) *Teresa of Avila: Doctor of the Soul*. London: Bloomsbury.
Tyler, P. M. (2015) 'Carl Jung: Friend or Foe of Christianity?' in *Vinayasādhana*, Vol. VI: 1. January 2015.
Tyler, P. M. (2016) *The Pursuit of the Soul: Psychoanalysis, Soul-making and the Christian Tradition*. Edinburgh: T & T Clark.
Tyler, P. M. (2017) *Confession: The Healing of the Soul*. London: Bloomsbury.
Tyler, P. M. (2018) 'Psychology, *Theosis* and the Soul: St. Teresa of Avila, St. Augustine, and Plotinus on the Western Picture of *theosis*' in *Mystical Doctrines of Deification: Case Studies in the Christian Tradition*, ed J. Arblaster and R. Faesen, pp. 152–64. London: Routledge.
Waaijman, K. (1999) *The Mystical Space of Carmel: A Commentary on the Carmelite Rule*. Leuven: Peeters.
Waismann, F. (1979) *Wittgenstein and the Vienna Circle*. Ed B. McGuinness. Trans. J. McGuinness. Oxford: Basil Blackwell.
Ward, B. (2012) 'The Spirituality of the Desert Fathers and Mothers' in *The Bloomsbury Guide to Christian Spirituality*, ed R. Woods and P. M. Tyler, pp. 42–56. London: Bloomsbury.
White, N. and C. Cook (2020) *Biblical and Theological Visions of Resilience: Pastoral and Clinical Insights*. London: Routledge.
Wittgenstein, L. (1958) *Philosophical Investigations*. Ed G. E. M. Anscombe and R. Rhees. Oxford: Blackwell.
Wittgenstein, L. (1961) *Tractatus Logico-Philosophicus*. Trans. D. F. Pears and B. McGuinness. London: Routledge and Kegan Paul.

Wittgenstein, L. (1967) *Letters from Ludwig Wittgenstein with a Memoir by Paul Engelmann*. Ed B. McGuinness. Oxford: Blackwell.
Wittgenstein, L. (1977) *Remarks on Colour*. Ed G. Anscombe. Trans. L. McAlister and M. Schättle. Oxford: Blackwell.
Wittgenstein, L. (1982) *Last Writings on the Philosophy of Psychology, Vol I*. Ed G. Anscombe and G. von Wright. Oxford: Blackwell.
Wittgenstein, L. (1984) *Notebooks 1914–1916*. Trans. G. E. M. Anscombe. Oxford: Blackwell.
Wittgenstein, L. (1988) *Lectures on Philosophical Psychology 1946–47. From the Notes of P. Geach, K. Shah and A. Jackson*. Ed P. Geach. London: Harvester.
Wittgenstein, L. (1993) *Philosophische Untersuchungen* in *Werkausgabe in 8 Bände*. Vol. 1. Frankfurt am Main: Suhrkamp.
Wittgenstein, L. (2000) *Wittgenstein's Nachlass: The Bergen Electronic Edition*. Oxford: Oxford University Press.
Scripture Quotations from the *New Revised Standard Version*. London: Harper, 2007, with modifications as necessary.

Index

A
Abraham 158, 215
abstractions 83
absurdity 39
abuse 187
abyss 141, 186
adversity 154, 165
aeronautics 169
Aesop Fables 212
aesthetics 18, 70, 171
ain es-Siah 125
Ales Bello, Angela 93, 99–100, 102, 203–4, 215
Allied bombing 126
altar 28, 157
ambiguity x, 62, 118–19, 153, 175, 194, 197, 210
Amsterdam 132
Anfang war die Tat 80–1
Angelic Doctor 105
anger 58, 189
Anglo-American discourse 199
Anglo-American mind 69
anima 183
animals 45, 47, 56, 64–5, 75, 108, 201, 217
Annunciation 157
Anschauung 70–1
Anscombe, Elizabeth 219–20
anthropology 79, 81, 86, 91, 100, 104–5, 136, 140, 145, 147, 164–5
   classic scholastic 140
   late medieval 142
   modern 83
   phenomenological 116

   spiritual 53, 69, 92, 113, 133, 165, 183
   theological 93
anthropomorphism 152
Antichrist 188
anti-essentialism 181
anti-intellectualism 36
anti-rationalism 36–7
   political 37
anti-Semitic riots 130
anti-Semitism viii, 186
Apollo 69–71
Apollo and Dionysos 71
Apollonian 69–71, 76
Apollonian cult 76
Apollonian life forces 89
apologia 5–6, 11
Apostles' Creed 150
apperception 85, 87, 100, 110–11
   unity of 60, 85
apprehension 48, 77, 141
archetypes 72, 77, 91, 100
Areopagite, Dionysius the xi, xiii, 116, 130, 133–4, 153, 216
Aristotelian logic 148
Aristotle 107
Arnold, Matthew 77
artists 69, 71–2, 154–5, 163, 202
Aryan 128
ascent 124, 138, 140–1
Aspect-seeing/the Dawning 148
astonishment 148, 189
atonement 8, 188
Attic Greece 74
Aufbau 79, 83, 86, 98, 215

Index

Augustine 84–5, 110–11, 117, 140, 150–1, 202
Augustinian anthropology 142
Auschwitz- Birkenau xi, 92, 152, 157, 190, 192, 217
Ausgelassensheit 77
Austro-Hungarian army 20
Austro-Hungarian Empire 20–1, 169
Avila xii, 26–8, 65, 116–17, 122, 124, 126–7, 144, 155, 219
Aylesford 125

B

Bacchae 72
baptism xvi, 28
Baruzi, Jean 132
Basel 216
Batzdorff, Susanne 187, 195
Bayreuth festival 89, 90
Beckmann-Zöller, Beate 93, 203, 213–14, 216
being 40–3, 45–6, 48, 51, 60, 62–4, 80–1, 83–7, 100–6, 128–9, 146–8, 157–8, 160, 181–2, 186–7
Belgium xiv, 129–30, 196
Bergen Electronic Edition 211, 220
Bergzabern 26–8, 113
Berkeley, George 33
Berlin 15, 169, 195, 216
Bethlehem 130
Betschart, Christof 30, 85, 93, 101, 103, 105–8, 203–4, 216
Bettelheim, Bruno 95–7, 216
Beuron Abbey 121–2, 128
Bewusstsein 88
Biberstein, Ernst 13, 187, 195
Biberstein (Stein) Erna 5, 7, 9, 11, 180
Bild 84–6, 116, 153, 157, 163, 210
Bildung 108, 110
birth 35, 68–76, 78, 90–1, 129, 132, 218
Black Forest 22, 26
borderlands of philosophy and psychology 106
Brahms, Johannes 169
Brentano, Franz 115

Breslau 3, 7, 10–13, 19–22, 24, 113, 127–30, 191–2, 195
Breslau theatre 12
Breslau University 15, 180
Breslau/Wroclaw 5
Bridges, Robert 156, 210
Britain 95
Britten, Benjamin 69
Brussels 4

C

Calcagno, Antonio viii, xv, 23, 24, 182, 189, 204, 216
Cambridge 169–71, 174–5, 216–19
carer of souls 10
Carmel 115, 121–6, 128, 130, 207, 216–17, 219
Carmelite habit 114, 128
Carmelite mystical theology 113
Carmelite Order 4, 79, 109, 113, 122–4, 207
Carmelite Rule 126, 219
Carmelite Spirituality xv, 113, 126, 218
Carmelites xi, xiv, 125, 129, 139–40, 192, 207, 219
Carpathians 21
Carr, David 34, 196
Cartesian epistemology 211
Cartesian *epoché* 41
Cartesian Meditations 34, 217
Carthage 150
Catalan 207
Catholic catechism 27
Catholic Church ix, 27, 31
Catholic education 79, 180
Catholicism 5, 8, 17, 28, 121, 123, 129, 169, 180
Cato 30
Celestial Hierarchy 134, 152, 154
centre 6, 57, 65, 75, 78, 101, 103, 105, 108, 126, 180
ceterum censeo 30–1
change of aspect 146, 148
Charlottenburg 169
Chemnitz 9

Chenu, Marie-Dominique 150–2, 154–5, 216
Chinese 197
choreography 111, 165
Christ, Jesus xv, 26, 85, 110–11, 115, 117–18, 126, 127, 131, 132, 153, 155, 156–9, 161–2, 188
  Christ's death 187
  Christ's name 187
  Transformation in 75
Christian and Jewish Perspectives 187, 217
Christian anthropology 84, 86, 108
Christian baptism 85
Christian life 29
Christian Mystical Tradition 91, 118, 219
Christian Mysticism 133, 217
Christian Philosophy xv, 218
Christian psychologists 84
Christian Spirituality 219
Christianity vii, 25, 55, 68, 75–7, 90–1, 93, 99, 101, 104, 112
Circumcision 27
Clermont-Ferrand 124
cogito ergo sum 40, 47, 198
Cologne xiv, 4–5, 113, 115, 122, 126–30, 188, 190
Cologne Carmel 115, 122, 126
Cologne Linderthal 126
Conrad-Martiuses 26, 101, 103, 216
Conrad, Theodor 15–16
conscience 8
  examination of 157
conscious mind 74
consciousness 39, 41, 48, 58, 60, 62, 74, 84, 87–8, 99, 171–2
  human 49, 74
  stream of 60, 87–8
  unified stream of 60
  unknown stream of 61
constitution, psycho-physical 65
contemplation 103, 125, 144
contemplation in action 32
contemplative life 32, 167
Continental Philosophy 3
continuity, psycho-physical 57

convent life xiii, 30–1
conversion 5, 8, 25–7, 31–2, 93, 99, 104, 113–14, 121–3, 167, 171
co-originality 63–5
core x, 48, 66, 89, 101–7, 181, 202
Courant, Auguste 7
Courant, Salomon 6
Courants 3, 6, 195
Covid-19 pandemic viii
creation 45, 112, 150, 153, 158, 160
creative 162
creative force 115, 159
creativity x, 115, 151
Creator Spirit 210
crisis of civilisation 212
Crisis of European Sciences 34
culture xii, 8, 13, 17, 69, 82, 150, 165, 168, 197, 217
  contemporary 185
Czechia 20, 169, 195
Czechs 21

D

Dali, Salvador xv, 131
dark knowledge 135
dark night 133, 135, 139–40, 145–46, 148, 208
darkness 76, 96, 137–8, 144, 161, 167, 180, 186
Darwin, Charles 92
Davies, Norman 194
death viii, xii, 26, 64, 131–47, 152, 155, 157, 160–1, 168–9, 193, 195–6, 210
dehumanization 185
Deification 219
Deleuze, Gilles 71, 216, 219
depression 138, 165, 208
Descartes, René, 39–43, 45, 47, 52, 198, 214
desert 124, 126, 139, 144
desert fathers, early 139
dialogue, analytical 18
Dilthey, Wilhelm 115
Dionysian 69–72, 75–6, 78, 84, 87, 89–90, 92, 115

Dionysian/Apollonian trope 201
Dionysian psychology 79
Dionysian Self 216
Dionysian symbolism 90, 152
Dionysian tradition 136
Dionysius the Areopagite xiii, 76, 108, 116, 130, 133–4, 149–55, 157, 163, 165, 216
Dionysius's mystical theology 135
Dionysos 67–92, 73, 201
Dionysos and Apollo 69
discernment 121, 123
dissociation 38
divine 32, 80, 84–5, 91, 112, 115, 141, 143, 158, 167
divine light 136, 138–9
dogmatic slumber 42
Dominicans 125, 190
Dominican sisters 29
dreams 4, 10, 69–72, 118, 217
drunken feast 75
dulzuras 144
Duns Scotus 158, 159, 215
Dutch Catholic Bishops 163
duty 29, 167–89, 218
    philosopher's 168

E
Easter 7, 29, 121
Eastern Front 171
Eaton, Mary xv
Ecce Homo 67–8, 90, 218
Echt 4, 22, 122, 129–32, 152, 192
Echt Carmel 131, 210
ecstasy 72
ecstatic abandonment 100
Edmund Husserl Archive xiv
ego 40–2, 64, 146–7, 198, 204
Einfühlung 17, 24, 55, 198, 213
Elbe 4
Elijah 124–5, 218
embodiment 135, 216
empathy 17–20, 22, 24, 52, 55–66, 98, 100, 103, 114, 194, 198
empiricists 41, 48–9, 56

Engelmann, Mother Ambrosia Antonia 210
enlightenment 14, 36, 69, 71, 81, 97, 138, 142, 172
entelechy 107, 206
Entfaltung 108, 110, 206, 211–12
epiphenomena 88
epistemology 14, 43
epoché 40, 47, 49–51
    universal 50
Erinnerungen 218
Erkenntnis 111, 215
eros 92, 151
eschatological 164
essence 50, 59, 109–10, 112, 126, 170, 181, 183
essentialism 181
ethics 18, 170–1
Euripides 72
Europe xii, xvi, 4, 34–7, 69, 95, 122, 126, 130, 161, 180
European culture 34, 68–9, 75, 92
everyday life 60, 83, 94
everyday world 43, 49
Ewigweibliche 91
existence 47, 56, 106, 124, 155, 157–9, 182
existential 38, 83
experience 17, 40, 42–3, 45–6, 48, 50, 55–60, 64, 87–8, 134, 138, 170–3, 176–7
    human viii, 166
    inner 211
    lived 99
    phenomenal 101
    phenomenological 117
    stream of 52, 61
extinction 37

F
faculties 14, 48, 134, 146, 184–5
    creative 154
    logical 148
    spiritual 184
faith viii, 8, 17, 32, 37, 78, 141, 143–4, 154, 207, 213

Falk laws 156
Faust 51, 78–80, 91, 216–17
Feldes, Joachim 196
fiat 157, 159
Fidelio 13
Fifth Mansion 114
First World War 13, 19, 77, 82, 87, 16870, 195
flesh 48, 62, 166, 201
fly-bottles 176
Fourth Mansion 114
France 124
Franciscan nuns 165
Franciscan tertiaries 156
Franciscans 125
Franconian countryside 90
Frankfurt-am-Main 23, 216–17, 220
freedom 80, 83–5, 143
Freiburg-im-Breisgau 3, 22–5, 27, 213, 218
Freiburg University 109, 128
Freud, Sigmund vii, 36, 66–9, 71–4, 75–9, 82–5, 87, 89–93, 95–7, 100, 146–7, 199, 204, 216–17
    English translation of Freud's work 95
    Freud/Jung Letters 217
    soul 96
    terms 96
Friedrich Wilhelm University 12
Friends of Sophia xv

G
Galilee 160
Gay Science, The 74, 202–3, 218
Geach, Peter 211
Gegeben 57
Gegebenheit 56, 58–9, 63
Geist 62, 83–4, 94, 100–3, 108–12, 117, 142–3, 154, 182, 184, 197, 202–3, 209
Geisteswissenschaften 67, 79, 94, 213
geistig 62, 65–6, 89, 97, 100–2, 108, 143, 182
Gemeinschaft 88, 100
gender stereotypes 24
genealogy 203, 218

genetic-psychological investigation 59
German citizens of Jewish origins 129
German cultural tradition 67
German drama 14
German idealism 81
German Institute for Scientific Pedagogy 79
German philosophy 74, 83
German Reich 20
Germanistics 13
Germany xiv, 4, 22, 24, 122, 126, 130, 180, 187, 190, 195
Gesamtkunstwerk 72–3, 90
Gestalt 182
Gestapo, xiii 131–2
givenness 50, 56, 58, 63
Gnostic Christianity 91
God xii, 27, 58, 75–7, 80–1, 84–5, 108–9, 111–12, 114–15, 122–3, 134–6, 138–41, 143–4, 146–7, 151–3, 155, 160, 166–7
    image and likeness of 106
    picture/image of 108
    tripersonal 109
God-head 84, 86, 106
Goethe, Johann Wolfgang von 71, 80–2, 91, 216–17
    Idealism of Goethe 82
Good Shepherd Sunday 123, 128–9
Goplana 169
Gorgias 40
Gorlice 21
Göttingen 15–16, 20, 22, 24, 26, 30, 169
Göttingen School of Phenomenology 16, 152
Götzen-Dämmerung 74
gozo 134
grace 80–1, 85, 105, 114, 142–4, 160
grammar 12, 177
    phenomenology is 173, 178
    third-person 177
grammatical questions 178
Greece 35–6, 197
Greek genius 89
Greek philosophy 36

Greek psyche 76
Greek purity 74
Greek scepticism 40
Greek tragedy 72
Greeks 14, 36, 39, 42, 69, 70, 75, 92, 150, 202
Grillparzer, Franz 12
ground of being 154, 160, 162
gustos 134, 144

H
Habilitationsschrift 79, 105
habitus 106, 108–9
haeccitas 159
Haifa 124
Hamburg 10–11
happiness, soul's 138
health 64, 182
heart 13–14, 29–30, 38–9, 68–9, 91, 93, 105, 107–8, 110, 116–19, 126, 144–5, 154–5, 157, 159–61
 right-believing 170
Heidegger, Martin 23, 83–4, 92, 201
Heraclitean Fragment 107
Heraclitus 99
Herbstrith, Waltraud 113, 163, 187, 189–91, 196, 211, 217
Herkenbosch 4
hermits 125
Hexentrank 72
Hillesum, Etty 190
Hillman, James 118, 165–6, 217
Hintikka, Jaakko 173, 217
Holland, xiv 4, 122, 130, 152, 162, 190, 192
Holocaust, ix 187
holocaustum 188
Holy Land 125, 207, 216
Holy Spirit 84, 162
Holy Year 187
homo capax 108
homo transcendens 162
Hönigswald, Richard 14
Hopkins, Gerard Manley x, 149, 155–62, 166, 210, 215, 217–18

Hranice 20
human beings xiii, 47, 106, 109–10, 179, 183, 186, 210
 complete 86, 185
human existence 138, 153, 155, 157
human life viii, 155, 157, 162
human person vii, x, 55, 83–6, 98, 108–9, 111–12, 182, 210, 216
human personhood viii, 84, 89, 91, 107, 115, 140, 186
human soul 84–5, 92, 112, 115, 162, 182, 210
humanism 95
humanity 35, 42–3, 48, 78, 82, 84–5, 90, 94, 108, 183, 186
humankind 84
Hume, David 33, 41–3, 48
humility 29, 162, 193
Hungarians 21
Husserl, Edmund viii–x, 15–19, 22–5, 33–3, 56, 69–71, 74, 91–2, 97–100, 113–15, 128–9, 171–2, 179, 196–8, 204, 215–17, 219
 critique 48
 early 52
 idiosyncratic practices 24
 interpretation 47, 211
 Krisis 34, 39, 172, 196–8, 217
 phenomenology 15, 171–2
Husserlian/phenomenological school 33

I
IASPES ix, xv
Ibsen, Henrik 12
Ichkern 65
Ichmenschen 145
Id 72, 92
idea-ism 41, 49
idealism 83–4, 86
 subjective 51
ideas 41–2, 65, 74, 83, 93, 101, 146, 163, 183, 202, 211
Id/Es 90
illusion 46, 96, 176, 178

image 47, 62, 84–6, 108–9, 112, 118, 140–1, 143, 153
image and likeness 210
imagination 46, 63, 165–6, 217
imago 108
implications 94, 148–9, 165
Indian cultures 197
Individualität 108, 110
individuality 72, 216
Individuation 215
infinity 35, 99
Ingarden, Roman 24, 51–2, 103
innate dispositions 89
inner awareness 80
insanity 90
inscape 158, 215
instincts 202
instress 157–8
intellect 82, 104, 111, 142, 145, 197
   cool Apollonian 72
   human 111
intellectus 110
intention 24, 46, 175
intentionality 39, 42, 47, 52
Interior Castle, The 116
interpretation 11, 18, 33, 51–2, 56, 69, 97, 133–4
intoxication 70, 72, 77
introspection 175
intuition 46
inwardness 176
   the lure of 176
irrationalism 36–7, 92
Isaiah, xii
Islam 124
Israel 124
Italians 21

J

Jackson, Andrew 211
Jaegerschmid, Sr Adelgundis 31, 188, 194
Jahrhunderthalle 13
Jammerinstitut 75
Jerusalem 125, 162

Jesuits 156
Jewish culture 14
Jews xiii, 8, 122, 162, 186–7, 192
   assimilated 14
John of the Cross, St 124, 126, 131–49, 194, 207, 209, 217–18
Jowett, Benjamin 156
joy xv, 75, 134, 193
Judaism 6, 8, 14, 26, 113, 123, 167
Jung, Carl Gustav 36, 51, 66–9, 72–4, 75–9, 82–4, 89, 91–3, 100, 199, 201, 217–19
Jungian anthropology 76
Jung's Reception 216
Jung's Reception of Friedrich Nietzsche 216

K

Kant, Immanuel 13–14, 37, 41–2, 47–9, 56, 60, 91
Katholische Frauenorganisation 182
Kaufmann, Fritz 16, 25, 30
Kent 125, 156, 159–60, 210
Kern 64–6, 89, 101, 105–7, 202
Khidr 124
Kierkegaard, Søren 176
Kingdom 163
Klimt, Gustav 169
knowledge 41, 43, 49, 51, 84, 87, 111, 114, 134, 136, 150, 153, 168, 171
   direct 178
   embodied 171
   head 171
   indirect 178
   objective 50
   obscure divine 135
   secret 135
   specialized 9
   supernatural 136–7
Kölnische Rundschau 191
Königsberg 33, 37, 42
Krakow 169
Kreuzeswissenschaft xiv, 154, 210, 215
Kristeva, Julia 202
Kunst Triebe 71

L
Lacan, Jacques 218
language 12, 47, 51, 73, 116, 130, 148, 170, 172–4
   contemporary 147
   everyday 173
   independent basis 173
   ordinary 172–3, 211
   primary 173
Latin 12–13, 32, 155, 196
   obligatory 12
Latin Vulgate xii
Lebensbild 218
Lebenskraft 60, 87–9, 119
Leib 48, 62–3, 111–12, 206
Leibniz, Gottfried Wilhelm 41
Leipzig 17, 22, 218
Leitmotiven 157
Lemberg 169
Leuven/Louvain xiv, 197, 214–15, 219
levels 59, 86, 93, 102, 125, 144, 186
   cosmic 157
   psychological 103
Leytonstone 156
libidinal creativity 116
libido 77–8, 119, 217
licentiousness 77
life, soulful vii, xi
life of consciousness 39, 41
life force 64–6, 87–91
life philosophy 30, 113, 121, 123, 125, 127, 129, 186
life in the world 179
light, xiii 84–5, 87, 104, 109, 122, 131–47, 152–3, 160, 169, 193
likeness 106, 151
Lima, Rodrigo xv
Linderthal, Cologne 126
Linz 170
Lipps, Hans 22
Lipps, Theodor 16–19, 58
literary elegance 154
Locke, John 33, 39, 41–2, 52
logical positivists 172
logical structure 173

logos 79–81, 84
love, xi 8, 20, 58, 111, 127, 137–9, 144, 153, 209, 217
Low Countries 128
Lubliniec 6
Lublinitz 6–7, 195
Lucifer 132
lumberjacks 9

M
Maastricht 131–2
madness 77, 82, 166
Madrid 216–17
magic 12–13
Mahler, Gustav 69, 169
Mährisch-Weisskirchen 20
Malebranche, Nicolas 41
Manchester xv, 169, 218
Mann, Thomas 69, 71–4, 76, 201, 218
Mary 157, 159
mass 28, 128, 186, 219
mass movements 100
material reality 152
materialist 85–86
mathematics 12, 40, 169, 171
matter 40, 45, 49–50, 57, 109, 111–12, 118–19, 123, 175–6, 183, 188
   dead 64
   objectified 50
   physical 100
McDonald, Archbishop Kevin xv
McGinn, Bernard xv
McGuinness, Brian 170, 218–20
me-centre 146
mediation 71–3
medieval laws of symbolism according to Chenu 151
medieval origins 155
medieval symbolic 150
melody 68
memory 47, 111, 140–1, 190, 219
Mensch xiii, 202, 209, 215
Menschlichen Person 79, 98, 215
mental gaze 98
mental health 12

mental life 96
mental phenomena 57, 174–5
  observing 175
mental processes 175, 179
me-person 145–6
Merleau-Ponty, Maurice 34, 216, 219
metanoia 85
metaphors 108, 124
metaphysical perspectives 101
metaphysical principles 140
metaphysical questions 86, 105
metaphysics 18, 83, 141, 216, 218
Middle Ages xii
mindfulness 161
mindset, contemporary psychological 136
Mitteleuropa xv
modern psychology 44–5, 51, 53, 99
modern self/soul 201
Moore, Thomas 94
Moravia 16
Morgan, Edwin xv, 131
Mosley, Joanne xv
Mothers, realm of the 51, 71, 91
Mount Carmel xii, 124–6, 138, 140–1
Munich 16, 196, 218
Münster 79, 122–3, 180, 218
music 13, 68, 73, 94, 218
Muslims 124
mystery vii, 26, 70, 107–9, 146–7, 150, 152, 155, 159
mystic/mystical 134–5, 171, 176, 217, 219
  mystical locution 134
  mystical marriage 145
  mystical mountain 124
  mystical quiet 134
  mystical space 125, 219
mystical theology 133–5, 14344, 148
myth 49, 75, 78, 92
  sacred 75
mythos 73, 78

N

naïveté 37
naivety, objective 37
Napoleonic occupation 126

National Socialist Party 92
natural attitude 35–6, 50
natural state 147
nature viii, 59–60, 62–4, 66, 80–1, 83, 86–7, 89–90, 97–8, 105–7, 109, 115–18, 172–4, 176, 182–3, 197–8
  human 29, 67, 84, 105, 139, 158
  inner 81, 143
  person's 80
nature and grace 105
Nazareth 159
Nazism 36, 73, 77, 91, 100, 132, 180, 190
  anti-Semitic policies 152
  Nazi Germany xiii, 30, 34
  Nazi ideology 184
  Nazi laws 132
  Nazi persecution 195
neo-Platonic spiritualizing 95
Netherlands 22, 130
Netherlands Red Cross 192
New Synagogue, Breslau 130
New York 216–18
Niemeyer, Max 216
Nietzsche, Friedrich x, 36, 66, 67–84, 89–92, 201–3, 216, 218–19
  Nietzsche and Philosophy 216
  Nietzsche's Dionysian 90
  Nietzsche's Dionysian revelation 74
  Nietzsche's life force 90
  Nietzsche's Philosophy 218
  Nietzsche's post-enlightenment programme 82
  Nietzsche's work 75
noche oscura 207
noche sosegada 135
nominalism 165
Norway 170
nous 85
nucleus 89, 105
Nuremberg 219

O

objectification 37
  scientific 35–6, 49, 99
objective world 43, 46–7, 50

objectivism 37–9, 43–4, 49
  modern 49
objectivity 43, 185
  naive 37
objects 39–40, 42, 45–7, 49–50, 58, 98,
  100, 158
Olomouc 20
Olympus 76, 202
ontic structure 50, 214
oppression, totalitarian 168
optimism 82
original sin 39–41
Other Minds argument 178
outsider status 169
Oxford xvi, 156, 217–20
Oxford Centre for Applied Carmelite
  Spirituality xv

P
Pacelli, Cardinal Eugenio 196
Palestine 130
pandemic xv
panic 201
Pâquier 131
Paris 196
Parmenides 158
Passion Sunday 188
passions 85, 122, 139, 154–5, 160, 165
pastoral care 94
Patmore, Coventry 156
Pentheus, King 72
perception 35, 46–9, 52, 56, 63–4, 110,
  117, 139, 148, 154, 177
perfection 81–2, 84–5, 138
person 62–3, 80–1, 85–6, 101, 103, 105–7,
  110, 112, 114–15, 145–7, 154–5,
  159, 177–8, 185, 215–16
  complete 185
  psychophysical 56
personality, xii 62, 71, 101, 103, 106, 108,
  147, 184
  human 118
personhood viii, 39, 66, 82–3, 93, 107,
  142, 162
Pfänder, Alexander 65, 115, 218

Pfister, Oskar 96–7
Phänomenen 195
Phänomenologie 214, 217
phantasy vii, 140
phase, atheistic 11
phenomenologists vii, ix, 6, 16, 34, 47, 57,
  99, 172, 181
phenomenology xv, 3, 16, 18, 20, 34,
  36, 41–3, 45, 171–3, 181, 184,
  216–19
phenomena 17, 35, 51, 55–7, 59, 64, 75,
  117, 172–5, 178–9, 199
phenomenological analyses 87, 93, 102
phenomenological approach viii, 37,
  59, 98, 173, 181, 211
phenomenological attitude 50
phenomenological circle 15
phenomenological interpretation 132
phenomenological investigation 45
phenomenological language 173, 211
phenomenological method 36, 38
phenomenological movement vii
phenomenological reduction 45, 56
phenomenological Research 152
physical 174
psychological 174–5
phenomenology and anthropology 3
Phillips, Jacob xv
philosophers of consciousness 171, 173
philosophia perennis 115
philosophical anthropology viii, 17, 25,
  30, 32, 79
philosophical duty 180
Philosophical Investigations, The 81, 147,
  175, 219
philosophical psychology 55, 94, 113, 220
philosophical theology 113
philosophy vii–x, xii–xiii, xv, 3, 13–16,
  18–19, 33–8, 42–3, 59–60, 66,
  102–3, 169–72, 186, 192–4,
  215–16
  idealistic 56
  modern 39–40
  modern Western 38
  natural 14, 172

perennial 59
scholastic 105
transcendental 43
philosophy of mathematics 169
philosophy of mathematics and logic 169
philosophy and philology 126
philosophy and psychology 16, 55, 67–8, 106, 149, 166
philosophy of psychology 174, 211, 213, 220
philosophy and theology, x 106, 132
physical bodies 40, 57, 61–2
physics 174–5
picture 84–5, 108–9, 112, 116–17, 153–4, 163, 176, 199
    body-soul-intellect 114
pitch 157–9
pitch of existence 157
Plotinus 219
Poland 20–1, 195
Pope Innocent Iv 125
Pope Pius Xi 187, 196
Pope St John Paul Ii xii
Pope Urban Ii 124
Posselt, Mother Teresia Renata 9, 25–9, 113, 121–4, 127, 129, 131–2, 187–8, 194, 196, 218–19
post-Freudian concepts 204
postmodern return 118
post-Nietzschean agenda 78
power xiii, 64, 80, 82, 85, 90–1, 110, 143, 180, 182, 184
    healing 91
Poznań, 6
Prague 34
prayer xv, 6–7, 123, 126, 141
prejudices 17, 38–9, 47, 179
prescientific 42–3
prophets, school of the 124
Protagoras 40
Protestant Theology 115, 196
Prussia
    Prussian character 17
    Prussian history 14
    Prussian Society 14, 180
    Prussian state 14

Prussian Ministry of Education 181
Przywara, Erich 27, 29, 31, 121
pseudo-sciences 51
psyche 89–90, 97, 99, 102–3, 110, 139, 161, 165–6, 199, 203, 212
psyche and spirit 165
psychic life 77, 199
    foreign 57
psychoanalysis 73, 75, 77, 83, 95–7, 194, 219
psychoanalysis and theology 95
psychological concepts 87, 177
psychological development 104
psychological grammar 177–9
psychological life 63, 97
psychological resilience 164
psychological therapies 73–4
    twentieth-century 72
Psychological Types 76
psychologism 33, 39, 44
    battle against 15
    supposed 41
psychologists ix, xii–xiii, 15, 62, 71, 82, 86, 95, 161, 174–5
    clinical 175
    modern 118
psychology x, 14–16, 33–4, 39, 41, 43–5, 49, 55, 59, 66–8, 96, 139–40, 174–5, 194–5, 219–20
    analytical 91
    bewitchment of 176
    contemporary 94, 162
    depth 67–8, 79, 147
    empirical 108
    metaphysical 108, 110
    neo-empirical 176
    objective 44
    positive 94
    traditional 47
psychology and anthropology 136
psychology and history 194
psychology and phenomenology 59
psychology and philosophy 66
psychology with soul 100
psychology without soul viii

psycho-physical individual 59, 62
psychotherapeutic process 78
psychotherapy 217
pure i 59

Q
Quaestiones disputatae 214
quietude 135–6

R
Raserei 77–8, 82
ratio 36, 70
rational arguments 37
rational/empirical 36
rational explanation 38
rational logicians 41
rationalism 36–7, 39
　bad 37
Rätsel 44
Realgymnasium 170
realist 175
realities 52, 118, 150–2, 154, 157–9, 164–5, 173, 179, 197
realization, empathetic 63–5
realty/reality 158
reason 10, 14, 17, 36–9, 71, 73, 76, 82, 84–5, 89, 91–2, 97, 100, 148, 150
rebirth 90, 92
Red Book, The 91, 218
Red Cross 21
reductionism 84, 86
　empiricist 110
Reich laws 123
Reich Literary Association 128
Reich Postal Service 191
Reich's censors 128
Reichskristallnacht 130
Reinach, Adolf 16–17, 26
Reinach, Pauline 23, 27
Reize/Triebe 146
religion xi, 14, 31–2, 75, 78, 95, 97, 122, 166, 170, 193–4
　classical 75
　modern 78
　mythic root of 78
　psychological 78
religion and theology 95
religious life 8, 22, 26, 32, 125, 167, 180
Renaissance 37–8
representation 39, 91, 151, 160
　remembering 60
resilience xv, 163–5, 216, 219
　spiritual xi
responsibility, social 179
resting qualities 104
Resurrection 26, 187
return of soul-language 119
revelations 32, 141
reverence 28, 188–9
revolution x, 33, 35
Ribot, Philip 207
Riesengebirge 13, 68
Ritterplatz 11
Roger, King 201
Romanians 21
Romanies 21
Roman Senate 30
Rome 27, 187, 215
rowdy behaviour 21
Russell, Bertrand 169
Russell, Lucy xvi
Russia 169
Russian enemy 170
Ruthenians 21

S
sabiduría mística 144
sabores 144
sacrifice 66, 127, 181, 188
sage 33, 37, 42
Salamanca 133
Salzburg 180
sapientia oscura 135
satyr 92
Sawicki, Marianne 23–4, 203–4, 213, 219
Scheler, Max 17
Scheuklappen 17
Schifferstadt 190, 216

Schopenhauer, Arthur 12, 19
Schutz, Alfred 34
Schwind, Canon Joseph, 28–29
Schwind, Dean Konrad 191
science 35, 38, 40, 42–3, 49, 51, 128, 130, 132, 134, 136, 149–66, 174
  fact-minded 38
  sacred 94
  universal 35, 53
science of psychology 174
scientia crucis 149, 210
scientific attitude 35, 43, 49
scientific materialism 165
scientific-medical establishment 96
scientism 174
scientistic approach 175
Second German Reich 3
Second World War xiii
Seele 57, 60, 62, 93–7, 100–3, 105, 107–12, 145, 147, 196, 198–201, 203–4, 206
  Seele/Kern 103
  seelische 61, 86, 96, 97, 102, 110, 116, 183, 200, 212
  seelisches Leben vii
Seelenburg, Die 112–13, 115–16
Seelentriebe 115, 146–7
Seelsorge 10
Seiendes 197, 214
Seins 215
self 59–60, 65, 81–2, 84–8, 91–3, 95–8, 100–3, 107–8, 110–11, 116–18, 132–3, 140–2, 144–6, 148–9, 162, 181–2, 204–5
  embodied 98
  human 84–5, 110–11, 116, 202
self knowledge 85, 111, 114
sensations 61–4, 98, 101
  bodily 62
  physical 62
sensory/sensual 138–9, 146
Seventh Mansion 115
sexism, old-fashioned viii
sexual differences 183
Shakespeare, William 12

shock tactics 176
silence 23, 164
Silesia 3, 19, 195
Sinn 80, 142–3, 215
Sinnbild 163
Sinnbildung 99
Slovaks 21
Slovenes 21
Smet, Joachim 126
Social Sciences 219
society 10, 73, 83, 88, 156, 167, 171, 179–81, 184–5, 216
Socrates 71, 90
Socratic-Alexandrian 92
Socratic dialectic 71, 89
solitude 126, 144
Solomon 218
soothsaying 75
sophistication 168
Søren Kierkegaard 176
Sorge 98, 101, 103, 114
soul 29, 43–4, 56–7, 60–6, 80–2, 85–7, 89, 93–112, 114–19, 133, 135–6, 138–41, 143–7, 161–3, 165–6, 181–4, 198–201, 216–17, 219
  soul-discourse 60, 118
  soul-guidance 29
  soul journeys 138–9
  soul-language 94–5, 101, 116, 118–19
    performative 118
  soul-life 58, 96
  soul-maker 119
    contemporary 118
  soul-nature 86, 102
  soul-person 146
  soul-perspective 148
  soul-psychology 91
  soul's life 82
  soul-states 165
  soul-work 118
  soulish 61, 96
South America 123
Southern beat music 61, 94
Speyer 28–9, 105, 114, 180, 190
Spinoza, Baruch 13, 41

spirit 145, 162, 165–6, 182, 193, 197, 202, 212
   created 112
spirit and psyche 102
Spiritual Canticle, The 135–6, 194
Spiritual Direction 10, 29, 121, 123, 218
Spiritual Exercises, The 27, 158
spiritual eye 85
spiritual life 11, 110–12, 133, 135
spiritual/mental 89
spiritual search 147
spiritual sleep 135
spirituality, viii 95, 161, 182, 219
spiritus 110
St Augustine of Hippo 84, 107, 110, 219
St Bernard of Clairvaux 134
St Bonaventure 134
St Cyprian 150
Stein, Auguste 6–10, 28, 72, 78–9, 127, 129–30, 139, 185, 198, 219
Stein, Edith vii–viii, 21–2, 24–6, 51–3, 57–62, 64–5, 80–9, 91–4, 97–100, 104–8, 110–12, 116–18, 130–2, 145–7, 149, 152–7, 161–9, 173–5, 179–81, 201–4 *et passim*
   Abitur 13
   anthropology 66, 93–121, 147
   birth 7
   canonization process 27, 187, 190
   convent life 8
   conversion to Christianity 5, 25, 27, 55, 93, 99, 104, 121, 156, 180
   deportation 210
   Gymnasium 10, 12
   intellectual apostolate 31–2, 114, 121, 180
   intellectual curiosity 171
   intellectual development xiii, 105, 181
   intellectual maturity 67
   Jewish origins 128
   profession, final 129
   Prussian allegiance 17

Salzburg lectures 183
secret bound by seven seals 193
secretum meum mihi xii, 11, 30
Teresia Benedicta a Cruce 211
women's rights activist 192
Stein, Rosa 7, 9, 129–32, 164
Stein-Courant family 7
Steinian approach 205
Steinian psychology 104
Steinian scholarship viii
Steinian sources 215
Steinian terms 148
St Elizabeth of Thuringia 161
Stephansplatz vii
Stern, William 14–15
St Ignatius Loyola 27
St John of the Cross x–xi, xv, 118, 128, 131–3, 143, 155, 163, 217
St John Henry Newman 5, 29, 31
St Ludger 123
St Ludger's Church 123
St Magdalena 29, 191
St Martin of Tours 28
stoicism 127
St Simon Stock 124
St Patrick's Cemetery 156
Strachey, James 95–6, 204
   Strachey's editorial choices 204
   Strachey's English translation of Freud 147
strangeness 3, 135
stranger god 69, 201
stream of life 88, 99, 172
Strietzel, Willy 14
St Stephen's Cathedral vii
St Teresa of Avila xii, 26–8, 65, 110, 113–14, 116–17, 122, 126, 127, 144, 155, 216–17, 219
St Thomas Aquinas xiii, 31–2, 86, 106–8, 110, 116–17, 128, 194, 202
   Thomistic categories 105
   Thomistic style 139
   Thomist tradition 61
   Thomist understandings 105

Stuttgart 217
subject 12–13, 17–18, 20, 26, 39, 44–6, 56–8, 108–9, 171–2, 174–5, 181, 183, 190–3
   psychophysical 98
   transcendental 49
subjectivity 43, 46, 99
   absolute 51
   enigma of 44
   knowing 43
substance 134
Sühnopfer 188
Sullivan, John xiv–xv
supernatural 31, 134, 140–1, 183
Swansea 175
Switzerland 130–2, 180
symbol 62, 73, 75, 114, 138, 150–5, 163–5
   symbol and myth 75
   symbolic 72, 133, 149–50, 152, 156, 160
   symbolic form 152, 154
   symbolic interpretation 160
   symbolic language 155
   symbolic mentality xi, 150–1, 154
   symbolic perspective 153, 155, 160–1
   symbolic sense of self 118, 157
symbolic theology, medieval 136
symbolism 150–2, 163, 173
sympathy 9
symptoms 165–6
synagogues 23, 124
synthesis 116, 128

T
tabula rasa 41
Tapferkeitsmedaille 169
Tarnow 21
Tatras 4
tear down the veil of Maya 72
teleological 106
telos 82, 106–7, 206
tensions, creative 116
Thanatos 92
theologia mystica 133–6, 140
theology x, xiii, 95, 119, 126, 132, 134–5, 149, 153, 163, 216, 218
   moral 134–5
theology and psychology 119
theōria 36
theosis 219
therapy 78, 185, 205
thinking 40, 47, 94, 96, 105, 143, 148, 170, 174–5, 177–8
Third Reich 168
Thompson, Liza xvi
thought 172–3, 176, 179, 181, 202
Thuringia 161
Toledo 155
Tractatus Logico-Philosophicus 22, 171, 220
tradition 33, 38, 81, 115, 124, 133–6, 165, 208
tragedy 68, 72–3, 76, 90, 92, 218
tragic muse 89
tranquility 135–6
transcendent 86, 88, 114, 117–18, 155, 161–2
transcendental 51, 119, 171
   transcendental category 88
   transcendental epoché, 49
   transcendental idealism 86
   transcendental presupposition 91
   transcendental reduction 51
   transcendental subjectivism 42
   transcendentalism 41–2
transcendent function 166
transcendent perspective 161, 165
transcendent reality 88, 151, 154
Transcendental Phenomenology 34, 52, 196, 217
transformation 10, 35, 77–8, 114, 143, 146, 217
transpersonal, contemporary 94
trees 47
Triebe 70, 82, 87, 115, 146
Trinitarian nature 84, 112, 115, 118
Trinity 85, 107, 110, 117, 196

Tristan 73, 218
Triune God 112, 210
truth xii, 31, 37, 50, 63, 71, 85, 147, 154, 160, 166
  objective 43, 51
turmoil 34, 186
typology 69, 139

U
Über-Ich 90, 147
Übersehen 197
Unbehagen 90
Unbewusste 90
unconscious bias viii
unconsciousness 77
union 109, 115–16, 141, 143
union with the beloved 138
United States 5, 128–9, 195
unity 60-2, 82, 84–7, 99, 102–3, 110, 118, 184
unity of perception 110, 117
unity of spirit and psyche 102
universe 160, 197
Upper Silesia 6
Utrecht 162

V
validity, ontic 40, 43, 50–1
Vatican 187, 190, 207
venereal diseases 20
Venice 69, 218
Vercelli 125
Vernunft 197, 202
Vienna, vii 16, 34, 95, 168, 172, 175, 180, 217
Vienna Circle 168, 172, 219
  Vienna Circle Manifesto 172
Viennese Golden Age 169
Viktoriaschule 22
vine, soothsaying God of the 85, 91
vineyard 124
Visconti, Luigi 69
Vistula river 169
vocation 31, 180, 185

vows, permanent 122
Vratislava 195

W
Wagner, Richard 13, 73, 89, 90
  Wagnerian music drama 72
Wagner, Winifred 217
Waismann, Friedrich 173, 219
Walzer, Abbot Raphael 121, 123, 128
Weimar Germany xiii
Weisskirchen hospital 21
Weltanschauung 175
weltlichen Seelsorgern 96, 204
Westerbork 190, 192
Western culture 34, 77
Western Monasticism 122
Wiener Kulturband 34
wisdom vii, 74, 144, 154, 171
Wissenschaft 163, 197
Wittgenstein, Ludwig, xi 20–1, 81, 99, 146–8, 161, 167–79, 185–6, 192, 211, 217–20
  anti-Philosophy 215
  disputes 175
  life 171
  Nachlass 220
  phenomenological issues 173
  philosophical problems 172
  rejection of phenomenological language 173
  style 176
  young 20
  war 171
Wolfe, Steven xv
Wollust 72–3, 82
women xi–xiii, 3, 9–10, 14–15, 23, 25, 27, 31, 32, 79, 122, 127, 180–1, 183–6, 189, 191, 194, 216
  women's Education 183
  women's equality 181
  women's intrinsic value 180, 185
  women's rights 13–14, 180, 183, 195
  women's rights movement 13, 180

work ix–x, 15–19, 29, 31, 36, 67–8, 71–2, 79–80, 88, 95, 128, 132, 146–7, 155–6, 162–3, 166, 168–70, 172, 197–9, 202
world viii–ix, 16–17, 32, 35–6, 38–40, 42–3, 45–6, 48–51, 56–7, 64, 71, 81–3, 85–6, 103–4, 106–8, 154–5, 160–1, 167, 169–71, 182
   phenomenal 57
Wotan 77, 85
Wroclaw 3, 195

Würzburg 217
Würzburg School 15, 217
Wyse, Hymie xv

Y
Yom Kippur 8

Z
Zarathustra 68, 74, 82
Zurich 182

www.ingramcontent.com/pod-product-compliance
Lightning Source LLC
Chambersburg PA
CBHW062137300426
44115CB00012BA/1961